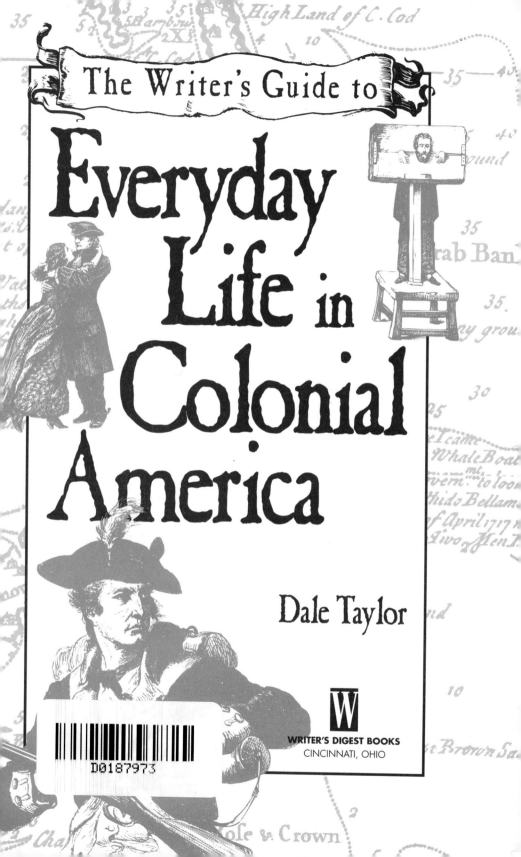

The Writer's Guide to Everyday Life in Colonial America

Dale Taylor

W
WRITER'S DIGEST BOOKS
CINCINNATI, OHIO

D0187973

Visit our Web site at www.writersdigest.com for information on more resources for writers.

To receive a free weekly E-mail newsletter delivering tips and updates about writing and about Writer's Digest products, send an E-mail with the message "Subscribe Newsletter" to newsletter-request@writersdigest.com or register directly at our Web site at www.writersdigest.com.

Other fine Writer's Digest Books are available from your local bookstore or direct from the publisher.

03 02 01 00 99   5 4 3 2 1

Library of Congress Cataloging-in-Publication Data

Taylor, Dale.
   The writer's guide to everyday life in Colonial America / Dale Taylor.
     p.   cm.
   Includes bibliographical references and index.
   ISBN 0-89879-942-2 (pbk. : alk. paper)
   1. United States—Social life and customs—To 1775—Handbooks, manuals, etc. 2. United States—History—Colonial period, ca. 1600–1775—Handbooks, manuals, etc. 3. Historical fiction—Authorship—Handbooks, manuals, etc. I. Title.
E162.T26 1997
973.2—dc21
                                         96-38093
                                           CIP

Photography by Dale Taylor
Edited by Jack Heffron and Roseann S. Biederman
Production edited by Amy Jeynes
Designed by Sandy Kent
Cover illustrations courtesy of Dover Clip Art Books

TO MY WIFE SUE,

AND ALL THE GHOSTS

WHO HAVE PERMITTED US

TO SHARE THEIR HOUSES.

ACKNOWLEDGMENTS

A book like this does not get written without the efforts of many people over a long period of time. It is impossible to name them all, but I owe a great debt to my college professors (one of whom, Joe Youngblood, recognized the merit in my unorthodox desire to remain relatively ignorant of post-colonial matters so I could more easily empathize with and assimilate the lost mental framework of this culture) and to the many individuals who professionally shared their knowledge and encouragement with me. To those like the staff of the African-American Interpretive Program at Carter's Grove and the several craftsmen who reviewed sections of the book to make sure they were not off base, I extend my deepest appreciation.

The people who really made this book possible are forgotten by all save a few historians. Every sailor, no matter how mean, who pulled an oar for a mapmaker whose name we remember; every farmer, no matter how base, who raised food for the townsfolk and for the manor houses which still stand as monuments to the upper classes; every slave, no matter how involuntary their work, who built those houses—all contributed effort and often a surprising amount of professional skill to the founding of the American colonies. Without them there would be no story to tell.

Lastly, my editors at Writer's Digest, Roseann Biederman and Amy Jeynes, and the copyediting and proofreading team know more about my bad habits than anyone including myself. They have graciously and tactfully changed a few of them for your benefit, readers, all the while remaining both gracious under the pressure of archaic terms, conventions and spellings and pleasant to work with. For that I am most grateful.

Table of Contents

INTRODUCTION

HOW TO USE THIS BOOK

Inevitably, this book has a huge amount of territory to cover. Historians tend to take isolated facts and examine them scientifically in narrow specializations. Those of us who tell stories, whether fiction or nonfiction, need themes and concepts to carry our tales; the facts become merely the trees alongside the road of ideas. As a result, you will find this book emphasizes interrelationships and ideas in a way historians' in-depth studies do not. Toward that end, I have employed a few techniques to help you find your way:

- Unusual PERIOD TERMS and COLLOQUIAL USAGES are set in small capitals.
- Visual references to selected films that further illustrate a topic are indicated by a special icon 🐦 and a page number. Follow the page number to the Appendix, which lists the films (all available on videocassette) and the specific related scenes.

SEQUENCE

The American colonies went through three fairly distinct periods, with blurred transitions and tangential excursions. These periods are (1) the Period of Settlement, roughly from 1607 to 1675, during which the colonies got on a firm footing, established economic bases, grew in population and solved the problems of colonization; (2) the Period of Organization, roughly from 1675 to 1750, during which the colonies solved their major political problems and gained strength; and (3) the Period of Revolution, ending in 1783, during which American cultural life was strongly influenced by the European powers' battles over their American colonies, first in the French and Indian War, then in the American Revolution.

I have used relative dating for many trends and changes. "Early" tends to stand for the Period of Settlement; "late" refers to the Period of Revolution. "Earlier" or "later" are relative to these or the other definitions I provide.

Period of Settlement

The early settlers faced innumerable difficulties, not only from the wild country, but also from their own lack of preparedness due to poor planning and unreasonable expectations. Spain had been so quick to derive bullion from Mexico City, Colombia and Peru that the rest of Europe thought the entire New World was a treasure chest awaiting only discovery to exploit. If that had been the case, the few colonists could have paid for the extensive support necessary to keep them alive. As it was not, they had trouble.

The early Virginia colonists were so certain they would soon be rich that they spent too much time prospecting and no time at all attending essential needs like planting crops for the winter, even though their landing in May gave them ample opportunity to do so. At least the Plymouth colonists had an excuse for their starvations. Traveling to an established area of Virginia, they were blown off course in a storm and landed, already in need, in the middle of a harsh New England winter.

English geographer Richard Hakluyt, among others, attempted to inform the colonists of what was needed. Hakluyt assembled a huge library containing accounts of exploration and the New World and offered recommendations of what to expect. Even though he was less realistic than he might have been, if any of the colonists had listened, they would have been better off than they were.

This period was characterized by the colonists unlearning what they thought they knew. English society might one day be transplanted, but not without far-reaching social casualties, except in those late additions to the Empire, Canada and Florida. Elsewhere, the rigid class structures had to bend a bit.

After the initial problems of survival were solved, new ones appeared. The Englishmen, anxious to solve their own ills, were not far-sighted about the effects of their actions upon the colonies. The Navigation Acts are only one example. The English also sent petty criminals and the poor to a colony like Georgia. The thinkers failed to think that those who would not work in England would not in America.

On the flip side, the labor shortage encountered in Virginia led to the headright system, which had a positive effect on the new country. The English poor who would sign up to labor for five to seven years in exchange for passage were the ones with the most initiative (often shut out by the established structures in England). Those that survived their indentures often proved to be the hardworking, independent lot from whom our national identity would finally arise.

During the earliest days of this period, a major concern was the Spanish Threat. Shortly, however, Spain incurred serious financial problems, and the threat became more manageable at the same time as the colonies grew and became better able to defend themselves. The threat became nothing more than a border skirmish, which occupied less attention in the latter part of this period than later.

Throughout this period, the lack of centralized (royal) governing authority meant the various colonies exercised control over their own areas, each benefiting or suffering from its own unique political formulae, methods of raising capital, and internal political rivalries.

Funding the colonies was a great concern. Most did not become self-sufficient for a long time and required continual infusions of colonists, supplies and other support from the home country. This required substantial investment, and few private companies created to accomplish the task for the government made any profit. This in turn meant few could provide the level of support necessary to the task.

The different colonies passed through this period at different times. The later the settlement, the shorter the period of settlement, because more resources were available and the basic problems were understood. In this regard, even Massachusetts showed a marked improvement over Virginia. Later colonies like the Carolinas could utilize the pool of colonists and other resources nearby in Virginia and Maryland. Tolerant colonies like Pennsylvania fared best of all by not alienating the Indians.

Period of Organization

The Period of Organization roughly corresponds to the time from the ascension of William and Mary through the Seven Years' War. During this period the colonies worked out internal problems, such as the boundary disputes between Virginia and North Carolina, and expanded their population and economic bases. Cultural institutions like the St. Cecilia Society were organized. Slowly, the various colonies solved their own disputes and began to work as one, willingly or not.

Although England was continually at war through this period, those wars were not as noticeable in the colonies, where disputes with the French and Spanish took the form of local garrisons or militias under colonial leadership involved in localized squabbles without much support from abroad.

As the colonies gained strength, certain elements such as piracy yielded to the law, and by the end of the period the individual colonies, although still fractious, were coordinated enough to work on real problems. Interestingly, at the beginning of this period, the religious New England colonies dropped out of communication with England, only to come back into the network on a mercantile basis just before the Period of Revolution.

Period of Revolution

European squabbles flowed over into the colonies during the French and Indian War. The massive problems posed by the French move to cut the colonies off from the interior required regular troops under British officers and intercolonial cooperation on a scale never before seen.

Although this period was short, it contained the most dramatic political change within the modern world in the colonies. The mostly aristocratic British officers quartered in local homes and working closely with colonial officers contributed not just to the military experience of men such as George Washington, but also to cultural exchange as institutions like amateur theater and the Band of Music (see page 171) were made available to the public for the first time. The problems of quartering these troops, and the taxes imposed by England, not only to win the wars but also to maintain troops here "for the colonies' defense" when the colonies were no longer threatened, led directly to the Revolution.

The colonies learned from their cooperation during the war against the French that they could accomplish more when they worked together, and they also began to realize they had shared interests.

To most people, "colonial America" refers to this short time period. Imported mahogany replaced native woods in furniture, local artisans created outstanding works, and the historical personages we all know took the stage. The colonies even exported artists like John Copley and Benjamin West. The colonial ball swirled to its greatest elegance, only to slam into the trauma of the Revolution.

Interestingly enough, after this period the new states passed into nearly a century of isolationism, cut off from cultural exchange with England by the heavy tariffs imposed to promote the long-neglected manufactures and to settle the war debt.

NATIVE AMERICANS

This book makes no attempt to cover the very different lives or views of the Native Americans in any detail, nor to present these peoples from a modern viewpoint. The Europeans were less than open-minded about people they generally viewed as heathen and primitive (one source from the 1690s refers to "the cannibals") and whom they most commonly called natives, savages or, later, Indians. To try to present a balanced perspective is beyond the scope of this book, just as it was beyond the ability of most colonists. Partly for reasons of size, and partly because of the need to help readers understand the cultural biases of an earlier day, this book takes the position of outlining the European view prevailing at the time. If your work requires a balanced view, further research is necessary.

GETTING STARTED

My goal has been to do what most traditional histories do not: synthesize the many facts available into concepts that help you understand the period without excessive study. In some twenty years of interpreting this period in living history museums, teaching other interpreters and making this history relevant to the general public, the concepts, trends and patterns have enabled me to tell the story of the colonies in an entertaining and understandable manner. The specific facts of school-book history, although important, are less so in telling a story, whether for a museum visitor or a reader.

Ultimately, nothing can substitute for your own research when you need to know specific facts. Toward this end you should read biographies and histories of the areas and times about which you are planning to write, visit museums that provide visual and documentary materials and, if you need details, check out some probate inventories in the clerk of the court's office or on microfilm at large research libraries. Living history museums are often willing to provide local detail provided you do not claim to have your story "authenticated" by them, simply because the fewer errors there are out there, the easier their job is.

Good luck, and keep writing!

TIME LINE

Up to 1625

1598   *France* Edict of Nantes decrees Catholic-Protestant coexistence in France.

1603   March 24: Death of Queen Elizabeth, ascension of James I.

1604   End of England's war with Spain.

1605   Gunpowder Plot against James I.

1607   *Virginia* May 19: First permanent English settlement in New World is founded at Jamestown by the Virginia Company. Named for James I, "King James His Towne."

1608   *Virginia* Jamestown burns, is rebuilt; first women arrive.

1608   Galileo constructs astronomical telescope.

1608   July 3: Samuel de Champlain founds Quebec.

1609   *Virginia* John Smith is injured in powder keg explosion, returns to England.

1609–10 *Virginia* Starving Time. Population of 550 people at Jamestown is reduced to 65 by starvation, cold. Winter hardship is comparable to that at Valley Forge. One case, apparently unique, of cannibalism: a man kills his wife, salts her away, is caught and burned at the stake.

1609   *New York* September 13: Henry Hudson sails up the Hudson to Albany.

1610   *Virginia* Colony is abandoned; colonists meet relief under new governor Lord Delaware, return same day.

1611   King James Bible is published; beginnings of standard English.

1612   *New York* Dutch use Manhattan as fur trading post.

1612   *Virginia* Tobacco is first planted.

1614   *Virginia* John Rolfe marries Rebecca (Matoaka, also known as Pocahontas).

1614   *New England* John Smith explores, maps and names New England.

1616   William Harvey announces circulation of blood in a lecture.

1617   Henry Briggs publishes first one thousand improved base-10 logarithms.

1617–19 *Massachusetts* Smallpox introduced by English and Dutch fishermen kills 90 percent of Massachusetts Bay Indians.

1618   Thirty Years' War begins in Europe.

1619   *Virginia* First elected assembly in New World.

1620   *Massachusetts* December 26: Pilgrims land at Plymouth, found Plymouth Colony.

1621   *Massachusetts* William Bradford becomes governor of Plymouth Colony.

1621	Dutch West India Company is formed.
1622	*Virginia* Opecancanough orders attack on English settlements March 22 after meeting with John Rolfe, who may have claimed Indian succession. Native Americans visit as they have for some time in homes of settlers, then on signal grab whatever is to hand and start killing. Out of some 600 English in James River Valley, 347 are killed. Jamestown colonists are spared because Christianized Indian Chanco warns them. Flowerdieu Hundred settlers warned by canoe from Jamestown.
1623	*New Hampshire* Little Harbor settlement is established by David Thomas.
1623	*New York* New Netherlands is formally organized.
1624	*Virginia* Virginia Company is dissolved, Virginia made Royal Colony.
1624	Henry Briggs publishes *Arithmetica Logarithmica* with thirty thousand more logarithms.
1624	England declares war on Spain.

1625–1649

1625	March 27: Death of James I and ascension of Charles I.
1627	*Massachusetts* William Bradford and seven others buy out the merchant adventurers who owned Plymouth Colony, then share it out.
1628	Assassination of the Duke of Buckingham.
1628	William Harvey publishes circulation of blood in *Exercitio anatomica de motu cordis et sanguinis in animalibus*.
1629	Charles dissolves Parliament, rules as monarch for eleven years.
1629	*Massachusetts* Massachusetts Bay Company is chartered.
1629	*New Jersey* Swedes settle Pavonia (Jersey City).
1630	Founding of Massachusetts Bay Colony.
1631	Roger Williams arrives in Massachusetts Bay Colony.
1631	First ship built in Massachusetts is launched.
1632	June 21: Maryland is chartered.
1633	Henry Briggs publishes *Trigonometrica Britannica* with logarithms for trigonometric functions.
1633	*Ark* and *Dove* set sail for Maryland.
1633	*Massachusetts* Smallpox decimates Indians, kills thirty-five English in the Plymouth colony.
1634	*Maryland* First settlers under Baltimore arrive.
1634	*Massachusetts* Peaceful Revolution results in representative government for lawmaking.
1634	*Connecticut* Smallpox epidemic transmitted by Dutch kills

95 percent of the Indians living along the Connecticut River, prompting settlement by English.

1635   *Massachusetts*   Roger Williams is banished from Massachusetts Bay Colony.

1635   *Massachusetts*   August 14: Great Hurricane eye passes between Boston and Plymouth. William Bradford reports, "It blew down many hundred thousands of trees" and many houses.

1636   *Rhode Island*   Roger Williams founds Providence, establishes first separation of church and state.

1636   *Massachusetts*   October 28: Harvard College is founded.

1636   *Connecticut*   Thomas Hooker founds settlement at Hartford.

1637   *New England*   First mounted mail service is inaugurated between Boston and New York.

1637   *Connecticut*   During Pequot War, New England troops attack Indians near New Haven.

1638   *Massachusetts*   Three hurricanes (August 3, October 5, October 19) in Boston area, including Rhode Island.

1638   Anne Hutchinson is banished from Massachusetts, moves to Rhode Island.

1638   *Connecticut*   New Haven Colony is founded by Theophilus Eaton and John Davenport.

1638   *New Jersey*   Swedes settle on lower Delaware.

1639   *Massachusetts*   First printing press in America is set up in Cambridge by Stephen and Mathew Day.

1640   *Massachusetts*   Publication of *Bay Psalm Book.* Population of Massachusetts reaches twenty thousand.

1641   *Virginia*   Lord William Berkeley is appointed Governor.

1641   Massachusetts recognizes slavery.

1641   *Canada*   October 14: Montreal is founded by Samuel de Champlain.

1642   August 22: Outbreak of the English Civil War.

1644   *Virginia*   Indians kill approximately three hundred colonists but colony is much larger than during the 1622 attack. Indians are defeated, driven to reservations.

1644   *Rhode Island*   Roger Williams obtains patent to lands around Providence, writes pamphlet *The Bloody Tenent of Persecution* which defends religious freedom for all mankind, including non-Christians.

1645   August 30: New Englanders sign peace treaty with Narragansett Indians.

1646   First Civil War ends with capture of Oxford by Parliamentary forces.

1646	First published mariner's charts using Mercator's projection, not quickly adopted.
1647	Quaker doctrine first preached.
1648	Beginning of Second Civil War because of disunion between Scots and Parliament, with the King allied this time to the Scots.
1648	End of Thirty Years' War.
1648–49	*Massachusetts* Very virulent smallpox and whooping cough sweeps hardest from Scituate to Cape Cod, and as far north as Boston and Roxbury. Towns of Scituate and Barnstable declare November 15, 1649, a "Day of Humiliation."
1649	January 30: Charles I is beheaded; end of Second Civil War.

1650–1674

1650	English invasion, conquest of Scotland.
1650	*Massachusetts* Harvard College is chartered.
1651	John Playford's *English Dancing Master*.
1652	Rhode Island recognizes slavery.
1652	*Massachusetts* June 10: John Hull establishes mint in Boston.
1652	*Massachusetts* October 29: Massachusetts Bay Colony declares itself an independent commonwealth.
1653	Oliver Cromwell is named Lord Protector.
1654	*Regensburg, Germany* Experiment demonstrates air pressure. Otto von Guericke uses vacuum pump to remove air from a hollow metal cylinder; sixteen horses cannot pull it apart.
1654	*New York* Jacob Barsimson becomes the first known Jewish settler in America.
1656	England and Spain at war. Jamaica is captured from Spain by Sir William Penn, the colonist's father.
1657	Chemist Robert Boyle's *Mechanica Hydraulica-Pneumatica*.
1657	*Massachusetts* William Bradford dies in office.
1658	Spain is defeated at Battle of the Dunes; war ends.
1658	*Massachusetts* May 29: The General Court bans Quaker meetings.
1658	September 3: Oliver Cromwell dies.
1660	May: Restoration of the Monarchy; ascension of Charles II.
1661–65	Punitive Clarendon Code is enacted, cutting Dissenters out of government and denying them the right to worship.
1661	Virginia recognizes slavery.
1662	Robert Boyle publishes law of gases in *New Experiments Physico-Mechanicall* and *Sceptical Chemist*.

1662	*New York* Iroquois smallpox outbreak kills more than one thousand people out of no more than ten thousand.
1663	Samuel Butler's *Hudibras.*
1663	March 24: The Carolinas are chartered.
1664	Charles Cotton publishes parody of *Book I Aeneid*, so popular it goes through six editions in his lifetime.
1664	*New York, New Jersey* September 7: Dutch surrender New Amsterdam. New Jersey granted to Duke of York.
1665	Great Plague of London kills 68,596.
1666	Great Fire of London.
1666	France and Holland declare war on England.
1666	Robert Boyle's *Origin of Forms and Quantities.*
1666	*Massachusetts* Boston's first major smallpox epidemic kills about forty of four thousand inhabitants.
1667	*Virginia* Hurricane comes up James River Valley; eye circles Jamestown without breaking out into calm. Secretary of Colony Thomas Ludwell recounts ten thousand houses blown down, almost all food crops lost.
1667	John Milton's *Paradise Lost.*
1667	July 21: Peace of Breda ends Second Anglo-Dutch War, establishes English control of New Netherlands.
1668	*New York* Outbreak of yellow fever kills many people, leads to a "General Day of Humiliation" in September because of high mortality.
1670	July 8: By Treaty of Madrid, England and Spain agree to respect each other's rights in American territories.
1673	Test Act of Parliament requiring officeholders to take Anglican sacrament, swear allegiance to the monarch, and confirm the monarch as head of the Church of England effectively bars non-Anglicans from office.
1674	*New York* Governor Edmund Andros arrives as agent for Duke of York.
1674	*New Jersey* Quakers buy Lord Berkeley's interest in New Jersey.

1675–1699

1675	*New England* King Philip's War, bloodiest colonial war. By year's end, out of 90 settlements in New England, fifty-two are attacked, twelve completely destroyed.
1675	*Massachusetts* August 2: Brookfield is attacked by Wampanoags.
1675	*New England* Hurricane; extensive tree, housing, shipping damage is reported in Connecticut, Rhode Island and Massachusetts.

1676	*Virginia* Bacon's Rebellion—Nathaniel Bacon leads rebellion against Governor Berkeley for failure to punish Indian attacks. Bacon drives Berkeley out, takes Jamestown, burns it. Bacon dies, the rebellion is put down. Bacon's lieutenants are executed, one possibly drawn and quartered. Indians are pushed west.
1676	*Massachusetts* February 10: Lancaster is attacked by Indians under King Philip.
1676	*Connecticut* June 12: Colonists under John Talcott defeat Indians under King Philip near Hadley.
1676	August 12: King Philip is shot, ending King Philip's War.
1676	*New Jersey* Quintipartite Deed divides New Jersey.
1677	*Virginia* Lord William Berkeley returns to England.
1677–78	*Massachusetts* Boston's second major outbreak of smallpox kills many more than in 1666, thirty in one day at the height of the epidemic.
1681	*New Jersey, Pennsylvania* William Penn buys proprietary rights to east New Jersey, is granted Pennsylvania.
1681	*New York* Governor Andros arrests the Governor of East Jersey in a jurisdictional dispute, is recalled to England.
1682	*Pennsylvania* William Penn arrives.
1682	La Salle reaches mouth of Mississippi and claims territory for France.
1683	*Connecticut* August 13: Hurricane with major flood of Connecticut River, which rises twenty-six feet above normal; all crops destroyed.
1684	Massachusetts Bay charter is revoked; Massachusetts becomes royal colony.
1685	February 6: Charles II declares himself a Catholic on deathbed, dies in bed of a stroke.
1685	Accession of James II.
1685	*Pennsylvania* Chief Justice Nicolas More is impeached.
1685	*France* Louis XIV revokes Edict of Nantes, which leads to 160,000 immigrants to England and elsewhere, bringing many skilled artisans and designers such as Daniel Marot with the latest designs. Many come to colonies.
1685	William Penn intercedes on behalf of Quakers with James II, gets immigration rights for prisoners to America.
1686	*New England* Edmund Andros is appointed governor of the new Dominion of New England.
1686	*South Carolina* Spain attacks from Florida, is driven off by a hurricane.
1688	November 5: Invasion of England by William III; flight of James II (The Glorious Revolution).

1688	*New Jersey* New Jersey is included in Dominion of New England.
1688	*Pennsylvania* Quakers publish first antislavery resolution.
1689	April 11: Ascension of William III and Mary; beginning of King William's War (England and the United Provinces versus France and Spain).
1689	Toleration Act allows Protestant dissenters to worship in areas licensed by Anglican bishops. Catholics are not tolerated.
1689	*New England* Governor Andros is arrested by Boston populace and transported to England in wake of Glorious Revolution, but is acquitted.
1690	John Locke's *Two Treatises on Government* and *An Essay Concerning Human Understanding*. *Treatises* establishes a precedent for the Declaration of Independence.
1690	*Massachusetts* First paper money is issued in colonies. Boston newspaper *Publick Occurrences* is first in colonies.
1690	English capture Port Royal, Nova Scotia. French and Indians destroy Casco, Maine.
1691	*Carolina* August 11: Carolina splits into two colonies.
1692	French invasion fleet is defeated at La Hogue.
1692	*Virginia* Edmund Andros appointed governor.
1692	Robert Boyle's *General History of the Air* is posthumously published.
1692	*Jamaica* June 7: Three earthquake shocks strike Port Royal, capital and largest English port in Caribbean, just before noon. Northern two-thirds of city slides under harbor, ships capsize, ground swallows people; nearly two thousand die. Kingston is built over old city.
1693	*Virginia* College of William and Mary is chartered, run by Anglican Church.
1693	John Locke's *Some Thoughts Concerning Education.*
1693	*Virginia* Hurricane on Eastern Shore changes many river courses, possibly affects Long Island.
1694	December: Death of Queen Mary from smallpox.
1695	Licensing Act is allowed to lapse, revoking old form of government censorship by issuing printing monopolies; government settles for postpublication libel laws. Beginning of free press.
1696	*Maryland* King William's School (St. John's College) is chartered.
1697	September 3: Peace of Ryswyk ends King William's War.
1697	*Virginia* Church authorities obtain recall of Edmund Andros.

1699	*Virginia* Fourth statehouse at Jamestown burns. Williamsburg (named for King William III of Orange) is founded, capital is moved there.
1699	*Massachusetts* King William's War ends locally with signing of treaty at Casco, Maine.
1699	*Massachusetts* July 6: Pirate Captain Kidd is captured at Boston, extradited to England for trial.
1699	*South Carolina* First positively identified Charles Town yellow-fever epidemic begins late August and kills between 170 and 191 people, or 3 to 7 percent. The receiver-general, the provost marshal, the chief justice and nearly half the assembly perish, causing considerable confusion.

1700–1724

1700	William, last surviving child of Duke of Gloucester and Anne, dies at the age of 11.
1700	William III assembles "Grand Alliance" and begins War of the Spanish Succession, called Queen Anne's War in America.
1700	*South Carolina* September 14: Hurricane strikes Charles Town. Two ships full of evacuees from a settlement of Scots in Panama are caught while waiting to cross the bar; over one hundred people are lost.
1701	Charles II of Spain dies, wills all of his domains to Louis XIV's grandson. French accept will instead of treaties; war escalates.
1701	Charter of the Society for the Propagation of the Gospel.
1701	*Connecticut* Yale University is chartered.
1701	*Virginia* July 24: Detroit is founded by French.
1702	March 8: William III dies of complications from a broken collarbone sustained in a riding accident; Queen Anne ascends.
1702	May 3: Queen Anne's War begins in Europe.
1702	*Florida* English force from South Carolina besieges St. Augustine, burns town.
1702	*New Jersey* East and West are united under one governor.
1702–03	*Massachusetts* Boston experiences outbreaks of both smallpox and scarlet fever, loses about 4 percent of population or three hundred out of seven thousand people.
1702	*New York* Yellow-fever outbreak kills 20 people daily, some 570 total, or about 10 percent of the population.
1703	*New Jersey* Charters are revoked, East Jersey and West Jersey are made royal colonies.

1704	Battle of Blenheim.
1704	*Massachusetts* Abenaki Indians attack Deerfield, kill over fifty people.
1706	*Pennsylvania* Philadelphia presbytery is organized.
1706	October 14–16, November 6: Two hurricanes. The first is in the Hudson River valley and causes the greatest flooding then known. The second is offshore and causes extensive damage, catching two fleets, one inbound, one outbound for Virginia; at least fourteen ships are lost, many more damaged.
1706	*South Carolina* Charles Town yellow-fever epidemic. The French and Spanish hear of the epidemic and send a fleet of five ships to demand the city's surrender. Governor Johnson stations the militia away from the city and repulses the attack with one loss. The fever, however, kills about sixty-five out of thirteen hundred people, including many prominent citizens.
1707	*North Carolina* Worst winter in local history.
1709	Act for the Naturalization of European Protestants becomes impetus for massive immigration by Palatines, others.
1711	*North Carolina* September 22: Beginning of Tuscarora Indian War.
1712	*Virginia* September: English naturalist Mark Catesby in Virginia studying natural history, cf. 1722.
1712	*Pennsylvania* Assembly bans slavery.
1712	*Carolina* Separation of North and South.
1713	*Massachusetts* Anglican King's Chapel in Boston gets first organ in colonies.
1713	April 11: Treaty of Utrecht ends War of Spanish Succession, leaves ambiguities in America.
1713	*South Carolina* End of Tuscarora Indian War.
1713	*South Carolina* September 16: Hurricane hits north of Charles Town, kills about seventy people. A ship is carried three miles inland.
1714	August 1: Queen Anne dies; ascension of King George I.
1715	*Carolina* Yamassee Indians kill several hundred colonists.
1716	*New England* Major storm, October 13–14, grazes Cape Cod, Martha's Vineyard, dismasts many vessels at sea.
1716	*Virginia* September: Governor Alexander Spottswood's Knights of the Golden Horseshoe return from successfully cresting the Blue Ridge.
1721	*Massachusetts* June 26: Smallpox inoculations are administered in a Boston hospital as Boston loses 844 people

out of 11,000, with 6,000 infected. Many flee Boston.

1722   Catesby returns for four years to finish collecting for his *Natural History of Carolina, Florida and the Bahama Islands.*

1724   *Virginia, Maryland* August 23: "The Greate Gust" damages most of tobacco and corn crops, causes flooding, possibly is followed by a second storm which destroys crops in South Carolina.

1725–1749

1727   *Massachusetts* Earthquake causes much commentary in Boston area.

1727   *New England* September 27: Connecticut, Rhode Island, Massachusetts, Boston and Marblehead report one fatality and several injuries, extensive home, crop and tree damage from hurricane. Trees are torn up by roots from Connecticut to Cape Ann.

1728   Border between North Carolina and Virginia is surveyed; Great Dismal Swamp is named.

1728   *Beggar's Opera* opens in London, runs thirty-two nights, an overwhelming success. It forces Handel to close down his operatic academy and spawns a multitude of copycat ballad operas, popular in the colonies.

1728   *South Carolina* August 13: Hurricane at Charles Town sinks twenty-three ships, destroys two thousand barrels of rice, kills several people and is reported as a disaster as far away as New York.

1728   *South Carolina* Charles Town yellow-fever epidemic kills many people, brings city life to a standstill as many flee to the country.

1729   *Maryland* Baltimore is officially founded.

1732   Painter and engraver William Hogarth's *Harlot's Progress* is published.

1732   *Virginia* George Washington is born.

1732   *Pennsylvania* Benjamin Franklin publishes *Poor Richard's Almanac.*

1732   *South Carolina* Charles Town yellow-fever epidemic kills 130 whites and an uncertain number of black slaves; many flee city to outlying plantations.

1733   *Georgia* James Edward Oglethorpe founds Savannah.

1735   William Hogarth's *The Rake's Progress* is published.

1735   William Hogarth successfully pushes for Engraver's Copyright Act.

1735   *South Carolina* *Hob in the Well* is first opera performance in colonies, in Charles Town.

15

1735	*Massachusetts* October 30: John Adams is born.
1736	William Hogarth's *Before and After* is published.
1737	*Massachusetts* Boston celebrates first St. Patrick's Day in colonies.
1738	*New Jersey* New Jersey gets own governor, no longer shares with New York.
1739	*South Carolina, Florida* War of Jenkins' Ear, a border dispute between England and Spain, breaks out. Governor James Edward Oglethorpe of Georgia besieges St. Augustine; Governor William Gooch of Virginia attacks Cartagena, Colombia. Both unsuccessful.
1740	*Pennsylvania* Charity School (University of Pennsylvania) is chartered.
1741	*American Magazine*, first American periodical.
1741	*Pennsylvania* Bethlehem is founded by Moravians.
1742	*Georgia* Spanish attack is repulsed in Battle of Bloody Marsh.
1743	*Virginia* Thomas Jefferson is born.
1743	*Pennsylvania to New Hampshire* November 2: Hurricane, usual extensive damage. Ben Franklin observed it traveled opposite direction of its winds—key to beginning to understand cyclonic nature of hurricanes.
1743	French and Indians begin King George's War with attacks on English settlements in Canada, Maine and New York.
1743	*New York* Between July 25 and September 25, 217 people die from yellow-fever outbreak.
1745	*New York* Another outbreak of yellow fever.
1745	William Hogarth's *Marriage a la Mode*.
1745–46	The Jacobite rebellion in Scotland is defeated, leading to the CLEARINGS in which inhabitants are forcibly removed to the New World; results in many Scots-Irish settling in western North Carolina, Virginia, Maryland and Pennsylvania.
1746	*New Jersey* October 22: College of New Jersey (Princeton) is founded.
1747	William Hogarth's *Industry and Idleness*.
1748	Treaty of Aix-la-Chapelle ends King George's War, restores Louisbourg and Cape Breton, taken by English, to French.
1748	*France* Baron de Montesquieu publishes *The Spirit of the Laws*, an influential book whose ideas are found in the Declaration of Independence and the Constitution.
1749	*North Carolina to Massachusetts* ca. October 18: Major hurricane grazes coast, uproots trees, cuts new inlets, causes

extensive flooding, killing many people and destroying many ships from Cape Hatteras to Boston. Norfolk is flooded as far as a mile inland.

1750–1774

1750   Jean-Jacques Rousseau's *A Discourse on the Sciences and the Arts.*

1752   September 2: England adopts Gregorian calendar; this date is redesignated September 14. New Year's is moved to January 1 from March 25.

1752   *South Carolina* September 15: Most severe hurricane in colonial times hits Charles Town. It destroys all shipping in harbor, entire wharf, warehouse district with all the goods, the forts around the town; all roads are impass-able, plantations are heavily damaged for thirty miles around, and most trees are blown down. Most of the populace is in imminent danger of drowning until water levels drop five feet in ten minutes, saving them.

1752   *South Carolina to Maryland* October 1: Another hurricane hits Charles Town and the North Carolina coast, comes inland in central Virginia and raises streams thirty feet. Many tobacco barns, crops, dams, bridges, etc. are lost.

1752   *New Jersey* After losing two brothers at sea en route to ordi-nation, John Frelinghuysen defies the Classis in Holland and opens a seminary in Raritan (Sommerville) to or-dain ministers in the New World. It later becomes Queen's College, then Rutgers.

1754   Jean-Jacques Rousseau's *The Origin of Inequality* introduces idea that primal man and nature are inherently good.

1754   *Virginia* Militia Major George Washington starts French and Indian War by attacking a French party in a dispute over French activity on land claimed by Virginia near Pittsburgh. He also builds and later surrenders Fort Necessity.

1754   *New York* King's College (later Columbia University) is chartered.

1755   *Virginia* General Edward Braddock marches on Fort Duquesne, is killed in ambush. Washington shows his mettle by organizing troops.

1755   *Maryland* Nine hundred French Canadians expelled from Nova Scotia arrive in Maryland; some twelve hun-dred are lost at sea.

1755   Samuel Johnson's *Dictionary.*

1755   Lisbon is destroyed by great earthquake felt in Boston, New

York and Philadelphia. John Winthrop of Harvard College recognizes wave functions long before official discovery.

1756   French and Indian War spills over to Europe, where it is known as the Seven Years' War.

1756   *New York*   August 4: French capture Fort Oswego.

1757   *New York*   August 9: French capture Fort William Henry on Lake George.

1758   *New York*   July 8: British lose two thousand in failed attack on Fort Ticonderoga.

1758   *Canada*   July 28: British capture fortress Louisbourg and six thousand French.

1758   *Virginia and Pennsylvania*   General Forbes builds a wilderness road from Carlisle to Bedford and, on November 26, takes Fort Duquesne (Pittsburgh), renaming it Fort Pitt.

1759   *New York*   Fort Niagara falls to British, breaking French lines to Ohio Valley; French abandon Fort Ticonderoga.

1759   *Canada*   September 18: Quebec falls to British under General James Wolfe who dies in battle.

1759   *Pennsylvania*   December 13: Michael Hillegas opens music store in Philadelphia.

1760   *Canada*   September 8: Montreal falls to British.

1760   *Virginia*   November 29: Detroit falls to British.

1760   *Virginia*   Bray School is founded in Williamsburg for free and slave black children.

1761   *Connecticut, Rhode Island and Massachusetts*   October 24: Major hurricane. Near Providence, "on both roads east and west so far as we have heard, the roofs of houses, tops of barns, and fences have been blown down, and it is said thousands of trees have been torn up by the roots by the violence of the above storm."

1762   Jean-Jacques Rousseau's *The Social Contract* establishes the idea that a government's authority rests upon the people, who could withdraw it.

1763   Peace of Paris ends French and Indian War. France trades Canada to England for captured sugar island of Guadeloupe; Spain trades Florida to England for Cuba.

1763   *Virginia*   May 7: Chief Pontiac attacks Fort Detroit.

1763   October 7: Proclamation of 1763 makes settlement west of Alleghenies unlawful.

1763   *Virginia*   Young Patrick Henry breaks precedent and speaks within first week of office as a burgess, delivers "Caesar and Brutus" speech at Williamsburg. (He did

	not say, "If this be treason, make the most of it.")
1763–64	*Massachusetts* Boston loses 170 people out of a population of about 15,000 to 20,000 to smallpox. Many are inoculated, including the poor. Disease spreads to Cambridge, but inoculation keeps mortality to six.
1764	*Rhode Island* College of Rhode Island (later Brown University) is chartered.
1765	*Virginia* Patrick Henry finds colony's books one hundred thousand pounds short after death of John Robinson, Speaker of the House and treasurer of colony; publicizes scandal and obtains first separation of powers. But Peyton Randolph, Robinson's successor and protégé, survives to be elected president of First and Second Continental Congresses. Randolph dies in office.
1765	March 22: Stamp Act is passed imposing tax on legal documents, newspapers, etc.
1765	College of Philadelphia opens first medical school in colonies.
1766	Oliver Goldsmith's *The Vicar of Wakefield.*
1766	March 18: Parliament passes Declaratory Act giving itself authority to pass laws binding upon the colonies, repeals Stamp Act after intense opposition from colonies.
1766	*New Jersey* November 10: Queen's College (Rutgers) is chartered.
1766	*New York* December 19: Parliament suspends the legislature for voting against the Quartering Act.
1767	*Massachusetts* June 6: John Hancock is accused of smuggling; his sloop *Liberty* is seized by British customs officials.
1767	June 29: Parliament passes Townshend Revenue Act, imposes duties on tea and other goods.
1768	*Massachusetts* May 17: Frigate *Romney* arrives to protect customs officials.
1768	*Virginia* June 27: Two days after a group of gentlemen take the dangerous and radical step of inoculating their families and friends against smallpox, the Norfolk population riots and destroys their homes.
1768	*Massachusetts* August 1: Boston merchants sign non-importation agreement.
1768	*Massachusetts* October 1: British troops land in Boston.
1769	*New York, New Jersey* Dividing Line is determined.
1769	*New Hampshire* Dartmouth is chartered.
1769	Comet visible throughout colonies, sparks much comment.
1769	*North Carolina to New Hampshire* September 8: Major

19

storm hits New Bern, Williamsburg, Annapolis, Philadelphia, New Brunswick, New York and Boston in twelve hours, destroying many trees, bridges and houses and causing many shipwrecks.

1769   Monthly mail packets begin between New York and Charles Town, South Carolina.

1770   *Massachusetts* March 5: Boston Massacre. Five colonists are killed by British soldiers.

1770   Another comet visible throughout colonies, sparks much comment; Philadelphia mathematician David Rittenhouse plots orbit.

1770   *South Carolina* College of Charles Town is chartered.

1770   *New England, Connecticut to Maine* October 19: Hurricane, with second highest tide of all time lacking one foot, at Boston. Much damage to wharves and goods.

1770   Oliver Goldsmith's *The Deserted Village*.

1772   *Rhode Island* June 10: British customs schooner *Gaspe* is set on fire near Providence by colonists.

1773   *South Carolina* First museum in colonies opens in Charles Town.

1773   April 27: Parliament passes Tea Act, which leads to Boston Tea Party.

1773   *Rhode Island* May 28: First service at Touro Synagogue, Newport.

1773   *Massachusetts* December 16: Boston Tea Party.

1774   Oliver Goldsmith's *She Stoops to Conquer*.

1774   March 31: First of the Intolerable Acts is passed as punishment for Boston Tea Party.

1775–1783

1775   *North Carolina to Pennsylvania* Early September: Hurricane exacts a higher toll on life than any previous one, as well as massive crop damage. Storm went up Chesapeake and kept going.

1775   *Canada* Mid-September: Hurricane hits Newfoundland, creates £140,000 damage to fishing fleets; four thousand sailors are lost, mostly Irish and British.

1775   *Massachusetts* April 19: Gunfire exchanged at Lexington and Concord; Congress dispatches Washington to command army.

1775   *Virginia* April 20: Lord Dunmore, last royal governor, seizes powder from Public Magazine in Williamsburg. Patrick Henry raises militia and demands return or payment. Dunmore pays.

1775	*South Carolina* Francis Salvador is elected to the South Carolina Provincial Congress, first Jew to hold elected office.
1775	*Pennsylvania* Society for the Relief of Free Negroes is founded in Philadelphia.
1776	*Virginia* January 1: Norfolk is burned by Lord Dunmore.
1776	January 10: Thomas Paine's *Common Sense* sells more than one hundred thousand copies in only a few months.
1776	*Virginia* May 15: Virginia declares independence, instructs delegation in Philadelphia to move the issue in a document written by Edmund Pendleton which becomes a draft for Thomas Jefferson's Declaration.
1776	*Virginia* June 12: George Mason's Virginia Declaration of Rights is adopted and becomes the basis for the Bill of Rights.
1776	*New Jersey* July 2: New Jersey grants women suffrage.
1776	*Pennsylvania* August 2: Declaration of Independence is signed.
1776	*Virginia* December 5: Phi Beta Kappa founded at William and Mary.
1777	*New York* Saratoga campaign.
1777	*South Carolina* May 20: Cherokees sign Treaty of DeWitts Corner, give up all land in South Carolina.
1778	February 6: France recognizes United States, becomes ally.
1778	*Pennsylvania* June 6: British peace commissioners arrive in Philadelphia.
1778	*North Carolina to New York* September 12: Hurricane breaks up encounter between British and French fleets, pummels troops at Newport after destroying much of the corn crop in North Carolina, driving prices to fifty shillings a bushel.
1779	June 21: Spain declares war on England.
1780	*Virginia* Capital is moved to Richmond to keep the British Navy from cutting off the political leaders in Williamsburg.
1781	*South Carolina, North Carolina* October 7 and 8: Hurricane at Charles Town during occupation by British troops causes moderate damage but destroys a valuable store of salt at Wilmington.
1781	*Virginia* Battle of Yorktown, Battle off the Capes are last major battles of Revolution.
1782	March: Parliament votes to negotiate peace with America.
1782	March 20: Lord North, prime minister of England, resigns under pressure for peace.

1782	August 7: Washington establishes Order of the Purple Heart.
1783	September 3: Treaty of Paris ends Revolution.
1783	November 2: Washington delivers "Farewell Address to the Army."
1783	November 23: Last British troops leave New York.

GENERAL BIBLIOGRAPHY

Black, Jeremy and Roy Porter, ed. *A Dictionary of Eighteenth-Century World History.* Cambridge, Mass: Blackwell Reference, 1994.

Davies, K. G. *The North Atlantic World in the Seventeenth Century.* Minneapolis: University of Minnesota Press, 1974. An excellent broad overview with many details, not only for the English colonies but for French and Spanish.

Gould, William, ed. *Lives of the Georgian Age, 1714–1837.* New York: Barnes and Noble Books, 1978. This is an excellent biographical dictionary for the period.

Hoffman, Ronald, and Peter J. Albert, eds. *Women in the Age of the American Revolution.* Charlottesville, Va.: University Press of Virginia, 1989. An excellent study with many tables, statistics and points of view.

Holliday, Carl. *Woman's Life in Colonial Days.* Boston: Cornhill Pub. Co.; 1922. Reprint, Detroit, Mich.: Omnigraphics, 1990. An old book, but the information is carefully qualified and based largely on primary sources. Note that it is mostly about wealthy women.

Horowitz, David. *The First Frontier: The Indian Wars and America's Origins, 1607–1776.* New York: Simon and Schuster, 1978.

Jennings, Francis. *The Invasion of America: Indians, Colonialism and the Cant of Conquest.* New York: Norton, 1976.

Noël Hume, Ivor. *A Guide to Artifacts of Colonial America.* New York: Alfred A. Knopf, 1970. An encyclopedic field guide to the rubbish of everyday life for archaeologists, this book details the changes in styles and the appropriate dates for just about anything found in the ground, including gun furniture, bottles, pottery, buckles, iron implements and hundreds more items.

———. *Martin's Hundred.* New York: Alfred A. Knopf, 1982. This book reads like a detective novel, not surprising since its archaeologist author writes them under a nom de plume. It details the excavations of one of Virginia's small settlements, destroyed in the Indian Massacre of 1622, but along the way includes a great deal of information about everyday life. A must read.

Quimby, Ian M.G., ed. *Arts of the Anglo-American Community in the Seventeenth Century: Twentieth Annual Winterthur Conference,* 1974.

Charlottesville, Va. University Press of Virginia, 1975. A series of papers about various aspects of the decorative arts. Especially useful for its extensive definitions of fabrics.

Raimo, John W. *Biographical Directory of American Colonial and Revolutionary Governors, 1607–1789.* Westport, Conn.: Meckler Books, 1980.

Riddel, Edwin, ed. *Lives of the Stuart Age, 1603–1714.* New York: Barnes and Noble Books, 1976. This is an excellent biographical dictionary for the period.

Smith, James Morton, ed. *Seventeenth-Century America: Essays in Colonial History.* New York: Norton, 1972. Essays on many aspects of early life including Native American relations, religion and demographics.

A SAMPLING OF CONTEMPORARY SOURCES: SHORT LISTINGS

Beverley, Robert. *The History and Present State of Virginia.*

Bradford, William. *History of Plymouth Plantation.*

Butler, Samuel. *Hudibras.*

Byrd, William. *Secret Diary of William Byrd of Westover.*

———. *Histories of the Dividing Line Betwixt Virginia and North Carolina.*

Chippendale, Thomas. *The Gentleman and Cabinetmaker's Director.*

Fielding, Henry. *History of the Adventures of Joseph Andrews.*

———. *The History of Tom Jones, a Foundling.*

Fithian, Philip Vickers. *Journal and Letters.*

Fontaine, John. *The Journal of John Fontaine: An Irish Huguenot Son in Spain and Virginia.*

Goldsmith, Oliver. *The Vicar of Wakefield.*

Hamilton, Alexander. *The History of the Ancient and Honorable Tuesday Club.*

Harrower, John. *The Journal of John Harrower: An Indentured Servant in the Colony of Virginia.*

Kalm, Peter. "Journeys in America."

Lawson, John. *A New Voyage to Carolina.*

Letters of Benjamin Franklin and Jane Meecham.

Letters of John and Abigail Adams.

Sheridan, Richard Brinsley. *The Critic.*

Woodford, William. *The Woodford Letter Book.*

The writings of John Smith, William Strachey, William Penn, Franklin and many other important people (mentioned in passing in the text) are available and provide entertaining first-person accounts of their days, as well as good examples of language at the time.

REGIONAL MATERIALS AND HISTORICAL OVERVIEW

State government museums, libraries and departments of historic preservation, as well as nonaffiliated historical societies, may have extensive publication programs including pamphlets, brochures, newsletters and books covering many subjects related to their areas. Call or write for a listing. Sample subjects include women, military activity, crime and punishment, music, architecture, famous personages and specific events. Also look into Federal Writer's Project works for each state.

W.W. Norton published a series of bicentennial histories for the American Association of State and Local History. There is one for each colony, and they provide good to excellent overviews.

OTHER RESOURCES

Historic Urban Plans, 201 Cliff Park Road, Ithaca, New York 14850, publishes reproductions of many early city maps and views. (607) 272-6277.

The Museum Directory, American Association of Museums, available in most good libraries and larger museums, is a good way to find local sources. It lists museums and historical societies by location with a topical index. Listings survey collections, libraries and services. The larger museums often have publication programs, lecture series and bookstores.

The National Park Service, Department of the Interior, has many colonial sites. They do local research and may have affiliated organizations which run bookstores. Most sites also have guidebooks and pamphlets.

State and local historical Societies, Commissions and Departments of Historic Preservation can be good contacts to find local materials. Check the telephone directories (available at most large libraries) for the capital cities of interest, and ask your reference librarian for guides to associations.

Reenactor organizations and newsletters: Reenactors vary in accuracy, but the best do meticulous research and provide a wealth of information about details of costuming, individual history and specific events. Becoming involved with a group is a good way to experience everyday life in the period. A growing number of museums host Military Through the Ages (MTA) programs, which collect reenactors from the Picts to Vietnam. These museums can provide contacts, as well as opportunities to see people living in the period of choice.

The Brigade of the American Revolution is one of the umbrella organizations for Revolutionary reenactors. Contact Mr. Walter Myer,

Adjutant, 27 Compton Avenue, Plainfield, New Jersey 07063-1105.

Smoke and Fire News. This newspaper for reenactors includes listings of events. Contact Ms. Donlyn Meyers, Publisher, P.O. Box 166, Grand Rapids, Ohio 43522. (419) 832-0303.

The Moderne Aviso is a bimonthly publication for reenactors and enthusiasts, including information concerning Europe and America during the Founding Age (1560–1705). Contact Mary Aist, 9512 Dubarry Avenue, Seabrook Maryland 20706.

Period art can show much about the period. Care must be used, however, to understand the artist's working methods (one self-portrait shows an artist painting a complex still life from nothing more than a blank wall) and the context and allegorical meaning of the objects shown. See Ivor Noël Hume's *Martin's Hundred* (bibliographical information on page 22) for more about this.

Contact the history faculty at your local college or university and make good use of the school's library.

Bay

20

5

y is very
ll of Flatts —
the Sea
ngerous
k and
t
or d
d We
tts in
place of
Vessells and
r here .

↑ Rocky ground

4

10 30

Plymouth
Bay
Cedar P. XI

Marks I.

4 7

Gurnet head

2 channel 10 way

Barnstable I.
reason of s
Run a Shoal

Monement
high Land

Browns Sunken
Islands

7 Note that the
Bars are but
are set down
Water, and
7 there is the

3

3

Plymouth

Barnsta
c.

3

ds Bay is very dangerous
g and Flowing is but small

3

12 F
7 F

Sandwich

XI

2

Bay .

Barnstable

Tucgguiset
Woods Pt

hole

North Chann
3 Coarse Sand 3
Southacks Chan
Horseshoe sand

rpolin Cove

5

Tucgguiset Point

3

PART ONE

Almanac

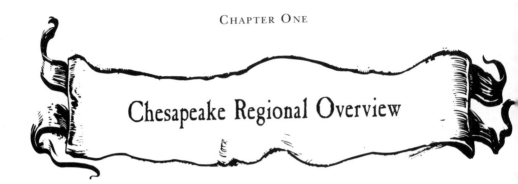

Chapter One

Chesapeake Regional Overview

The Spanish began to colonize the New World shortly after Columbus's first voyage. Within fifty years, Spain had brought back enough bullion to increase the net wealth of all Europe by a factor of between two and five. This money created severe financial problems, but Philip II offset the effect by using the money to raise vast fleets and armies to fight for the Catholic faith and the Holy Roman Empire, both threatened by the Protestants in the north. England, the low countries and even Catholic France, with its large Huguenot population, all desperately needed cash to fight back. This need drove the first colonial efforts. Only later, in New England, did colonization take on a religious motive.

Spain claimed all the New World north of Mexico as part of La Florida, and any other countries were seen as interlopers, especially if they threatened to pick off Spanish treasure ships as the French did from Fort Caroline (at modern-day Jacksonville) in 1563. Spain brutally destroyed this settlement, killing nearly eight hundred men, women and children, even after taking them prisoner. It was impossible to hold a number of prisoners equal in size to one's own force, and unlikely the prisoners could be fed on the end of a supply line which might run three years between visits. An early colonial venture was a winner-take-all gamble. Thus, the Spanish threat became a major concern for colonial planners well into the eighteenth century, and numerous forays were mounted from both sides.

In a sense, then, the colonies must be seen as an integral part of European nation-states' struggle for emergence, such as France under Richelieu, England under Elizabeth and Buckingham, Sweden under Gustavus Adolphus, and Germany under Frederick the Great.

The Chesapeake region was the first in which the English established permanent settlements, having explored it from the ill-fated Roanoke colonies in the 1580s. This region was ideally suited for communication with England and defense against the Spanish threat. Many geographers insisted the Northwest Passage to China must be found near this area, placing the English, in theory, in a perfect position to dominate this revolutionary trade route.

The dominant feature of this region is the Chesapeake Bay, one of North America's largest and most fertile marine estuaries. The deepwater navigable coastline of the bay in the early period must have exceeded 3,000 miles, with some rivers extending over 150 miles inland before reaching the fall line. This area is characterized by sandy soils, long rivers and peninsulas with easy access to deep water, and a temperate climate.

Unlike New England, the Chesapeake was settled for economic gain. From 1612, when John Rolfe developed a marketable tobacco that grew well here, until just before the Revolution, tobacco was the only cash crop of the region. Then, due to a history of unstable economies and price wars between Virginia and Maryland, many planters expanded to wheat, flax, corn and even iron and other manufactures.

Until the eve of the Civil War, the average plantation in the Chesapeake region consisted of a single family who lived in a one-room house some 16' × 20' or 20' × 20' on 50 to 250 acres. If lucky they had one or two slaves, who each cost up to five years' gross income. The house was usually frame with riven siding and dirt floors.

Servants were usually indentures or slaves. The headright system (see page 33) was imitated throughout the region after its success in encouraging immigration to Virginia.

Because tobacco consumed so much land, the population was decentralized. Large plantations took the place of towns, providing the essential trades of coopers, blacksmiths and shoemakers, as well as jobbing the smaller planters' shipments together and selling imported goods. Towns existed only for governmental purposes, or in locations where they were necessary for trade, such as the fall line of rivers.

Before the growth of slash-and-burn tobacco agriculture, the waters of the Chesapeake were deep and clear. When the Jamestown settlers tied their ships to trees on shore, the ships were in thirty-six feet of water, and large schools of huge sturgeon and other fish existed.

The insular nature of the Chesapeake isolated many areas, allowing communities of free blacks and pockets of pirates to exist.

Although not technically part of the Chesapeake, northern North Carolina is included in this chapter because of similarities between the Albemarle and the Chesapeake and the existence of tobacco as the major cash crop there. This area was in fact settled from Virginia largely before the establishment of the Carolinas as colonies. It did not get the subsidies for colonization that the southern portions did. The Albemarle was too shallow, so Norfolk served as northern North

APPROXIMATE POPULATION OF REGION	
1688	75,000
1715	145,200
1765	720,000

Carolina's port. (For information on Norfolk's ties to northern North Carolina, see page 181.)

The southern forests were largely yellow pines and mature hardwoods, with trees such as white oaks, chestnuts and walnuts reaching over ninety feet tall with branches spreading as wide. Trunks were often sixteen to twenty feet in circumference, and limbs often did not branch out until twenty or more feet in the air. Some areas, like coastal North Carolina and Virginia, had large stands of pitch pines and cypresses forming pine barrens, which became more common the farther south one went. Early accounts from Virginia speak of riding horseback through the forest without concern because the undergrowth was so sparse and the tree limbs so high.

The first European settlers sought a marketable commodity to use as the basis of an economy, and they carefully studied the forests for any candidates. Even with all the commercial interest, one thing that comes through the early documents, and even later accounts by travelers and immigrants, is the awe at their first encounter with the virgin forests. Most Europeans had never seen anything like them anywhere, because Europe, and particularly England, had seriously depleted its forests by the 1400s.

In their search for commercial commodities, early settlers evaluated pitch and tar from pine trees, exotic woods for cabinetry and musical instruments, caged birds, lumber, wines, medicinals, precious metals and stones, dyestuffs, foods and beverages, furs, fishing, and industries requiring large amounts of wood to sustain them, such as iron founding, glassmaking and shipbuilding.

VIRGINIA

Governors (With Dates of Service in Virginia)
1607, Edward Maria Wingfield; 1607–8, John Sicklemore (Ratcliffe); 1608, Matthew Scrivener; 1608–9, John Smith; 1609, 1627–29, Francis West; 1609–10, 1611–14, George Percy; 1610, 1611–14, Sir Thomas Gates; 1610–11, Thomas West, Lord De La Warr; 1611, 1614–16, Sir Thomas Dale; 1616–17, 1619–20, 1626–27, Sir George Yeardley; 1617–19, Sir Samuel Argall; 1619, Nathaniel Powell; 1621–26, 1639–42, Sir

Francis Wyatt; 1629–30, John Pott; 1630–35, 1637–39, Sir John Harvey; 1635–37, John West; 1642–44, 1645–52, 1660–61, 1662–77, Sir William Berkeley; 1644–45, Richard Kemp; 1652–55, Richard Bennett; 1655–57, Edward Digges; 1657–60, Samuel Mathews Jr.; 1661–62 Francis Moryson; 1677–78, Herbert Jeffreys; 1678–80, 1680–82, Sir Henry Chicheley; 1680, 1682–83, Thomas, Lord Culpeper; 1683–84, Nicholas Spencer; 1684–89, Francis, Lord Howard of Effingham; 1689–90, Nathaniel Bacon; 1690–92, 1698–1705, Francis Nicholson; 1692–98, Sir Edmund Andros; 1705–1706, Edward Nott; 1706–10, Edmund Jenings; 1710–22, Alexander Spottswood; 1722–26, Hugh Drysdale; 1726–27, Robert Carter; 1727–40, 1741–49, William Gooch; 1740–41, James Blair; 1749–50, Thomas Lee; 1750–51, Lewis Burwell; 1758, 1768, John Blair; 1758–68, Francis Faquier; 1768–70, Norborne Berkeley, Baron de Botetourt; 1770–71, William Nelson; 1771–75, John Murray, fourth Earl of Dunmore; 1775–76, Edmund Pendleton; 1776–79, Patrick Henry; 1779–81, Thomas Jefferson; 1781, William Fleming, Thomas Nelson Jr., David Jameson; 1781–84, Benjamin Harrison.

Religion

Anglican Church membership was required for the right to vote, called franchise. Some toleration for Protestants was established later. Catholics were generally suspect until very late. A fairly large Jewish community developed (late) in Norfolk and Richmond. The Shenandoah Valley saw sizable populations of Mennonites and other Germanic religions. Quakers were common. French Huguenots created settlements, and one member was influential enough to accompany Governor Spottswood on his expedition to the crest of the Blue Ridge as a Knight of the Golden Horseshoe. The Baptists took the colony by storm in the later period.

Franchise

Those qualifying for franchise were white, male, free (of indentures, apprenticeships, etc.), at least twenty-one years of age, owners of one hundred acres or fifty developed acres or holdings of similar value in town, and members of the Church of England. From 1619, an assembly comprised of two burgesses from each county met. After 1763, elections were triennial.

Towns

Jamestown; Williamsburg (earlier Middle Plantation, designed as a capital); Richmond (earlier Henricus); Fredericksburg, Alexandria and Petersburg (trading towns on the fall line); Norfolk (the port for northern North Carolina). An act of 1680 established twenty customs ports for tobacco inspection and duties collection: Bermuda Hundred,

APPROXIMATE POPULATION OF VIRGINIA

Year	Total	Slave	Indentured
1607	104	-	-
1618	1,000	-	-
1624	1,275	-	487
1640	8,000	-	-
1645	15,000	-	-
1670	40,000	2,000	6,000
1700	62,000	-	-
1715	95,000	23,000	-
1756	293,472	120,156	-
1775	500,000	200,000	-

Cobham, Hampton (earlier Kecoughtan, largest port in Virginia until 1750), Jamestown, Kinsale, Nansemond Town, New Castle, Norfolk, Northampton, Onancock, Patesfield, Powhatan, Queensborough, Queenstown, Tappahannock, Tindall's Point, Urbanna, Varina, West Point and Yorktown. Marlborough was added by act in 1691.

Population and Area

Virginia was the largest of the colonies and had about one-eighth of their Revolutionary population. It was also, until shortly before the Revolution, the wealthiest colony. As first claimed, Virginia extended from Maine to Florida and west to the Pacific. With time this area was narrowed by royal acts. Before the French and Indian War, the claim still ran to the Pacific and north to the Great Lakes, but after the war, Virginia ended at the Mississippi and included parts of today's Wisconsin, Michigan and Pennsylvania. Up to the 1680s, the Virginia population grew only because of immigration. In the five years before 1624, mortality ran approximately 75 percent.

In 1619, 811 servants were imported. Between 1623 and 1637, of 2,675 immigrants, 2,094, or 78 percent, were servants. This rate probably continued to about 1666, then dropped to about 1,500 a year for the rest of the century.

Virginia was named for Elizabeth the First—"The Virgin Queen"— by Sir Walter Raleigh. Originally settled by younger sons of titled families, Virginia saw itself as the breeding ground for the leadership of the American colonies. Running large plantations gave these sons practical experience. A heavy emphasis was placed on ties to England,

and many sons were schooled at the Inns of Court. The colony's government, and hence its law, were aristocratic, loyal to the monarchy but not strongly favoring Tory policies.

During the English Civil War (1642–1649) and Commonwealth (1649–1660), Virginia was a haven for loyalists. When a warship sent by Oliver Cromwell arrived in 1652 to demand the surrender of the colony to the Parliament, surrender was duly given, although the political impact was minimal.

In 1609 Sir George Sommers and Captain Christopher Newport were on their way to Virginia when they discovered Bermuda by running into it. In addition to inspiring *The Tempest*, this escapade provided the economically depressed English with a more attractive destination than Virginia, which was famous for the VIRGINIA BUG (actual disease or diseases unknown) and other maladies that killed a large number of immigrants in their first two years. Immigration shifted to Bermuda, only returning to Virginia in midcentury when Bermuda was incapable of handling more population.

To combat this loss of manpower, Virginia instituted the HEADRIGHT SYSTEM, in which a colonist was granted fifty acres of land for each person's passage to Virginia they paid for. Under this system, an aspiring planter would buy indentures, not land, and obtain both land and labor to work it. Between 1623 and 1637, out of some 2,675 immigrants to Virginia, at least 2,094, or 78 percent, were indentures.

The Indians of Virginia included about forty tribes, but over thirty were held together as a form of military dictatorship under the authority of Wahunsunacocke, or Powhatan. Powhatan played power politics with the new colonists in 1607, recognizing that a mere 104 settlers did not represent a major threat to his holdings. The colonists carried new weapons, however, and Powhatan used the colonists' lack of political alliances with other tribes in the area to settle some old scores.

At the same time, the great chief extended a helping hand to the English colonists, who often responded with an imperiousness based on their beliefs in their religious and cultural superiority belied by their own tenuous existence. Demanding and stealing food when it could have been acquired in a more civilized way, or planted, the settlers brought on themselves alternating periods of good relations and devastating starvation when they were not able to leave the safety of their forts to hunt.

The small amount of material known about the Powhatans yields some tantalizing clues, the significance of which will probably never be fully known. An early writer tells us that one of Powhatan's people came over the mountains from Mexico. No other evidence substantiates this claim, but based on existent trade routes, a single official escaping from the Spanish conquest of Mexico City could have come to act as an advisor to Powhatan, and certain elements of Powhatan's society are more reminiscent of the Aztecs than of the rest of the Algonquian eastern woodland Indians.

Another debated issue concerns Don Louis, the Indian boy kidnapped by the Spanish from a mission on the York River in the late sixteenth century, taken through the Caribbean to Spain, educated and then returned to his people, whereupon he instigated an attack upon the mission. It has been suggested that Don Louis was Opecancanough, Powhatan's brother and successor, who hated the English, but evidence does not support the assertion. Don Louis may have been a member of Powhatan's circle of advisors, however, giving Powhatan some firsthand knowledge of the European scene.

The Indians alternately helped and fought the English, until on March 22, 1622, they rose against the settlements along the James River and killed half the population of Virginia. This attack may have been prompted by English claims on the succession of Powhatan. Indian society was matrilineal, meaning power and property descended in the mother's line even though it was exercised by the men. Pocahontas, one of the many daughters of Powhatan, had married John Rolfe, an Englishman. Rolfe returned from an audience with the King in England and met with Opecancanough. Shortly thereafter the attack occurred. After a period of recovery, Opecancanough and his people were forced back. The attack was repeated in 1644 after Rolfe's son came to Virginia and met with Opecancanough, but the English were numerous enough to drive the remaining Indians onto reservations. Incursions by some outlying groups caused a war in 1676, after which the Indian threat to the colonists on anything other than a local level was virtually nonexistent.

Indians still residing in the settled areas continued to play a limited and local role, often as guides, trackers and interpreters on military and exploratory missions. Those living over the mountains were protected by the British, who, reacting to Indian concerns about westward expansion, in 1763 issued a proclamation declaring the ridge of Allegheny Mountain the westward limit of colonization. Due to this proclamation, the Indians sided with England in the Revolution, and the land-poor settlers supported the patriot side, which sought to expand.

MARYLAND

Governors (With Dates of Service in Maryland)
1634–43, 1644–45, 1646–47, Leonard Calvert; 1643–44, Giles Brent; 1645, Richard Ingle; 1646, Edward Hill; 1647–49, Thomas Greene; 1649–52, 1652–54, William Stone; 1652, 1654–58, a group of commis-

sioners appointed by Parliament; 1658–60, Josias Fendall; 1660–61, Philip Calvert; 1661–69, 1679–84, Charles Calvert, third Lord Baltimore; 1676, Jesse Wharton; 1676–79, Thomas Notley; 1684–88, a council of deputy governors; 1688–89, William Joseph; 1689–90, John Coode; 1690–92, Nehemiah Blakiston; 1692–93, Lionel Copley; 1693, 1694, Sir Edmund Andros; 1693–94, Nicholas Greenberry; 1694, Sir Thomas Lawrence; 1694–98, Francis Nicholson; 1698–1702, Nathaniel Blakiston; 1702–04, Thomas Tench; 1704–09, John Seymour; 1709–14, Edward Lloyd; 1714–20, John Hart; 1720, Thomas Brooke; 1720–27, Captain Charles Calvert; 1727–31, Benedict Leonard Calvert; 1731–32, 1733–42, 1747-52, Samuel Ogle; 1732–33, Charles Calvert, fifth Lord Baltimore; 1742–47, Thomas Bladen; 1752–53, Benjamin Tasker; 1753–69, Horatio Sharpe; 1769–76, Robert Eden; 1775–77, Daniel of St. Thomas Jenifer; 1777–79, Thomas Johnson; 1779–82, Thomas Sim Lee; 1782–85, William Paca.

Government

The FREEMEN of Maryland were required to attend the assembly, send a proxy, or meet in their HUNDREDS (a hundred was a grant of enough land to support one hundred fighting men) to elect burgesses to represent them in the assembly. Failure to perform their obligations resulted in a fine of twenty pounds of tobacco up to 1642. The custom of proxy disappeared about 1658. From 1689 to 1715, the colony was held by the crown, then restored to a Baltimore who was a Protestant. Assemblies were held throughout the period, with elections set for every three years.

Towns

Although Maryland shared many social features with Virginia, Maryland made a greater effort to create towns during the colonial period. There were town acts in 1668, 1669, 1671, and again in 1706, 1707 and 1708, but some of the towns created by act were never actually founded. As a result, it is difficult to list towns or dates. If your work requires this, see Reps's *Tidewater Towns* (bibliographical information is on page 38) or local histories. The first settlement and capital of Maryland was St. Mary's City (1634). Annapolis was created and the capital moved there in 1694. Baltimore was organized as a town of sixty one-acre lots in 1730 at the request of Charles and Daniel Carroll. In 1752, it contained only about twenty-five houses, but by the end of the period it became the largest port in the Chesapeake region and by 1790 the fifth largest city in the country.

Population and Area

Between 1633 and 1680 about twenty-one thousand indentures arrived, averaging about five hundred per year.

APPROXIMATE POPULATION OF MARYLAND

Year	Total	Slave	Indenture
1633	200	-	-
1660	8,000	-	-
1670	18,000	-	2,000
1707	33,833	4,657	3,000
1715	50,270	9,530	-
1755	153,564	46,200	5,400
1775	320,000	-	-

Maryland was chartered on June 20, 1632, a grant from Charles I to Cecilius, Lord Baltimore. Baltimore envisioned the colony as a haven for English Catholics but extended his official toleration to all religious sects. It was named for Henrietta Maria, sister of Louis XIII of France and Charles I's queen, and first settled in 1634 at St. Marie's Cittie. Maryland was originally envisioned for the area south of Virginia but was moved north to limit Dutch activity in the lower Delaware. The colony began at St. Mary's City, in a good location along the eastern Potomac on land purchased from Indians.

The king created tensions with Virginia to the south by removing a large part of Virginia's land but more importantly by granting Maryland all the fishing rights on border waterways, making the line the high-water mark on the Virginia side. These conflicts continued as the two colonies could not agree on a unified policy on tobacco production or quality control, resulting in price wars and general damage to the overall market. Religious issues were also a factor, as was Maryland's need to navigate through Virginia waters.

Typical of these concerns was the action of staunchly anti-Catholic William Claiborne, formerly a member of the Virginia Council. Claiborne had established a trading post on Kent Island in the bay. In 1630 he went to England with the hopes of thwarting Baltimore's efforts and obtaining funding for his own venture. He was partially successful, obtaining funds from a small group of London merchants. After his return in 1631, he transformed his trading post into a full-fledged colony with agricultural and mercantile facets. Baltimore approached diplomatically, offering a certain autonomy for loyalty to his claim. Claiborne refused. Virginia refused to get officially involved, recognizing that Claiborne had no legal claim. Virginia also worried about fueling an effort by the Virginia Company to regain their charter. But Claiborne found support among his backers and friends in

Virginia. Armed conflict ensued in 1635, but in 1636 Claiborne was recalled by the merchants, who surrendered the island to Baltimore. Claiborne returned, however, and for nearly twenty-five years did everything he could to bedevil Maryland.

During the Commonwealth, Claiborne and others who had allied themselves with the Parliamentary forces made use of ambiguity in their commission to obtain the surrender of Virginia (or the Chesapeake) and imposed their anti-Catholic views on Maryland. A period of strife ending in armed civil war occurred in Maryland, again with Kent Island and St. Mary's City as the poles.

The Head of Elk, east of Havre de Grace, became a strategic communications center, located at the overland ford from the South River, a tributary of the Delaware River to the Elk River that flowed into the Chesapeake Bay. Washington and Rochambeau used this route on their way to Yorktown.

NORTHERN NORTH CAROLINA

Governors (With Dates of Service in Albemarle County)
1664–67, William Drummond; 1667–70, Samuel Stephens; 1670–72, Peter Carteret; 1672–75, 1676–77, 1680–81, John Jenkins; 1675–76, Thomas Eastchurch; 1677, Thomas Miller; 1677–79, none; 1679, John Harvey; 1682–89, Seth Sothel; 1689–90, John Gibbs.

Carolina was chartered by the same group who chartered West Jersey, and the early governments were similar. As early as the 1650s, there were explorations and small settlements in North Carolina, but just when it was formally settled is difficult to say. Before the grant of a charter in 1663, Carolina should be viewed as part of frontier Virginia. Even after the grant of a charter, most Virginians looked down their noses at the poor, rural North Carolinians in this area.

Northern North Carolina extended down to near the bottom of the Albemarle region. It was settled by immigration from Virginia before Carolina existed. The area grew most of the same crops as Virginia but had serious problems delivering them to market, as the shallow waters of the Albemarle were hazardous for oceanic shipping. Thus, North Carolina suffered from a shortage of goods and markets for many years, and the governor hosted Blackbeard and other pirates (from whom North Carolinians filled their needs) much to the indignation of Virginia, on whose shipping these pirates largely preyed.

Looking for a group of resourceful settlers who would be relatively self-sufficient, the proprietors invited the Moravians from Pennsylvania to move to the area. They did, founding Salem and several surrounding towns, which became an economic asset to the part of western

North Carolina accessible from the Great Valley of Virginia.

Much of the Albemarle region in North Carolina was tied to the deep-water port of Norfolk, Virginia, along a trade route that went by road around the Great Dismal Swamp, then much larger than it is today. In the late period, George Washington and others formed a company to drain the swamp, reclaim land and build a canal to enhance commerce. Unfortunately, they were able to build only one drainage canal to Lake Drummond and could not do much to further communications. Incidentally, the Great Dismal Swamp was named by William Byrd, who never set foot in the real swamp. The swamp was famous for snakes, of which there were actually very few.

BIBLIOGRAPHY

Andrews, Stephenson B., ed. *Bacon's Castle*. Richmond, Va.: Association for the Preservation of Virginia Antiquities, 1984. An excellent study of an important early house.

Bridenbaugh, Carl. *Myths and Realities: Societies of the Colonial South*. Westport, Conn.: Greenwood Press, [1981] c1952.

Cometti, Elizabeth. *Social Life In Virginia During the War for Independence*. Williamsburg, Va.: Virginia Independence Bicentennial Commission, 1978.

Craven, Wesley Frank. *The Southern Colonies in the Seventeenth Century, 1607–1689*. Baton Rouge: Louisiana State University Press, 1949.

Hariot, Thomas. *Thomas Hariot's Virginia. A Briefe and True Report of the New Found Land of Virginia*. 1590. Reprint, New York: Dover Publications, 1972.

Middleton, Arthur Pierce. *Tobacco Coast: A Maritime History of Chesapeake Bay in the Colonial Era*. Baltimore: Johns Hopkins University Press, 1984.

Reps, John William. *Tidewater Towns: City Planning in Colonial Virginia and Maryland*. Williamsburg, Va.: Colonial Williamsburg Foundation, 1972.

Rountree, Helen C. *The Powhatan Indians of Virginia: Their Traditional Culture*. Norman: University of Oklahoma Press, 1989.

Tate, Thad W., and David L. Ammerman, eds. *The Chesapeake in the Seventeenth Century: Essays on Anglo-American Society*. Chapel Hill: University of North Carolina Press, 1979. Good essays about many aspects of daily life.

Wust, Klaus German. *The Virginia Germans*. Charlottesville, Va: University Press of Virginia, 1969.

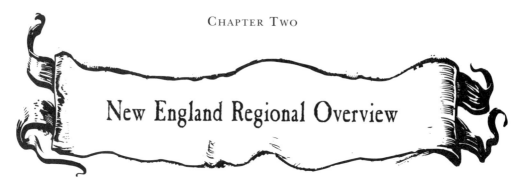

CHAPTER TWO

New England Regional Overview

T hat New England was settled when it was an accident. The Pilgrims were headed to Virginia but were blown off course. They were running out of beer and nearly in mutiny when they landed and decided to settle at what became Plymouth. Because their charter was not valid at that latitude, they drew up the Mayflower Compact to give themselves some legal basis. As it turned out, they were happier there than among the Cavaliers. The feeling was mutual. The dissenting religious nature of their colony placed them at odds with the loyalist and therefore strictly Anglican views of the Virginians.

The Plymouth Colony they founded in 1620 continued, but in 1630 the Massachusetts Bay Colony was founded under John Winthrop near Boston and became the driving force for all of New England.

New England benefited from a steady influx of immigrants. Lacking a commodity, however, like the tobacco that made the South successful, its economy was less stable for a long time. The bulk of the populace were content to survive, awaiting the day they could return to England and take with them the secrets to building the perfect society.

Their day came when Parliament overthrew the monarchy and established the Commonwealth. A wave of reverse immigration ensued, emptying much of New England. After the Commonwealth collapsed, there was little interest in emigration to New England and little contact between the remaining Dissenters and the restored monarchy. In 1686, with an eye to crushing the hostile Puritan theocracies in New England, James II created the Dominion of New England, which was later extended to include the Jerseys and New York, where many Dissenters had moved. The region suffered in isolation.

As early as the 1640s, the merchants established control of the coastal towns, and these towns soon differed greatly from the rural, poorly capitalized and vulnerable towns on the interior. The coastal towns were modern, in touch with current trends, and wealthy, while the interior ones even allowed the "Old Deluder Satan" to have sway, not bothering to educate their children as their doctrine required; they were too busy fighting Indians and poverty. The bloodiest colonial conflict, King Philip's War, was fought exclusively in New England near the end of the century. By about 1700, when the old religious theocracy had seen several generations—and the old ardor—pass, the more worldly merchants assumed control of the government. Over the next sixty years or so, they would strive to bring New England back in touch with the mother country. Thus, New England was closer to England on the eve of the Revolution than it had been for one hundred years.

Boston became a shipping hub and a major manufacturing center, making chairs shipped throughout the colonies. Its merchants brokered most of the textiles for the region. Furniture made in Boston in the late period, like that made in Philadelphia, was heavily decorated at the expense of being substantial or built to last. It was designed for self-made, self-important men, with neither the Puritan's respect for simple quality nor the Southern gentry's view toward the long run.

When James II ascended the throne, he did not forget that the New England colonies had engaged in political activities contributing to the execution of Charles I. He exerted royal authority over all New England, creating the Dominion of New England to purge the religious leaders. The religious theocracy in the colonies had begun to break down enough that when Joseph Dudley (a native of Roxbury, Massachusetts and son of John Winthrop's colleague Thomas Dudley) was sent to England to ward off revocation of the charter, he secretly advised the king to revoke it. In 1685 he was awarded the presidency of the Council of New England seated in Boston. In 1686 Governor Andros arrived and enacted five major threats to New Englanders: He taxed by executive order, dispensed with the elected assemblies, closed town meetings, denied the towns the right to collect tithes to pay their clergy and revoked all grants of land, threatening QUITRENTS (annual rents) of one pound per eight hundred acres on land previously held in fee simple. Essentially, New England was on the verge of becoming another Ireland in governance and instability. In 1689, when it became known that the Glorious Revolution had replaced James II, the citizenry arrested Governor Andros and reaffirmed the old charters.

The Glorious Revolution redeemed England in the eyes of the religious, proving it would not become a papist state. With that done, the religious theocracy was willing to quietly concede the growing mercantile basis of the region and begin to hand off power. Unfortunately, the deep-seated, local power structures of New England did not change as easily as the leadership.

New England based its society on the township, a minimum of twenty families and a minister. In accordance with policies against

SOLITARY LIVING, land was not granted to lone individuals. New England towns in the early period were centralized, with farms radiating from the town proper. One symptom of the decay of the old Puritan theocracy in the later seventeenth century was the establishment of townships with decentralized farms straggling back from the Connecticut and other rivers.

Because the congregation and the township were virtually synonymous in the early years, little difference existed between discipline for religious and for temporal transgressions. The church, however, did not proceed with the same rights as the courts. Excepting some capital crimes, in both cases transgressors were entitled to rejoin the community if they displayed suitable humility, modesty, patience, repentance and some evidence of reformation, and if they properly petitioned the authorities. As the final decision often lay in the congregation's majority vote, the situation worked similarly to many homeowners' associations today to create an inviolable community standard. The community thought any transgression, moral or temporal, was its business. Arguments in both temporal and religious cases frequently contained biblical quotes.

Indian populations throughout much of New England were largely decimated by one or more epidemics of smallpox contracted from European fishermen and traders before the settlement period began. While smallpox killed a relatively small percentage of Europeans— they had some natural immunity from previous exposure—it could kill 90–95 percent of native populations which had no immunity. As a result, large amounts of territory became available for settlement without significant resistance. The few Indians who survived had to take a more conciliatory view toward the colonists.

Additionally, the inability of Indian healers and priests to stop the epidemics may have caused religious doubts that possibly made survivors more accepting of Christianity and more willing to work with Christians, who happened to be more resistant to the disease. In any event, with a few exceptions, settlers and Indians worked together, the Indians teaching the colonists how to plant, hunt and fish in the strange new world. Only after population pressures exerted by the English grew and the Indian societies had recovered their numbers somewhat did frictions become explosive.

In 1675 the Indian leader Philip, spurred by increased distrust and English demands for land, rose against the Plymouth Colony in a desperate last bid to prevent the destruction of his people. The war spread to all the surrounding colonies, although the Iroquois refused to become involved in the Albany area. When it was over, New England had suffered badly, but the Indians were virtually all killed or sold into slavery in the Spanish colonies.

41

APPROXIMATE POPULATION OF REGION	
1688	75,000
1715	162,150
1765	600,000

The northern forests included many large white pines, white birches and red maples, as well as nut trees such as walnut, butternut, oak and chestnut, and fruit trees such as cherries. The timber of these forests was the basis for many industries, although perhaps too much has been made of England's laying claim to towering pines (King's trees) for masts for the Royal Navy. Some were undoubtedly marked and a few harvested, but most spars for the Royal Navy came from the Baltic, and New England was a reserve in case the Baltic might be closed. Local production, though, utilized local materials.

MASSACHUSETTS

Governors (With Dates of Service in Massachusetts)
1630–34, 1637–40, 1642–44, 1646–49, John Winthrop; 1634–35, 1640–41, 1645–46, 1650–51, Thomas Dudley; 1635–36, John Haynes; 1636–37, Sir Henry Vane; 1641–42, 1654–55, 1665–72, Richard Bellingham; 1644–45, 1649–50, 1651–54, 1655–65, John Endecott (or Endicott); 1672–79, John Leverett; 1679–86, 1689–92, Simon Bradstreet; 1686, 1702–1715, Joseph Dudley; 1686–89, Sir Edmund Andros; 1692–94, Sir William Phips; 1694–99, 1700–01, William Stoughton; 1699–1700, Richard Coote, Earl of Bellomont; 1701–02, 1715 (February 4 to March 21), 1757 (April 4 to August 3), Massachusetts Council; 1715–16, 1730, William Tailer; 1716–23, Samuel Shute; 1723–28, 1729–30, William Dummer; 1728–29, William Burnet; 1730–41, Jonathan Belcher; 1741–49, 1753–56, William Shirley; 1749–53, 1756–57, Spencer Phips; 1757–60, Thomas Pownall; 1760, 1769–74, Thomas Hutchinson; 1760–69, Francis Bernard; 1774, Thomas Gage; 1774–75 (October 1774 to July 1775), Provincial Congress; 1775–80 (July 1775 to fall 1780), Council of State; 1780–85, John Hancock.

Franchise and Government
Massachusetts Bay Colony elected the governor, deputy governor and eighteen Assistants in annual elections of assembled freemen. The last election of this sort took place on May 12, 1686, just before the colony was made royal. Plymouth operated similarly, ending its reign in June 1691. During the tenures of Dudley and Andros, the appointed council

APPROXIMATE POPULATION OF MASSACHUSETTS

Year	Total	Black
1620	102	-
1630	2,000	-
1645	18,000	-
1670	60,000	-
1700	80,000	-
1725	110,000	-
1750	122,000	2,000
1776	338,667	5,249

was the only legislative power in Massachusetts Bay. After the royal charter of 1691, government was vested in the governor, council or assistants, and a General Assembly of freemen representing their towns. Towns of over 120 FREEHOLDERS could elect two, smaller towns one, and Boston alone four. In 1643 only about 1,938 people (or about 11 percent) were enfranchised citizens.

Settlement in Massachusetts began in December of 1620, when the settlers of Plymouth Colony landed in distress at Plymouth. Plymouth remained a separate colony until 1690 when a new charter was written consolidating it with the Massachusetts Bay Colony that settled Boston in 1630. Plymouth Colony was a loosely organized group of settlers, including many who were not religiously motivated.

By comparison, the Massachusetts Bay Colony was well-organized. They had reconnoitered and were one of the best funded colonial efforts. In 1630 the Massachusetts Bay Company sent seventeen ships with fifteen hundred settlers and by 1635 had sent over eight thousand settlers. During the 1630s, immigration averaged about two thousand per year. It is not surprising that the dynamic Boston-based colony became ascendant.

New England's individualistic creeds led to small, localized government of both church and state. Anything else could not have led to consensus. These facts were evident as early as the Anne Hutchinson trial in 1638, when Hutchinson had the backing of Governor Henry Vane and the Reverend John Wheelwright, both members of the establishment. Her views were clearly heretical to both Puritans and Anglicans, in that she claimed direct revelation from God, dangerously close to the divine revelation of the Catholics. After Vane left, both Hutchinson and Wheelwright were tried. Hutchinson's banishment from Massachusetts Bay led her to take a contingent of followers to Rhode Island, while Wheelwright's banishment on charges of sedition and contempt of authority caused him to emigrate to New Hampshire with a small contingent.

The late 1630s and particularly the 1640s saw a drop in immigration as Puritans became hopeful of their chances in England. This led to economic depression in Massachusetts, which in turn led to the rise of government controls. In the 1640s Bradford in Plymouth complained of the decay in the moral structure due to material success. During this time, and with the extension of government authority, society changed from a fairly colorful, open and expressive one to a more strict, rigid and puritanical one. Some independent parties always existed, even within New England. Most of the merchants and the Gloucester and Marblehead fishermen were not Puritans.

A dichotomy arose between the merchants in the coastal cities and the rural farmers inland. The material wealth and the quality of the goods enjoyed by the merchants is proving through archaeology to be considerable, rivaling or exceeding even the finest homes of Virginia. Not much of that wealth, however, made it to the interior, as the merchants' and ship captains' principal clients were outside the region. Thus, valid generalizations for the colony, or the region, are difficult to make.

CONNECTICUT

Governors (With Dates of Service in Connecticut)
New Haven: 1639–58, Theophilus Eaton; 1658–60, Francis Newman; 1660–64, William Leete. Hartford: 1639, 1640, 1641–42, 1643–44, 1645–46, 1647–48, 1649–50, 1651–52, 1653–54, John Haynes; 1640–41, 1644–45, 1646–47, 1648–49, 1650–51, 1652–53, 1654–55 (absent), Edward Hopkins; 1642–43, George Wyllys; 1655–56, 1658–59, Thomas Welles; 1656–57, John Webster; 1657–58, 1659–76, John Winthrop, Jr.; 1676–83, William Leete; 1683–87, 1689–98 Robert Treat; 1687–89, Sir Edmund Andros; 1698–1707, Fitz-John Winthrop; 1707–24, Gurdon Saltonstall; 1724–41, Joseph Talcott; 1741–50, Jonathan Law; 1750–54, Roger Wolcott; 1754–66, Thomas Fitch; 1766–69, William Pitkin; 1769–84, Johnathan Trumbull.

Government
The Hartford and New Haven colonies coexisted early. New Haven established a government based on the liveries of London, with freeholders electing a committee of eleven who in turn elected seven to meet as a court. In 1643 the General Court adopted a set of

APPROXIMATE POPULATION OF CONNECTICUT		
Year	*Total*	*Black*
1645	5,500	-
1670	20,000	-
1700	30,000	-
1725	50,000	1,500
1750	100,000	2,000
1774	191,342	6,464

"Fundamental Orders" that provided for election of a governor, deputy governor, magistrates, secretary and marshal. In 1638 Hartford, which became Connecticut proper, drafted Fundamental Orders providing for a governor, deputy governor and six magistrates to be chosen by the freeholders. The Royal Charter of 1665 which consolidated the two colonies provided for the same officers with the addition of twelve assistants. General courts met in May and October. Between 1687 and 1689, the government was solely in the hands of Andros.

Population and Area

The Connecticut colonies followed the Connecticut River, which runs north and south through the middle of Connecticut. The separate colonies of New Haven (near the mouth of the river) and Hartford (further inland) were founded by splinter groups from Massachusetts. New London was founded and governed by John Winthrop Jr., son of the governor of Massachusetts Bay Colony. The area along the river north of central Connecticut was the richest farmland in New England.

At the same time, the relative isolation from Boston allowed the Connecticut River region to develop a highly individual culture. Locally produced "sunflower" chests and "heart and crown" chairs are instantly identifiable.

The Connecticut River colonies, including Deerfield, Massachusetts, were hit particularly hard during the wars with the Indians, as these colonies were the closest to the Iroquois and the most incursive into Indian lands. The towns of Hadley, Northampton and Hatfield surrounded themselves with defensive stockades. In the Pequot War of 1637, the English surrounded the main fortified Indian town, burned it and shot most of the inhabitants as they tried to escape, killing six hundred to seven hundred in a half hour. The survivors were sold into slavery. The pious colonials could not contain their joy at the victory. The other tribes did not forget.

Although the Congregationalist ideals of New England applied here as well, the remoteness of the area and the religious views that led individuals to leave Massachusetts and found colonies in Connecticut allowed an earlier breakdown in some aspects of traditional New England society, including the township. Isolated houses did exist in Connecticut, and the later townships established along the river centered along and sprawled back from the river. Baptists and Quakers were more common in Connecticut and on Long Island (socially part of Connecticut) than in Massachusetts.

Connecticut was founded by a group from Plymouth Colony, which settled Windsor and was bought out by seventy dissatisfied Congregationalists from Dorchester in 1633. Shortly, settlements were formed at Wethersfield (1634); Hartford (1635) by the Dutch as a trading post, then taken over by a group from Massachusetts under Thomas Hocker in 1636; Saybrook (1638); and Milford and Guilford (1639). After this, so many towns were settled it is impossible to list them all. The bibliography contains a source with a reasonably complete listing.

In 1662 John Winthrop Jr. obtained a charter to all of Connecticut, combining the separate colonies into one. That charter was a source of pride, and when Sir Edmund Andros came to Connecticut to assume power, it was spirited away from under his very nose and hidden in an oak tree until the end of his reign. William and Mary confirmed the old charter upon their ascension.

Connecticut was the home of the largest and longest spate of witchcraft hysteria in New England. The first person tried, convicted and executed for witchcraft was Alice Young of Windsor in 1647. The years 1662 and 1663 saw a panic with a number of executions. The last occurrences were after the Salem incidents in Massachusetts.

In 1752 the Spanish ship *Saint Joseph and Saint Helena*, with a cargo in gold, silver and goods worth some four hundred thousand Spanish dollars, anchored off the Connecticut coast in need of minor repairs. By the time the pilots brought the ship into port, it had been run on the rocks twice and dismasted. Public opinion was that the pilots were intentionally trying to damage the ship so they could claim the cargo. The governor, Roger Wolcott, appointed executors to protect the ship and its cargo. Unfortunately, the Spanish cargo master, Joseph Miguel de San Juan, was taken in by two unscrupulous New Yorkers, Henry Cayler Jr. and Henry Lane, and refused to accept the governor's protections, seeking to have one of the New Yorkers given control of the cargo. In the end, through a series of confusions that read in summary like the plot of a Shakespearean comedy, Wolcott did give the cargo to Cayler, whereupon the silver disappeared. The gold had already been stolen. Wolcott lost reelection on the fears the colony would be held responsible to Spain for a value near one million pounds.

From about 1760 until the Revolution, Connecticut and Pennsylvania disputed lands in northern Pennsylvania, settled in part by residents of Connecticut through the Susquehanna Company. The issue was checked somewhat by the Treaty of Fort Stanwix of 1768 that limited the western incursion into Indian lands, after an attack on the settlement area in 1763. The conflicting claims were finally settled in favor of Pennsylvania at a court sitting in Trenton in 1782.

RHODE ISLAND

Governors (With Dates of Service in Rhode Island)

Prior to 1654 the governors were judges or presidents of cities: Portsmouth judge 1638–39, Newport judge 1639–40, Portsmouth and Newport governor 1640–47, 1651–53, William Coddington; Portsmouth judge 1639–40, William Hutchinson; Portsmouth Chief Judge 1644–47, Roger Williams; 1647, John Coggeshall; 1648–49, Jeremiah (Jeremy) Clarke; 1649–50, Providence and Warwick president 1652–53, John Smith; 1650–51, Portsmouth and Newport president 1654, Nicholas Easton; Portsmouth and Warwick president 1651–52, Samuel Gorton; Portsmouth and Newport president 1653, John Sanford; Providence and Warwick president 1653–54, Gregory Dexter.

1654–57, Roger Williams; 1657–60, 1662–66, 1669–72, 1677–78, Benedict Arnold; 1660–62, 1666–69, William Brenton; 1672–74, Nicholas Easton; 1674–76, 1678, William Coddington; 1676–77, 1686, 1696–98, Walter Clarke; 1678–80, John Cranston; 1680–83, Peleg Sanford; 1683–85, William Coddington Jr.; 1685–86, 1690, Henry Bull; 1686, Joseph Dudley; 1686–89, Sir Edmund Andros; 1689–90, John Coggeshall Jr.; 1690–95, John Easton; 1695, Caleb Carr; 1698–1727, Samuel Cranston; 1727–32, Joseph Jenckes; 1732–33, William Wanton; 1733–40, John Wanton; 1740–43, Richard Ward; 1743–45, 1746–47, 1748–55, William Greene; 1745–46, 1747–48, Gideon Wanton; 1755–57, 1758–62, 1763–65, 1767–68, Stephen Hopkins; 1762–63, 1765–67, Samuel Ward; 1768–69, Josias Lyndon; 1769–1775, Joseph Wanton; 1775–78, Nicholas Cooke; 1778–86, William Green Jr.

Government

Rhode Island was settled in scattered towns, and each elected the officials it deemed necessary, most often judges and magistrates. The original charter for the colony was issued under the Commonwealth, and in 1647 elections were held for a president, four assistants, a recorder, a treasurer and a "general sargant," but soon the colony split, and each faction elected its own assembly, governor and two assistants. In 1654, the old government was reinstated. For a period ending in 1650,

APPROXIMATE POPULATION OF RHODE ISLAND		
Year	Total	Black
1655	1,200	-
1675	3,000	-
1688	6,000	-
1701	8,000	-
1726	10,000	-
1755	40,636	4,697
1774	59,678	3,761

all laws were placed under public referendum. In 1663, under Charles II, a new charter was obtained. This document called for a governor, deputy governor and ten assistants. In addition, a legislature was formed, comprised of four deputies from each of the original towns except Newport, which was allowed six, and two from any other towns. This assembly met regularly between 1686 and 1690.

Rhode Island was settled by various groups with different goals. True to the New England model, each new colony was founded as a town. Roger Williams arrived after he dissented with the Dissenters of Massachusetts Bay and was exiled. He founded Providence in 1636 on land given him by the Indians, with whom he remained on friendly terms. Anne Hutchinson settled Pocassett in 1638. William Coddington settled Newport; William Arnold, Pautuxet; and Samuel Gorton, Shawomet. At some point these towns had to think regionally and realized their location on Narragansett Bay gave them their own unique identity. Given the stubbornness of the individual colonists, this realization took some time. In their first four years, Providence had two schisms, Pautuxet one. Later, other settlers came with the intent of expanding the hegemony of Massachusetts Bay. These others were the first common enemies. As most of the settlers had serious differences with Massachusetts, they did not want to be run off their land by their old enemies.

Roger Williams finally obtained a charter, in part to protect himself from the threat of being run out again by the faction loyal to Boston obtaining one first. In setting up his colony Williams established the first clear and absolute separation of church and state. He believed that no civil government could compel adherence to a religious doctrine without endangering free will, and thus being repugnant to God. Thereafter Rhode Island became a destination for Quakers, Baptists and others who came into conflict with the other New England authorities.

The first Jewish settlers in Rhode Island arrived in Newport by 1677, when there were enough Sephardic families to obtain land for a burying ground. The community declined after 1690 but was rejuvenated in 1730 with the arrival of a ship from Curaçao, and more Spanish and Portuguese Jews arrived in 1740.

Rhode Island's problems were not over yet. After the Restoration, Connecticut attempted to claim all the land to the western shore of the Narragansett. Support from King Charles II and some quick maneuvering preserved Rhode Island's boundaries. Then Sir Edmund Andros arrived, and Rhode Island chose to hide its charter from him.

During this period the colony was forced to recognize that it had greater concerns than those of the individual towns, and the government forced a larger view on the settlers. As a result Rhode Islanders decided the future lay in trade, and anything that got in the way of that trade was avoided as stubbornly as they had earlier avoided seeing eye to eye. Rhode Islanders became known for shipping ventures that required ENTERPRISE. This usually amounted to smuggling, high-risk trading (such as slaves), or other ventures the rest of the colonies saw as shady. Even farmers underwrote parts of voyages much the way we buy stock today. Rhode Islanders harnessed their disrespect for the law and government with a hard-driving capitalism to become wealthy. After 1764 the Rhode Island populace, as ever at odds with the British government, was more united in the movement toward independence than virtually any other colony.

The slave trade killed some of the tolerance Williams had bestowed on the early colony. By 1760 some 15 percent of Newport's population were slaves, while in other areas it reached 17 percent.

By the 1740s pig iron was being produced in Rhode Island, although never in large quantities. Cocoa beans were ground at several chocolate mills, making Rhode Island the chocolate capital of the colonies. In the 1760s whaling off of Martha's Vineyard drove the spermaceti industry, and Rhode Island became the chandler to the colonies.

NEW HAMPSHIRE

Governors (With Dates of Service in New Hampshire)
1680–81, John Cutt; 1681–82, Richard Walderne (Waldron); 1682–85, Edward Cranfield; 1685–86, Walter Barefoote; 1686, 1702–15, Joseph Dudley; 1686–89, Sir Edmund Andros; 1689–90, each town exercised local self-government; 1690–92, Simon Bradstreet; 1692–97, John Usher; 1697–98, 1700–02, William Partridge; 1698–99, Samuel Allen; 1699–1700, Richard Coote, Earl of Bellomont; 1715–16, George Vaughan; 1716–23, Samuel Shute; 1723–28, 1729–30, John

APPROXIMATE POPULATION OF NEW HAMPSHIRE

Year	Total	Black
1675	4,000	-
1709	5,150	-
1726	7,000	-
1749	30,000	-
1775	81,050	656

Wentworth; 1728–29, William Burnet; 1730–41, Jonathan Belcher; 1741 (May to December), New Hampshire Council conducted executive affairs; 1741–67, Benning Wentworth; 1767–75, John Wentworth; 1775–76, Matthew Thornton; 1776–85, Meshech Weare.

Government

Each of the detached settlements that comprised early New Hampshire was granted the authority to rule itself, and each elected a governor, while some also elected assistants. After the royal takeover in 1679, a council was formed under the governor, and a call went out for election of an assembly. Assemblies met every year but the period from 1686 to 1692, during a part of which time the crown took considerable action to break up the dissenting local governments.

Population and Area

New Hampshire began in 1621 as a series of five grants to Captain John Mason, Governor of Newfoundland from 1615 to 1621. Mason, who teamed up with Sir Ferdinando Gorges on four of the grants, founded the Laconia Company in 1622 to establish settlements. The underfunded company soon dissolved, but Mason retained his original grant of land between the Merrimack and Piscataqua Rivers and, as proprietor, named it New Hampshire. Gorges took the remaining four grants in Maine, which area remained part of Massachusetts until 1820.

The Laconia Company started a settlement at Strawbery Banke (later Portsmouth), one of the finest harbors in New England. By 1633 the towns of Northram, Hampton and Exeter existed. John Wheelwright, banished from Massachusetts, purchased the land for Exeter directly from the Indians, causing some confusion in title. By 1640 about one thousand people lived in the colony. In 1641 the populace, unable to agree about government after the death of Mason in 1635, asked Massachusetts to govern them. They remained affiliated until the crown separated them again in 1679. In 1685 New Hampshire was included in the Dominion of New England, until 1691 when it was again made its own colony but had only 209 qualified voters.

The problems of land ownership, boundaries and responsibility created by the Mason grants and the on-again, off-again relationship with Massachusetts came to a crisis in 1715, when Massachusetts Lieutenant Governor George Vaughan (with special authority for New Hampshire) chose to ignore the orders of his absent governor, Colonel Samuel Shute. The problem exacerbated dissension between the merchants of Portsmouth and the farmers of the newer towns.

In 1717 the crown appointed John Wentworth to replace Vaughan, and he turned the situation around with his personal interest in promoting settlement. In 1719 a new group of one hundred Scots-Irish Presbyterian families from North Ireland arrived and established themselves in the area just over the Massachusetts border, where they produced flax and linen. By 1722 their town of Londonderry was formally recognized.

New Hampshire wanted to settle the boundary with Massachusetts but could not take the matter up in England because of the expense. Meanwhile, Massachusetts continued to tax areas already taxed by New Hampshire, and residents did not know which laws to follow. Finally in 1740 the crown granted New Hampshire the disputed counties along the coast as well as the area west of the Connecticut River that later became Vermont. This grant was known as the New Hampshire Grants. Benning Wentworth was named the colony's governor, and in 1746 Mason's descendants sold their interests to twelve Portsmouth men who quit their claim to rights within the established towns and chartered thirty-seven new towns. The Portsmouth men administered the remaining two million acres of their grant relatively fairly.

The remaining problem was created by the New Hampshire Grants. Technically, after the land had been taken from Massachusetts, New Hampshire extended to New York. The settlers of the Connecticut valley, today's border between New Hampshire and Vermont, were more aligned to Connecticut and Massachusetts, however, and New York also exerted interests in the area. In 1764 the King decreed that the west bank of the Connecticut River was New Hampshire's western border. Unfortunately, some of the settlers in the grants did not want to belong to New York, and the matter continued to be a problem as Ethan Allen and his Green Mountain Boys engaged in virtual guerrilla war in the region, agitating for independence.

In 1771 the original province was divided into five counties: Rockingham, Strafford, Hillsborough, Cheshire and Grafton, and all five were running by 1773.

New Hampshire was settled by men with knowledge of fishing and lumbering, and lumbering and shipbuilding became major industries.

Locally designed GONDOLAS or GUNDELOWS were flat-bottomed, low boats suitable for carrying heavy loads up inland streams and under low bridges. Shipyards in Portsmouth, Kittery (then part of New Hampshire; later part of Maine), Dover and Exeter also produced ships up to three hundred tons. The growth of American shipbuilding may have been one reason for the Navigation Acts, as England feared the colonists, with better access to raw materials, could too easily smuggle goods and shut down the English shipbuilding industry.

By the 1630s water-powered sawmills appeared at the fall line on the Piscataqua, and by 1700 there were ninety in the region. The mills produced lumber for shipbuilding, cabinetmaking and export. Other people went straight to the trees to obtain wood for cooperage, making shoe pegs, spools, clothespins, toothpicks and baskets. They gathered chestnut for ship's blocks, maple for burning to make potash and pearl ash, and bark for making birchbark containers. But the fortunes made in New Hampshire were made by trade.

BIBLIOGRAPHY

Bailyn, Bernard. *The New England Merchants in the Seventeenth Century.* Cambridge, Mass.: Harvard University Press, 1955.

Carroll, Charles F. *The Timber Economy of Puritan New England.* Providence, R.I.: Brown University Press, 1973.

Cronon, William. *Changes in the Land: Indians, Colonists and the Ecology of New England.* New York: Hill and Wang, 1983.

Deetz, James. *In Small Things Forgotten: The Archaeology of Early American Life.* Garden City, N.Y.: Anchor Press, 1977. An excellent, readable treatment of a subject that is rarely covered, the transformation of the world from medieval to modern. A classic.

Main, Jackson Turner. *Society and Economy in Colonial Connecticut.* Princeton, N.J.: Princeton University Press, 1985.

McManis, Douglas R. *Colonial New England: A Historical Geography.* New York: Oxford University Press, 1975.

Miller, Perry. *The New England Mind: From Colony to Province.* Cambridge, Mass.: Harvard University Press, 1953.

———. *The New England Mind: The Seventeenth Century.* Cambridge, Mass.: Harvard University Press, 1954.

New England Begins: The Seventeenth Century. Boston: Museum of Fine Arts, 1982. The catalog of an exhibit, it contains excellent articles on diverse subjects like Mannerism, Indians and society.

Roth, David M., ed. *Connecticut History and Culture: An Historical Overview and Resource Guide for Teachers.* Connecticut Historical Commission, Eastern Connecticut State University, 1985. Good summary of basic issues, resources, listing of settlement dates for towns.

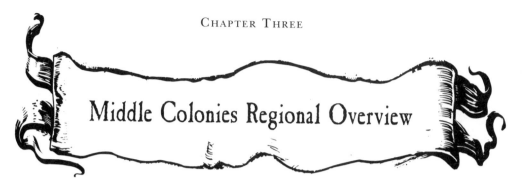

Chapter Three

Middle Colonies Regional Overview

The settlement of the middle colonies followed two waterways, the Hudson and the Delaware. As settlement proceeded up these rivers simultaneously, it is appropriate to discuss the general trends here in the regional section. The area was first settled by the Dutch about 1623. The center for the Delaware colonists was Fort Nassau near modern-day Gloucester, New Jersey. Atlantic colonists centered around New Amsterdam, later New York, but went up the river as far as Albany. Late in the seventeenth century, a center near the Delaware Water Gap was connected to the Hudson by an Indian trail from Kingston. This trail was known as the Old Mine Road but was not developed as a road until the early eighteenth century.

The Swedes came to the Delaware about 1638, settling first in the area between Fort Christina (Wilmington) and Philadelphia. As early as 1640, the land in New Jersey from Raccoon Creek to Cape May was granted to Peter Ridder. For a time the Swedes and Dutch existed in an uneasy truce, but in 1655 the Swedes, about one hundred in all of New Jersey, were near starvation and in poor health due to a lack of support from Sweden, and they surrendered to the Dutch.

The Dutch holdings were the most feudal of all New World colonies. The patroon system granted huge tracts of land (as much as three million acres) to a few who worked it with tenants.

In 1664 the English assumed control of all Dutch holdings in North America in exchange for the captured sugar islands of Surinam. Despite Peter Stuyvesant's famous foot-stomping, the bulk of the settlers welcomed the English because the English were more serious about development than the Dutch were, and the English system offered more opportunity for the tenants. Dutch policy had emphasized trapping and trade with the Indians, and thus discouraged settlement.

New York was the major colonial player in the fur trade, although significant numbers of furs came from New Jersey and Pennsylvania.

APPROXIMATE POPULATION OF REGION	
1688	42,000
1715	99,300
1765	580,000

This area had large tracts of cedar trees that had particular use in furniture and musical instruments. Long Island was a major exporter of black locust wood, used throughout the colonies for fence posts and boatbuilding due to its near imperviousness to water and insects.

NEW JERSEY

Governors (With Dates of Service in New Jersey)
New Jersey: 1664–65, Richard Nicolls; 1665–72, 1674-76, Philip Carteret; 1672–73, John Berry; 1673–74, Dutch occupied.

East Jersey: 1676–80, 1681–82, Philip Carteret; 1680–81, 1688–89, Sir Edmund Andros; 1682–84, Thomas Rudyard; 1684–86, Gawen Lawrie; 1686–87, Lord Neil Campbell; 1687–88, 1689–98, 1699–1703, Andrew Hamilton; 1698–99, Jeremiah Basse; 1699, Andrew Bowne.

West Jersey: 1676–81, board of commissioners; 1681–84, Samuel Jennings (Jenings); 1684–85, Thomas Olive (Ollive); 1685–88, 1689–90(1), John Skene; 1688–89, Sir Edmund Andros; 1692–98, 1699–1703, Andrew Hamilton; 1698–99, Jeremiah Basse; 1699, Andrew Basse.

New Jersey: 1703, 1719–20, 1731–32, 1738–46, Lewis Morris; 1703–08, Edward Hyde, Viscount Cornbury; 1708–09, John Lovelace, fourth Baron Lovelace of Hurley; 1709–10, Richard Ingoldesby; 1710, William Pinhorne; 1710–19, Robert Hunter; 1720–28, William Burnet; 1728–31, John Montgomery; 1732–36, William Cosby; 1736, John Anderson; 1736–38, John Hamilton; 1746–47, John Hamilton; 1747, 1755–58, John Reading; 1747–57, Jonathon Belcher; 1757, Thomas Pownall; 1758–60, Francis Bernard; 1760–61, Thomas Boone; 1761–63, Josiah Hardy; 1763–76, William Franklin; 1776–90, William Livingston.

Religion and Government
Anglican membership was nominally required for franchise, but many Presbyterians (College of New Jersey), Dutch Reformed, New England Congregationalists and Baptists were accepted. The Provincial Council was the upper house and the governor's advisors. The Assembly was the lower house. The houses first met after the surrender to the crown in 1703 and continued regularly.

APPROXIMATE POPULATION OF NEW JERSEY	
1680	5,000
1700	15,000
1750	60,000
1775	120,000

Towns

In addition to the towns listed below, New Jersey had a number of towns by 1750: Trenton (developed as a trading post on the falls of the Delaware), New Brunswick (1731), Salem and Freehold.

Population and Area

The population in the late period was approximately 50 percent English in origin, 16 percent Scots-Irish, 16 percent Dutch, 10 percent German, and 8 percent African (mostly slaves). A small percentage were Swedish and French. More than 60 percent of the population lived in the northern counties.

New Jersey was still thinly populated when the English took over the region. Most Dutch attempts to settle had been driven back to Manhattan by the local Leni-Lenape Indians. In 1642, 1651 and 1655, small contingents from the New Haven Colony established themselves near Salem. None stayed long. In 1664 the Duke of York, brother of Charles II, received a patent to all the land between the Connecticut and Delaware Rivers. Shortly, the area experienced a large influx of people, mostly from Long Island and New England. By October 1664, Elizabethtown had been founded, and in April 1665 the Monmouth tract was established, creating Middletown and Shrewsbury. In 1666 Robert Treat of the New Haven Colony was granted land and founded Newark. The same year, another group of New Englanders founded Piscataway and Woodbridge. In addition, the Dutch village of Bergen was confirmed with a charter in 1668.

Unfortunately, after the Duke of York sent his own governor, he regranted much of the colony to Sir George Carteret and John, Lord Berkeley, as Proprietors. This led to confused and duplicated land titles, failure of the populace to pay quitrents, and ultimately the arrest by one governor (Andros, for the Duke) of the other (Carteret, cousin of the proprietor) for governing as an impostor.

The proprietors created a constitution known as the Concessions and Agreement of 1665. It allowed full freedom of conscience and created a legislative, elected assembly with full authority for taxation. A headright system different from Virginia's was specified, in which the settlers of new towns, within three years of founding, could receive 60 to 150 acres, plus additional acres for any servants. The goal of the proprietors was to establish a colony that could pay taxes, and liberal governmental and religious policies encouraged immigration. The settlers, however, never received full title to the land. Instead they were required, starting in 1670, to pay quitrents, annual rents of a half penny to a penny per acre, to the owners. Those who acquired their land by purchase from the Indians or by grant from the Duke insisted they were not required to pay quitrents.

The quitrent problem boiled over into a rebellion in 1672 and never died out until after the Revolution. In 1673 the Dutch captured and held New York for a year. By 1674 Berkeley had sold his interest in the colony to a Quaker, John Fenwick, and in 1676 the Quintipartite Deed was drawn up dividing New Jersey into East Jersey and West Jersey along a line from Little Egg Harbor to the northwest corner.

Carteret held East Jersey exclusively. A tentative stability returned but was upset when Andros arrested Carteret, and subsequently the inhabitants rebelled again. But this time, William Penn and eleven others bought the colony in 1682. Soon they brought another twelve proprietors in, six from Scotland. Twenty of the twenty-four were Quakers. The government fell to the Scots.

Under the new proprietors, large grants of land, as much as 17,500 acres per proprietor, were given. Large, freely held estates opposed quitrent tenants, and the land quarrels continued. At this time there was significant immigration from Scotland, leading in time to the Presbyterian bent of the colony. Population moved to Perth Amboy, founded in 1683, which became the capital of East Jersey.

The Quakers had built up West Jersey, founding Burlington in 1678 and establishing it as the capital. A large part of the population were artisans. Farms ran about three hundred acres, larger than in East Jersey but without the huge estates. The settlement of West Jersey occurred backward, moving east from the Delaware in a wide strip of fertile land but leaving the Pine Barrens undeveloped. The government of West Jersey was also highly democratic and tolerant. Like East Jersey, it was plagued by legal questions of land and authority.

The crown tried to deal with New Jersey's problems. First, the Domain of New England was created and both Jerseys placed within it, effectively ending the proprietary government. Next, on April 15, 1702, after a period of rioting and litigation based on the land questions, Queen Anne combined both East and West Jersey into one royal colony and revoked the charters of the Proprietors; however, the strong tradition of self-government survived.

Tensions resurfaced in 1738, when proprietor Lewis Morris was named governor. The Proprietors began ejection suits against people who held land grants earlier, and in 1745 they arrested Samuel Baldwin for cutting timber on land to which he held apparently legal title. On September 19, supporters broke into the Newark jail and freed Baldwin. When three men were arrested for aiding his escape, three hundred turned out and fought with militia guarding the jail. The assembly refused to take action. Riots spread through the northern counties, and were not quelled until the French and Indian War provided a common enemy.

Farming was the major industry in the state. Major crops included wheat, corn, oats, rye, flax, hemp and cranberries. Serious crop failures occurred in 1682 and 1687. Iron production was also important. The first commercial glass house was established by Caspar Wistar in Salem County in 1739 and operated until 1776.

New Jersey's Swedish population was dispersed, ranging from Raccoon (modern-day Swedesboro) to Great Egg Harbor on the Atlantic. By 1695 about nine hundred, isolated, poor and illiterate, lived in an area characterized as wild, and they became isolated and impoverished, with a high incidence of emotional and social instability. Most were employed in the lumber trades, and many were CEDAR CHOPPERS who mined downed cedar trees from the mud of the swamps that had preserved them for many years. With the establishment of their own church at Raccoon in 1705, these settlers achieved a long-sought break with their more affluent Pennsylvania brethren. The cultural gap thus created between the two sides of the river in part inspired America's first ballad opera, *The Disappointment*, published in 1767.

New Jersey was the most fought-over colony in the Revolution. Aside from the major battles (Princeton, Trenton, Monmouth, etc.), the proximity of New York made the area around the harbor prime scavenging territory, and British COWBOYS routinely raided cattle and other provisions and were ambushed by local militia. For a short time Philadelphia caused similar effects along the Delaware.

PENNSYLVANIA

Governors (With Dates of Service in Pennsylvania)
1681–82, 1695–99, William Markham; 1682–84, 1699–1701, William Penn; 1684–88, 1690–93, Thomas Lloyd; 1688–90, John Blackwell; 1693–95, Benjamin Fletcher; 1701–03, Andrew Hamilton; 1703–04, Edward Shippen; 1704–09, John Evans; 1709–17, Charles Gookin; 1717–26, Sir William Keith; 1726–36, Patrick Gordon; 1736–38, James Logan; 1738–47, George Thomas; 1747–48, Anthony Palmer; 1748–54, 1759–63, 1771, 1773, James Hamilton; 1754–56, Robert Hunter Morris; 1756–59, William Denny; 1763–71, 1773–76, John Penn; 1771–73,

APPROXIMATE POPULATION OF PENNSYLVANIA		
Year	Total	Black
1682	3,000	-
1685	8,200	-
1701	15,000	-
1730	45,000	4,000
1750	190,000	-
1775	300,000	-

Richard Penn; 1776, David Rittenhouse; 1776, Samuel Morris Sr.; 1776–78, Thomas Wharton; 1778, George Bryan; 1778–81, Joseph Reed.

Government
Penn's charter for the colony (including Delaware) required freemen to assemble in 1682 and elect members of an assembly (nine from each county) and a council (three from each county) to meet the following year. In 1696 the number sent to the council was reduced to two from each county. In the Charter of Privileges granted in 1701 and in force until the Revolution, council members were appointed.

Population and Area
Pennsylvania was granted to William Penn as settlement by King Charles II of debts owed to William's admiral father in wartime. Since it was a proprietary, not royal, colony, Penn was free to organize as he pleased. Being a Quaker, he espoused religious toleration and peaceable relations with the Indians. Consequently, Pennsylvania was able to attract ambitious skilled labor from many parts of Europe and became a successful trading and manufacturing center.

Pennsylvania was a haven for settlers from the Palatinate in Germany (the "Dutch"), who settled in the fertile lands of the southeastern part of the colony, and the Moravians from Czechoslovakia, who settled Bethlehem. Both groups proved to be extremely hardworking and stable, so much so that the leadership of North Carolina asked the Moravians to move there.

Philadelphia became a major debarkation point for Germans, Scots-Irish from the Clearings, and others, while retaining its original Swedish settlers and English Quakers. Ultimately, the Great Wagon Road opened from Lancaster County down the Shenandoah Valley to North Carolina, and this became the immigrants' main route to western North Carolina and the Cumberland Gap. After the French and

Indian War, Forbe's Road became the major route west into the Ohio Country until the Erie Canal was built. During the Revolution, Philadelphia was the largest of the colonies' cities.

Pennsylvania inherited a highly developed network of Indian trails, and many of its early roads followed them. Forbe's Road was built in a straight line over the mountains from the end of such a road protected by a string of forts at Fort Loudon, Fort Littleton and Fort Bedford. Later it was turned into a water-level route. Travelers today can gain some idea of the difficulty of the project by following U.S. Route 30, which parallels the old road. Other portions of the old roads survive. Though not a major route, Shade Gap became known as "The Shades of Death," because travelers claimed the gap was so dark you could not see your hand in front of your face at noon, making it a popular place for ambushes.

The Quaker influence both shaped the character of Pennsylvania and became one of its greatest problems. The complete abhorrence of war, even when thrust upon the population, allowed the frontier areas to be virtually denuded in the French and Indian War, as the Quakers, the new merchant class and professional government fought over how to deal with Indian attacks. What began in the War of Jenkins' Ear (1739) ended in 1756 when the Quakers abdicated power, and thence their influence was more tempering than driving. As late as the Revolution, Quaker influences prevented theaters from being built and music from becoming an institution, but the King overruled many prohibitive laws. Their aversion to the Revolutionary War saw many labeled Tories when they sought only to remain neutral.

Basic and grammar education was important to the Quakers, and they established many schools, including schools for poor children, but higher education was not important. Subjects in the public schools included fair writing, grammatical rules, merchants' accounts, and mathematics, including navigation and surveying.

The Quakers stayed close to Philadelphia. The Germanics, however, moved relentlessly over the mountains and built the larger state of Pennsylvania. Originally the area around Pittsburgh was part of Virginia. In the 1730s German settlers in the Lancaster area created the "Pennsylvania rifle" by combining the short German jaeger rifle with the long English fowler. It proved a popular weapon for frontiersmen in western Pennsylvania, Maryland, Virginia and North Carolina.

NEW YORK

Governors (With Dates of Service in New York)
1664–68, Richard Nicolls; 1668–73, Francis Lovelace; 1673–74, Dutch occupied; 1674–77, (sir) 1678–81, Edmund Andros; 1677–78, 1681–83,

Anthony Brockholls; 1683–88, Thomas Dongan; 1688–89, Francis Nicholson; 1689–91, Jacob Leisler; 1691, Henry Sloughter; 1691–92, 1709–10, Richard Ingoldesby; 1692–98, Benjamin Fletcher; 1698–99, 1700–01, Richard Coote, Earl of Bellomont; 1699–1700, 1701–02, John Nanfan; 1701, William Smith; 1702–08, Edward Hyde, Viscount Cornbury; 1708–09, John Lovelace, fourth Baron Lovelace of Hurley; 1709, 1719–20, Peter Schuyler; 1710, Gerardus Beekman; 1710–19, Robert Hunter; 1720–28, William Burnet; 1728–31, John Montgomerie; 1731–32, Rip Van Dam; 1732–36, William Cosby; 1736–43, George Clarke; 1743–53, George Clinton; 1753, Sir Danvers Osborn; 1753–55, 1757–60, James DeLancey; 1755–57, Sir Charles Hardy; 1760–61, 1761–62, 1763–65, 1774–75, Cadwallader Colden; 1761, 1762–63, Robert Monckton; 1765–69, Sir Henry Moore; 1770–71, John Murray, fourth Earl of Dunmore; 1771–74, 1775–80, William Tryon; 1777, Pierre Van Cortland; 1777–95, George Clinton; 1780–83, James Robertson.

Government

Under Dutch rule the colonists had neither elective nor legislative power. Occasionally councils were appointed to advise during crises, but they were short-lived. In 1664, with the arrival of the English, writs were sent to all Long Island towns for elections of two deputies from each town by the freeholders, English or Dutch. Under the code they rubber-stamped (the Duke's Laws), which lasted until 1691, only local officers were elected. During the Dutch rule of 1673 and 1674 again only local officers were elected. In 1674 the Duke of York obtained a new charter, and in 1680 a petition was forwarded requesting an assembly. It met and drafted a constitution which was not ratified. Andros's arrival vested all authority in the governor and council. After Andros was imprisoned, Lieutenant Governor Leisler took power and called an assembly, but the arrival of Sloughter, bearing an order from William and Mary for an assembly, saw Leisler's execution for usurpation.

Population and Area

With the ascension of George I of Hanover to the English throne in 1714, the problems of a small group of German states became concerns of England through their shared monarch. Before that time, family relations had tied the two areas together. The American colonies became part of a solution that took a mass of poor but hardworking tenant farmers from the land-poor provinces of Germany and sent them under state aegis to the colonies. In 1710 the British government sent 3,200 Germans to New York, and other colonies would get later shipments. The Germans proved hard workers and good farmers willing to take the risks inherent in expanding the settled area to obtain tillable land. They probably proved useful for the government because

APPROXIMATE POPULATION OF NEW YORK

Year	Total	Black
1664	7,000	700?
1670	11,000	-
1700	20,000	-
1725	40,564	6,171
1749	73,448	10,692
1771	168,007	19,883

of the linguistic similarities to the Dutch already present.

The Dutch established New Amsterdam on Manhattan Island in 1624 and used it as a trading base. During attempts to settle outside the immediate area, a conflict soon became apparent between the colonists, who wanted to farm and develop the land, and the Indian traders and fur trappers, who wanted only limited settlement so as to disrupt the land and their trade the least. Ultimately, the traders and trappers won, and New Amsterdam stayed a small, if thriving, trading center. The old town of Manhattan was below modern-day Wall Street, and farms spread out into the area around Fourteenth Street.

As the Dutch expanded into the lower Delaware Valley, they threatened the Virginia colony and forced the creation of Maryland where it is today. The Duke of York took action, sending a military force to obtain the surrender of the Dutch in 1664, which was confirmed in a treaty. In 1673 the Dutch sent a fleet and again took over New York and New Jersey for a year, but little changed during that period.

New York was located astride the Hudson River, one of the most strategic waterways in North America. Wide enough for an oceangoing ship to sail as far as Albany, the Hudson penetrates far into the mountainous interior. Above Albany, it could still be used by small boats and was an easier route than overland. Passing up a side creek to Lake George, and then to Lake Champlain by way of a short ford, which emptied into the St. Lawrence River, it provided a relatively easy route from the middle colonies to the interior of Canada, saving thousands of miles over the sea route.

This route was so obvious that a major stone fortress, Ticonderoga, was built by the British on Lake Champlain to protect the colonies from invasion from Canada. During the French and Indian War several campaigns were fought along this route. The first major American victory of the Revolution, which prompted France to recognize the new country, took place when the British attempted to cut New England off from the rest of the colonies by seizing the Hudson route. The British plan was unnecessarily complex, consisting of three different armies intended to converge on Albany. The Americans were able to defeat each in detail, keeping the valley open. Afterward, the British were content to hold New York, threatening the valley and denying the Americans the central harbor.

The Hudson was the major axis of settlement and in the early days allowed easy communication with the Iroquoian tribes in the interior from whom the Dutch purchased most of their furs. From the Hudson, another valley opened out toward the western edge of New York, passing through Fort Stanwix and Oriskiny. This route ran near many Iroquoian towns as well as Fort Niagara, the major defense of the Niagara portage. The cold climate of the interior meant the furs obtained by New Yorkers were of better quality than those obtained farther south.

Although not now associated with New York, oysters were a major source of food in the harbor, being plentiful enough into the twentieth century to feed by the bushel to hogs as waste food. Huge sturgeon were plentiful until they were killed for roe after the colonial period.

New York benefited from several factors that made it more accommodating than some colonies. Founded by Dutch merchants, for whom business was everything (and by whom anything which might disrupt business was avoided) New York enjoyed toleration in religious matters due to the assimilation of the Dutch church into the English empire. With the exception of several royal governors who did not understand these important precepts, the colony was noncommittal about many things, even failing to instruct its delegation to the Continental Congress in much of anything.

One incident that had little political import but created quite a controversy was the tenure of Governor Lord Cornbury, who was given by Queen Anne the choice of going to debtor's prison or taking the governorship of New York and New Jersey. Deciding to represent the Queen literally, he dressed in gowns and entertained so lavishly his debts piled up again. Finally, upon complaints, the Queen removed him from office, whereupon he was immediately seized and imprisoned for debt. He was saved by the death of his father, the Earl of Clarendon, whose title brought with it immunity from prosecution. His return to England brought a comfortable political career to him and much relief to the colonists.

A major factor in the development and politics of New York were the Iroquois who lived in the upstate area. Historians differ widely as to when the Iroquois confederation for the mutual benefit of various tribes occurred, some placing it several hundred years back, others placing it during the colonial period. What is indisputable is that the large, well-organized and political nation, which numbered some twenty thousand warriors at first contact, was a major force in colonial life. The Iroquois continued to exert a strong influence up to and through most of the Revolution, until a punitive expedition led by General Sullivan burned towns and fields, removing the Iroquois from the equation. Even then, the strength of the much-depleted nation (maybe one thousand warriors) was such that it continues with a strong identity to the present day, and much of what is known about other eastern Indians is related to or inferred from Iroquois practice.

The Iroquois, in understandable self-interest, took the side of whichever European power was most inclined to leave them alone. At first these were the Dutch and French, both of whom limited settlement and provided the Indians with arms in exchange for furs. After the English conquest of New Amsterdam, some tribes later aligned with the Iroquois joined with the French and were a major thorn in the side of the English government until it defeated them in the French and Indian War. At this point, reacting to Indian concerns, the English refused to grant the colonists the land in the Ohio Valley promised on defeat of the French, and instead issued the Proclamation of 1763 limiting colonization. European settlements that violated this order were burned by royal troops. Thus, the English secured the friendship of the Iroquois and alienated many of the small farmers who would become Patriots. The Iroquois influence would grow to include many tribes outside the five nations living in upstate New York and affected colonists in Pennsylvania, Vermont, Connecticut and western Massachusetts.

DELAWARE

Governors (With Dates of Service in Delaware)
1775–77, John McKinly; 1777, Thomas McKean; 1777–78, George Read; 1778–81, Ceasar Rodney; 1781–82, John Dickinson; 1782–83, John Cook; 1783–86, Nicholas Van Dyke.

Originally settled by the Swedes in 1638, taken over by the Dutch in 1655, conquered by the English as part of New Amsterdam in 1664 and then granted to both Maryland and Pennsylvania, Delaware did not become its own entity until 1775. An English court in 1685 granted the area to Penn, who considered it his three southern counties and protection for his access to the ocean. The court reflected his concerns, giving him land north and east of a line going from Cape Henlopen on the ocean, west midway to the Chesapeake, thence due north to the arc twelve miles from the center of New Castle (formerly, New Amstel under the Dutch) that forms the border with Pennsylvania today.

In 1703, using authority to hold their own assembly instead of sending delegates to Philadelphia, the Delaware territories started their own legislature in New Castle, which met under virtually the same rules as the Pennsylvania one.

Delaware contained the northern end of the strategic portage to the Chesapeake, starting at the mouth of the South River, continuing to its headwaters, over the portage to the Head of Elk, and thence to the northern Chesapeake.

Delaware had good farmland for grain crops, although much of the land was not cleared. It also was fine orchard land and produced peaches, cherries and apples. The extensive salt marshes proved to be suitable pasture for cattle, and the colony's extensive lumber industry, particularly oaks, produced enough tanbark for a major tannery at Cutwell's Bridge built by the Corbitts. Lumber went to shipyards at Johnneycake Landing (today's Frederica). The fall line of the Brandywine became a major milling site late in the period.

Towns

Wilmington, founded in 1730, eclipsed New Castle in size by the 1750s. The first bridge across the Brandywine was built in 1760 on the road from Philadelphia to Wilmington. New Castle, Dover and Lewes were the county seats. Fast Landing (Leipsic) was founded about 1723.

BIBLIOGRAPHY

Condon, Thomas J. *New York Beginnings: The Commercial Origins of New Netherland.* New York: New York University Press, 1968.

Heckewelder, John. *History, Manners and Customs of the Indian Nations Who Once Inhabited Pennsylvania and the Neighboring States.* 1876. Reprint, New York: Arno Press, 1971.

McCormick, Richard Patrick. *New Jersey From Colony to State, 1609–1789.* Newark: New Jersey Historical Society, 1981.

Penn, William. *William Penn's Own Account of the Lenni Lenape or Delaware Indians.* 1683. Reprint, with an introduction by Albert Cook Myers and a foreword by John E. Pomfret. Somerset, N.J.: Middle Atlantic Press, 1970.

Pierce, Arthur D. *Iron in the Pines: The Story of New Jersey's Ghost Towns and Bog Iron.* New Brunswick, N.J.: Rutgers University Press, 1957.

Raymond, Eleanor. *Early Domestic Architecture of Pennsylvania.* Princeton: Pyne Press, 1973.

CHAPTER FOUR

Deep South Regional Overview

The Deep South was settled in two movements. First the Carolinas were settled together, about the same time as Pennsylvania. Early in the next century, Georgia was added. Settlement went fairly smoothly, due in part to its late date and proximity to Virginia and the Caribbean colonies. Carolina was chartered in 1663 as a proprietary colony but then split into two colonies about 1712.

The Carolinas found neither the tobacco of the Chesapeake nor the sugar of the Caribbean to be effective crops. After a period of experimentation which mirrored that in Virginia, rice and indigo were found to be complementary. They were more valuable than tobacco, less so than sugar. In the earliest plans for settlement, the colonists understood the climate would allow cultivation of crops that might be killed by frosts elsewhere. Olives were tried, as were raisins, wine grapes, silkworms, capers, currants and various oil-producing crops.

Until the late period most of the region was held by wealthy men residing in England, many members of Parliament, who used overseers to maximize returns. The overseers themselves intended to stay for a short time, hoping to obtain enough return to purchase land and go back to England before dying of malaria or other local diseases. About the time of the Revolution, a resident planter class became established, first in the cultural center of Charles Town, then fanning out into the countryside. Most of the grand homes of the region date from after the war. The region focused on Charles Town, the only major city.

High labor mortality, high crop prices and an exploitive economic scenario led this area to become especially dependent on a steady supply of slave labor. The slaves in the best condition left over from the Caribbean were sold here for top dollar. Because of the rigors of a two-season cultivation in swampy fields (among alligators, alligator snapping turtles, water moccasins, malarial mosquitoes, jungle rot and danger from tools like machetes), slaves here experienced harsher and

APPROXIMATE POPULATION OF REGION	
1688	8,000
1715	27,950
1765	340,000

shorter lives than did those sold farther north.

The establishment of Carolina resulted in the construction, starting in 1672, of the Castillo de San Marcos in St. Augustine to protect the Spanish border. Tensions were aligned three ways as Spain claimed all the territory, France moved to protect its waterways with the establishment of New Orleans, and traders from Carolina moved west and south, hoping to break both parties' hold. The English were good at winning Indian support, in part because they had more trade goods than Florida, which was seriously underfunded by the crown.

About 1700, when Louis XIV claimed the Spanish throne for his grandson, the War of Spanish Succession (called Queen Anne's War in America) threatened an alliance between France and Spain, and an attack upon Carolina. Governor Moore of Carolina preemptively besieged St. Augustine in 1702. The Castillo barely held, but the town was burned to the ground. Moore was discredited and lost his office, but the campaign stopped any Spanish-French incursion into Carolina.

From then through the early eighteenth century, the frontier became an area of border warfare, small in total size but large in proportion to the resources of both Florida and the South. (The siege had seen about five hundred English and five hundred Indians against about three hundred Spanish, only twenty of whom were considered fit for a pitched battle.) Charles Town became the counterpoint of French New Orleans, while Georgia became the buffer for Florida.

SOUTHERN NORTH CAROLINA

Governors (With Dates of Service in North Carolina)

Carolina north and east of the Cape Fear River: 1690, Philip Ludwell; 1690–94, Thomas Jarvis; 1694–99, Thomas Harvey; 1699–1703, Henderson Walker; 1703–05, Robert Daniel; 1705–06, 1708–11, Thomas Cary; 1706–08, William Glover; 1711–12, Edward Hyde.

North Carolina: 1712–14, 1722, Thomas Pollock; 1714–22, Charles Eden; 1722–24, William Reed; 1724–25, 1731–34, George Burrington; 1725–31, Sir Richard Everard; 1734, 1752–53, Nathaniel Rice; 1734–52, Gabriel Johnston; 1753–54, Matthew Rowan; 1754–65, Arthur Dobbs; 1765–71, William Tryon; 1771, James Hasell; 1771–75, Josiah Martin;

APPROXIMATE POPULATION OF NORTH CAROLINA

Year	Total	Slave
1677	4,000	-
1715	11,200	3,700
1732	36,000	6,000
1752	30,000	10,000
1774	270,000	-

1775–76, Cornelius Harnett; 1776, Samuel Ashe; 1776, Willie Jones; 1777–80, Richard Caswell; 1780–81, Abner Nash; 1781, Thomas Burke.

Government

The charter of 1663 granted proprietors the right to pass laws "with the advice, assent and approbation of the freemen of the said province or the greater part of them or of their deputies." It also allowed full authority when no assembly could be called. In the charter of 1665 the authority was granted to subdivide the colony into counties, baronies and colonies. This authority was ultimately used to separate North and South Carolina. The colonists agreed to elect thirteen persons, from whom six councillors and a governor would be elected. The freeholders, or two deputies from each division elected biennially, could pass laws subject to proprietary abrogation within one year. Until 1712 there was one governor for both Carolinas. In 1731 the first assembly under royal authority met and followed prior custom. In 1716 the parish rather than the county became the election district.

Population and Area

Southern North Carolina looked to South Carolina for leadership and to Charles Town as its cultural center. In many ways, North Carolina was indistinguishable from South Carolina.

Along the mountain fringe the Cherokees were different from many other tribes. They occupied the mountain areas in far western North Carolina, thus placing them farther out of the way of a much slower expansion than the Indians had to contend with in many other areas. Influence over areas reaching into the trading routes between the colonists and other tribes was ceded to South Carolina by treaty, and so conflict was kept to a minimum during the colonial period.

Equally important were the Scots-Irish immigrants, most of whom came down the Great Wagon Road from Pennsylvania, Virginia and Maryland after being removed during the Clearings for their parts in the Jacobite Rebellion of 1745. Having rebelled against the English king, and consequently forbidden to wear tartans or kilts or play the pipes, they were loyal, but only to the extent called on under the old clan hierarchy. Their involvement in the Revolution was generally limited, and they returned home as soon as the patriots gave them a good reason to do so. Mostly they were interested in free land, readily available in western North Carolina, and in being as far as possible from the government, which the remote back country ensured. The climate reminded them of home even if it was less severe, and the mountainous terrain was similar to the Highlands, with the advantages of being more fertile and less rugged than home. They formed communities that remained isolated and traditional into the twentieth century.

SOUTH CAROLINA

Governors (With Dates of Service in South Carolina)
Carolina south and west of the Cape Fear River: 1670–71, William Sayle; 1671–72, Joseph West; 1672–74, Sir John Yeamans; 1674–82, 1684–85, Joseph West; 1682–84, 1685–86, Joseph Morton; 1684, Sir Richard Kyrle; 1684, Robert Quary; 1686–1690, James Colleton; 1690–92, Seth Sothel; 1692–93, Philip Ludwell; 1693–94, Thomas Smith; 1694–95, 1696–1700, Joseph Blake; 1695–96, John Archadale; 1700–03, James Moore Sr.; 1703–09, Sir Nathaniel Johnson; 1709–10, Edward Tynte; 1710–12, Robert Gibbes.

South Carolina: 1712–16, Charles Craven; 1716–17, Robert Daniel; 1717–19, 1730–35, Robert Johnson; 1719–21, James Moore Jr.; 1721–25, Francis Nicholson; 1725–30, Arthur Middleton; 1735–37, Thomas Broughton; 1737–43, William Bull Sr.; 1743–56, James Glen; 1756–60, William Henry Lyttelton; 1760–61, 1764–66, 1768, 1769–71, 1773–75, William Bull Jr.; 1761–64, Thomas Boone; 1766–68, 1768–69, 1771–73, Lord Charles Greville Montagu; 1775, Lord William Campbell; 1775–76, Henry Laurens; 1776–78, 1779–82, John Rutledge; 1778–79, Rawlins Lowndes; 1782–83, John Mathewes.

Government
When the 1716 statute making the parish the electoral district was revoked by the Proprietors in 1719, citizens rebelled and appealed to the King, who sent a provisional royal governor in 1721. The Proprietors, with the exception of Lord Carteret, sold their interests to the crown and were confirmed by act of Parliament.

Population and Area
Charles Town (it did not become Charleston until after the Revolution), founded about 1680, became the largest city in the South and,

APPROXIMATE POPULATION OF SOUTH CAROLINA

Year	Total	Slave	Indentured
1682	2,500	-	-
1703	7,150	3,000	200
1715	16,750	10,500	-
1737	47,000	22,000	-
1751	65,000	40,000	-
1769	125,000	80,000	-

just before the Revolution, the wealthiest colonial city. Located at the confluence of several rivers and creeks, it was the focal point for not only South Carolina, but also North Carolina, which was landlocked by the shoal waters of the Albemarle. Many planters avoided their plantations for entire seasons and established more or less permanent residences in Charles Town. Already a fairly stable city by the 1730s, it produced a level of culture unknown among other southern cities.

Close ties existed between Charles Town and England, in part because so many planters were or were related to members of Parliament. Like in Virginia, the work of Charles Town cabinetmakers is virtually indistinguishable from English work, except on microscopic examination of the wood. Stability meant music teachers, concerts, theater and other cultural events existed. Charles Town may have been the most English of American cities. Little wonder that the crown mistakenly felt South Carolina would be staunchly Tory during the Revolution.

While coastal Carolina became known for rice and indigo, trade with the Indians was increasingly dominated by Charles Town merchants. The port was closer to the hunting grounds of the Catawbas and Cherokees, and the mountains gave way to more penetrable terrain in southern North Carolina. War with the Westo Indians in the 1680s temporarily halted progress, but their defeat led to rapid expansion of a trade that became a large part of Charles Town's wealth. Conflict with the French of New Orleans followed, and ultimately the Tories who traded with the Indians removed to St. Augustine during the Revolution, causing headaches for the southern patriots.

As a result of the extensive Indian trade, a number of small trading settlements formed far into the interior, several of which became the focus of the southern campaign in the Revolution.

Beef also was a major export, as it was easily raised with little need to provide winter forage to the ranging cattle. As early as 1682 many planters reported herds of seven hundred to eight hundred head.

APPROXIMATE POPULATION OF GEORGIA

Year	Total	Slave
1733	152	-
1751	2,120	420
1765	11,300	4,500
1775	32,000	15,000

GEORGIA

Governors (With Dates of Service in Georgia)
1733–43, James Edward Oglethorpe; 1743–51, William Stephens; 1751–52, Henry Parker; 1752–54, Patrick Graham; 1754–57, John Reynolds; 1757–60, Henry Ellis; 1760–71, 1779–82, Sir James Wright; 1771–73, James Habersham; 1775, 1776, William Ewen; 1775–76, 1779–80, George Walton; 1776–77, Archibald Bulloch; 1777, Button Gwinnett; 1777–78, John Adam Treutlen; 1778–79, John Houstoun; 1779, John Wereat. Provincial Governors: 1780, Richard Howley, Stephen Heard; 1780–81, Myrick Davies; 1781–82, Nathan Brownson; 1782–83, John Martin; 1783–84, Lyman Hall.

Government
The original government of Georgia held all authority within an appointed council called "Trustees for establishing the colony of Georgia in America." Under chaotic conditions in 1751, an assembly was called, but it had no real authority. In June 1752 the trustees surrendered their charter, and the colony was ruled by a royal governor and council, with election of an assembly in 1754. For a while during the Revolution, Georgia was almost totally in British hands, and it was the only state of the Union in which a Tory assembly met during the war.

Georgia was conceived to fulfill a number of purposes. As the southern border of the colonies, a settlement on the Savannah River was seen as a military barrier to protect the Carolinas. Landholding was defined in small units to produce a contiguous line of citizenry for defense. Georgia provided as an opportunity to do good, particularly in light of the corruption then rampant in English government. Chartered in 1732 by General James Oglethorpe, Lord Percival, first Earl of Egmont, and others, Georgia was intended to "carry off the numbers of poor children and other poor that pester the streets of London."

Immigrants were carefully selected and only those of good, working character were allowed. Any people already supporting themselves in

England were forbidden to settle, as they were a benefit to England where they were. Names of potential emigrants were published in the English papers so creditors and abandoned wives could make claim before departure. Only about a dozen debtors were imported at first, and these showed promise of working on arrival.

Many of Georgia's early problems came from a well-intended but ill-informed altruism among the English aristocratic proprietors. Similar and yet different from the New Englanders and the Quakers, the proprietors intended Georgia to be a pragmatic, middle-of-the-road utopian experiment. Unfortunately, policies were based on poor information and then enforced as if they were moral dogma. The colony was planned less for what it could do for itself and more for what it was intended to do for England. Little had been learned from over a century of colonizing. England in the 1730s, in terms of expectations and adaptability, seems little advanced over that of 1607.

The original plan for Georgia was based on strictly controlled land ownership by small farmers of the English working class who were left out of the system in England. Admission of slaves to the colony was forbidden up to 1750 when, in a desperate attempt to save a faltering colony, the proprietors allowed slavery. The failure of the colony lay in the arbitrary restrictions imposed by the proprietors. A family could receive only fifty acres of land, and the largest landholdings allowed by law were five hundred acres. Land could be neither sold nor inherited by women. Much of the land consisted of pine barrens and so was too poor to support a family. The major crop, rice, required massive capital investment to build dikes, which the average farmer could not afford. Finally, the populace was said as early as 1739 to have been "useless in England" and "inclined to be useless in Georgia likewise."

In late September 1740, during the War of Jenkins' Ear, Governor Oglethorpe unsuccessfully besieged St. Augustine. His force of two thousand men included eleven hundred Indians, two hundred settlers from Georgia, and the rest Highlanders and from South Carolina. They were prevented from passing the inlet because of Spanish galleys and were suffering from disease, so he retreated.

In July 1742, fifty Spanish ships with eighteen hundred soldiers and one thousand sailors left Havana to attack St. Simon's Island in Georgia. A detachment of some two hundred Spanish were trapped and defeated by the Highlanders, some of Oglethorpe's five hundred men, at the Battle of Bloody Marsh. A French spy told the Spanish how weak Oglethorpe was, but Oglethorpe became aware of the spy and asked him to work for the English and keep the Spanish around for another few days so his reinforcements and a British fleet might destroy them. The Spanish decided to leave. Oglethorpe's ruse worked. There were neither reinforcements nor a British fleet.

In 1743 Oglethorpe moved on St. Augustine again, but when the Spanish would not come out to fight him, he returned to Georgia. These actions were important because they ended conflict between Spain and England along the border.

In 1763, after the French and Indian War, the Indians signed a treaty with Georgia ceding many of their lands in the interior. As this land was better than the coastal pine barrens, the 1770s saw extensive immigration from Virginia, North Carolina and Germany down the Great Wagon Road. At this time the Germans became the second largest ethnic group in Georgia.

Georgia's major trading partners were the islands of the Caribbean, from which Georgia obtained slaves, rum, sugar, molasses and furs in exchange for local rice, pork and barrel staves.

ENGLISH FLORIDA

During the French and Indian War the British captured Havana from Spain, and in the Treaty of Paris it was traded for Spanish holdings in Florida, securing England's southern continental flank. Florida was an affluent colony from 1763 until 1786, when it was given back to Spain.

Spain had not attempted to develop Florida into anything more than a military outpost based on the Castillo de San Marco in St. Augustine, in part because the royal treasury was often unable even to supply the garrison properly. The English, however, knew how to profit from the area and moved rapidly to develop it. Within a short time many productive plantations were in operation.

Although England promised to tolerate Catholics who remained when Spain evacuated, most of the population left. Most properties were left in the hands of one agent, who agreed not to sell until values rebounded. Almost all the four hundred homes in St. Augustine were a single story of TABBY (a poured shell aggregate) and in poor condition. Many were torn down for materials early in the English reign. The new colonists fixed the rest, adding wooden second stories and fireplaces (the Spanish had use braziers for heat).

The impetus for development in East Florida was Governor James Grant (who served from 1764 to 1771), a man with strong connections to Charles Town. He actively recruited major planters to move to Florida and develop plantations, winning them with promises of seats on the Council—a necessity since, without them, Florida did not have enough aristocracy to hold council meetings.

Grant was extremely well liked and never called legislative elections. Under his rule, plantations were developed along the coast as far south as the St. Johns River was tidal, and they began exporting indigo and orange juice. Plantations were granted in lots of up to twenty thousand acres and worked almost exclusively with slave labor. White indentures were not counted on even to provide their own food.

Grant governed with a strict adherence to social rank but held weekly balls and created a social life unequaled except in Charles Town. He built a sloop, the *East Florida*, to convey prospective planters and to ship their wares out. Because of his genuine concern for Creek interests, he was able to build strong relations with the Indians. By 1771 the Twenty-first Regiment was available, the government paid for schoolmasters, merchants congregated, and there were two Masonic lodges. St. Augustine, the capital, had become a little Charles Town.

John Moultrie replaced Grant. During his tenure (1771 to 1774) excellent roads and new public buildings were built and population increased. Dissension grew over the need for an elected assembly.

Moultrie was succeeded by a military man, Patrick Tonyn (who served from 1774 to 1786), who misread the situation as rebellious. Tonyn alienated the populace: He strictly adhered to rank and privilege, exhibited poor manners and poor hospitality, and kept not a wife but a mistress who reportedly ran the colony savagely, including abusing slaves rented from other landowners.

Tonyn's fortunes changed with the outbreak of hostilities. East Florida, as the southernmost colony and the only one south of Canada fully loyal to England, became the base for raids into the backcountry of the South, a refuge for Tories from the rebellious colonies (enough so that Tonyn finally authorized an assembly), and a military and ship-servicing post. Ultimately, though, East Florida was just a bargaining chip in the larger settlement and was returned to Spain.

West Florida, including Mobile and Pensacola, was more of a military outpost throughout the period.

BIBLIOGRAPHY

Arnade, Charles W. *The Siege of St. Augustine in 1702.* Gainesville: University of Florida Press, 1959.

Davis, Richard Beale. *Intellectual Life in the Colonial South 1585–1763.* Knoxville: University of Tennessee Press, 1978. In three volumes.

Martin, Harold H. *Georgia: A Bicentennial History.* New York: Norton, 1977.

Weir, Robert M. *Colonial South Carolina: A History.* Millwood, N.Y.: KTO Press, 1983.

Wright, Louis B. *South Carolina: A Bicentennial History.* New York: Norton, 1976.

Bay

5   20

ay is very
ll of Flatts
n the Sea   ↑ + *Rocky ground*
angerous
ck and   4
nt   4   7   10   30
Plymouth
Bay   Marks I.   4 *Gurnet head*
Cedar P. XI   7 *channel to way*
5 6

Monemeat   3   7 *Browns Sunken*   *Barnstable*
high Land   2   2   3   *Islands*   *reason of*
3   *Run a Shoa*

7 *Note that th*
Bars are bu
are set down
Water, and
7 *there is the*

Barnst
C.

ds Bay is very dangerous
g and Flowing is but small   3   ↗

Sandwich   12
7 F   XI

Barnstable
2

Tucgguiset
Woods Pt.

hole   2

North Chann
2 *3 Coarse Sand 3*
foot   *Southacks Chan*
Horseshoe sand
5   2 *Tucgguiset Point*   3

PART TWO

Everyday Life

CHAPTER FIVE

Food & Drink

GENERAL OVERVIEW

Housewives and professional cooks began their day early, sometimes around four o'clock. They built the fire, hauled water, gathered ingredients from the kitchen garden, smokehouse and dairy, and slaughtered and cleaned fowl. When the fire was ready they prepared a heavy breakfast, which was served after the rest were at work for about two hours. The main meal of the day was dinner, served about two o'clock, with a light supper, often of cold leftovers, in the evening. Baking day often had lighter meals to allow full attention to the week's baking. In the early period Fridays were still mandatory fish days, not because of religion, but to promote the English fisheries. In Maryland, religion kept this practice going. Elsewhere in the colonies, it may have been continued locally.

The opening of the New World brought a terrific influx of foodstuffs into Europe, and the development of a commercially based economy meant these foods were increasingly available to the public. The colonies benefited from this in several ways. They were local producers; they received new products from other areas, such as those under Spanish dominion, which they could then produce locally; and they were slowly acclimated to a larger dietary base. Diet contributed to most native colonists being substantially taller than new immigrants (despite what many say, average heights in the colonial period were very close to those of 1970), stronger, and with better complexions and greater longevity, something Europeans frequently commented on. The fact that the colonists had traveled to new areas and personally experienced many new foods meant that after a while they were more open to new foods than were the Europeans.

One aspect of the early colonists that is hard for us to understand is the difficulty with which they accepted new and nutritious foods, even when at the point of starvation. Tomatoes, potatoes, oysters and others were all rejected in various parts of the world as either inappropriate for their class or poisonous. It was late in the seventeenth century before England began to accept oysters, and the nineteenth century before France accepted potatoes. Tomatoes were widely held to be poisonous into the nineteenth century, even though they formed a major basis of the diet of Central Americans.

This phenomenon grew in part from several sources. During the period a change occurred in eating habits. Whereas European diets were previously similar within a social class, the rise of nationalism and the effects of writers commenting with disgust on other nations' and peoples' foods led to the establishment of national styles, which left little tolerance for those of other areas. As a result, most sedentary people became suspicious of anything outside their own country. When the foreigners were savages, there was even less reason to give them credit for taste. Americans today have similar attitudes; workers abroad tend to eat American food rather than the local foods and live within the expatriate community rather than experiencing the local lifestyle. We are not that far removed from our colonial ancestors.

Garbage and trash were thrown outside for livestock, scattered on the lawn, used to fill ravines or thrown into a TRASH PIT, often dug for clay for building.

AVAILABILITY OF FOODS

The Americas contributed a long list of foods to the world: potatoes and tomatoes (which were not accepted until after the period, although Thomas Jefferson grew potatoes), turkey, maize, avocado pears, "French" beans, pumpkins, pineapples, lima beans, scarlet runner beans, chocolate, peanuts, vanilla, green and red peppers, cranberries (craneberries), Jerusalem artichokes, and sweet potatoes (commonly called potatoes), to name just a few. In addition, it brought into common use foods that were more restricted in England, such as oysters and venison. New cooking techniques were introduced, including the clambake and the barbecue.

Venison had been available only to the upper class in England, and this created problems early on. Few settlers had experience hunting deer, and those who did had often been passive participants in organized hunts (🖈 *page 287*) which took little skill. For the lower classes it took some time to acclimate to the freedom to hunt deer. With time, venison became a staple in areas that had not been cleared.

Conversely, oysters were lower-class food in England, and it was hard for early settlers to break social barriers even when they were starving.

Later, they would eat oysters with gusto when they were not feeding them to their hogs.

Game birds, including turkey, passenger pigeon, goose, quail, Eskimo curlew (called dough bird in New England), woodcock, canvasback duck and other ducks, were so common throughout the period that they literally darkened the sky as they passed. In 1736 passenger pigeons were six for a penny in Boston. In 1770 one hunter killed 125 with a single shot. John James Audubon saw one man net six thousand in a day. Still, as early as 1692 a commentator remarked, "of late they are much diminished," and in 1708 part of New York imposed a closed season on heath hens, grouse, quail and turkey.

Game animals included deer, bear (a good source of fat), raccoon, rabbit, boar (escaped domesticated pigs), muskrat, opossum, beaver (the tail was fried or broiled), turtle and squirrel (traditionally part of Brunswick stew). Bison were not hunted, as larger animals created problems with preservation. It was easier to preserve local pork than to bring home a five-hundred-pound bear or a ton of bison.

Fish were common in the deep, clear rivers. Sturgeon in excess of two hundred pounds were common; scales excavated from the Jamestown fort measure up to three inches across. On the Hudson, sturgeon were called Albany beef. Eels could be caught with the bare hands and stingray speared with a sword. In New England after a storm, six-foot lobsters piled up on the beach. Crabs and clams were plentiful throughout, oysters up to fourteen inches fed two people, salmon spawned in rivers, and many others like the lowly shad were so common they provided reliable food supplies.

Settlers also brought foods to the New World. Peaches and apples were popular with the Indians; apricots remained more of a colonist's food. Wheat and rye failed to produce as well as corn and were not important until late. Turnips, beets, purslane, lettuce, cabbage, lentils, cauliflower and asparagus were the staple vegetables for the colonists. Honeybees were called English flies by the Indians. Pigs, chickens, beef cattle, sheep and goats were all imported. Africans brought black-eyed peas. Rice was introduced about 1720. Carrots were imported, then escaped to their wild form, Queen Anne's lace.

Foreign Influences

The low countries (today's Belgium, Holland, Denmark and the surrounding area) provided several influences on the colonies. The Pilgrims had spent time in Holland. Many English were involved in trade with the low countries. The Dutch and Swedes first settled the Middle Atlantic states. The other Germanic immigrants passed through this gateway and went on to people much of Pennsylvania, western Virginia, Maryland and North Carolina. Holland was one of the first states in northern Europe to establish a mercantile bourgeoisie. Rhenish taste in foods, beers and wines influenced the colonies greatly. Like the Germans, the Dutch liked sausage, cabbage, coleslaw, lentils, rye bread and soups. Unlike the Germans, they imported and grew much exotic fruit, a fashion that spread in the colonies until it became symbolic of both hospitality and a successful trading voyage. The Dutch also gave us cookies and waffles.

French colonists, particularly the Huguenots after 1685, brought a new and more refined cuisine that included such foods as chowder. Canada had a certain continuity of French culture, but it came mostly from the lower classes, fur traders and soldiers who subsisted on dried peas, black tea and not much else. Later, during the Revolution, some cultural exchange occurred with the army stationed here, but it is difficult to quantify beyond a few officers. Men like Thomas Jefferson, who took his cook to learn French cooking on his embassy to Paris, brought back the new ideas, but the range of dissemination was small, and most such contacts occurred at the end of our period.

A few colonists came from Italy, but their numbers were so small that any influence was local. A large number of Minorcans settled in British Florida after 1763 and ensured continuity of Mediterranean cooking in St. Augustine and its environs. This cooking relied on olive oil, vinegar, herbs, seafood, goat products, wine, vegetables and fruits. Pasta had probably not been introduced yet.

TYPICAL DIET

Traditionally the English viewed first mutton and then beef as their principal meat. Chop houses or steak houses were popular places to congregate. During several invasion threats in the middle and late periods the English caricatured the French as starving and coveting English beef. (In reality the French thought the English ate too much meat.) Beef became a symbol that unified the English, and this was probably known in the colonies through prints and magazines. Thus it appears surprising that pork became the colonials' staple, but there were good reasons.

Pigs (pork, brawn) were allowed to run wild, particularly if an island could be secured from predators. They survived well on the MAST (acorns) available from the forest. Cattle need more maintenance, although they also were turned loose. By the early eighteenth century, pork accounted for the majority of the meat in the South and a significant portion in New England.

Most English cooking in the seventeenth century was done in one pot. This meant a lot of stews, or pot roasts with vegetables. Puddings, bread or plum, could be steamed in a fabric bag in or over the pot.

RECEIPT FOR A PLAIN BOILED PUDDING

"Take a pint of new milk, mix with it six eggs well beaten, two spoonfuls of flour, half a nutmeg grated, a little salt and sugar. Put this mixture into a cloth or bag. Put it into boiling water: and half an hour will boil it. Serve it up with melted butter."

Susannah Carter, *The Frugal Housewife* (Boston, 1772)

RECEIPT FOR A BATTALIA PIE

"Take four small chickens, and squab pigeons, four sucking rabbits, cut them in pieces, and season them with savory spice, lay them in the pie, with four sweetbreads sliced, as many sheeps tongues and shivered palates, two pair of lambs stones, twenty or thirty cockscombs, with savoury balls and oysters; lay on butter, and close the pie with a lear."

Susannah Carter, *The Frugal Housewife* (Boston, 1772)

Meat was either boiled or broiled. Frying was uncommon. The middle period saw the beginning of more refinement, as the growth in material culture allowed for more variety in utensils and technique.

The main dish in English cooking was roasted or boiled meat by the middle period, with puddings of many varieties common. These puddings are difficult to define, because they could be steamed, boiled or baked, using a variety of ingredients. Pies and pasties were also common, being essentially stews set in pastry crusts and baked. Many regional variations existed, but most emphasized meat and tubers, the principal components of the diet. Bread was important to the lower classes, who could not afford meat. Vegetables were boiled, cooking much of the nutrition out, and served salted, peppered and swimming in butter. Beer remained the principal drink until late.

At the court level a wider variety existed, but whereas France continued to use as the basis for its cookery the old medieval dishes once common in upper-class England, these dishes were no longer known in England, and French cooking was viewed with contempt. Along with the new cooking came a new myth: The traditional strength of the English came from the simple, hearty fare they ate.

The English had a passion for sweets which they gratified with cakes, candies such as rock candy, candied fruits, marzipan and, late in the period, ice cream. Ice cream was known from the 1740s in private dinners of Governor Bladen of Maryland, but the first public sale was in 1777 in New York. Cakes were common in the RECEIPT (recipe) books of the day. They ranged from Sally Lunn, an egg bread like

---

RECEIPT FOR QUEEN'S CAKE

"Take a pound of sugar, and beat it fine, pour in yolks and two whites of eggs, half a pound of butter, a little rose water, six spoonfuls of warm cream, a pound of currants, and as much flour as will make it up; stir them well together, and put them into your patty pans, being well buttered; bake them in an oven; almost as hot as for manchet for half an hour; then take them out and glaze them, and let them stand but a little after the glazing is on, to rise."

Susannah Carter, *The Frugal Housewife* (Boston, 1772)

---

challa, to heavy recipes like Queen's cake or Twelfth cake, similar to a holiday fruitcake. These cakes required pounds of flour and butter and numerous eggs. But they were large and served many.

A diet based on corn alone lacked certain essential vitamins. As vegetables were relatively uncommon during the period, colonists made up this deficiency with fats, as the Indians did. A diet heavy in fat was not unhealthy as long as the eater worked hard, burning off the harmful parts before they built up. Under sedentary conditions, though, the effects of eating too much meat were thought to contribute to the gout.

Nuts were more important to the diet than at first assumed, especially during wartime. The vast stands of nutwoods have all but disappeared; today, on Jamestown Island, the deer herd numbers about 150 and needs supplemental food in a bad winter. In early colonial times, deer herds numbering over 250 were reported, and the area was reported to be fairly denuded by tribute hunting for Powhatan; the deer lived on the mast alone. Acorns can be used to make a flour, but were not eaten much by the colonists. Black walnuts, chestnuts, hickory, beech and pecans, however, grew wild and were eaten.

COOKING TECHNIQUES AND EQUIPMENT

Most cooking was done in a large fireplace, with a fire kept blazing for boiling and a source of coals for broiling. Later, as trivets (three-legged stands) became common, coals were raked out under individual pots, gaining more control of heat and a neater working environment. At first fireplaces had a simple lug pole across the throat of the flue to suspend pots by pothooks or trammels. Later, a crane allowed the cook to remove the pot from the fire before lifting it, a great improvement in safety. Still, about 25 percent of all women were killed by cooking accidents, notably burns from long dresses and active fires. Many women hitched up their skirts, petticoats and aprons, tucking them

The kitchen of Shirley Plantation, Charles City, Virginia, shows a variety of implements comprising a fairly complete kitchen without the clutter of later or more expensive tools. Included are a number of brass utensils (very common among the Dutch and those who traded with them) including a funnel, pans, a skimmer, lantern, saucepan and pitcher; an iron balance beam with pans; wooden bowls, rolling pins and lemon juicer; horn spoon; skillet; and a dresser, or shelf, to hold service ware in the back corner. This kitchen fed a large plantation. Smaller homes could, and often had to, make do with less.

into their waistbands when cooking. Many also worked in a state of undress. The kitchen was not a "decent" place to visit, leading in part to the low opinion of scullery maids and kitchen maids.

Later a very few coal grates (☞ *page 288*) came into use, for both heating and, less commonly, cooking. Kettles were rounded pots of cast iron (occasionally brass, especially among the Dutch settlers) with three short legs. They weighed up to forty pounds when full. They were used for boiling, rendering, simmering, thickening and curing. Frying was done on spiders (frying pans set on three legs) often with a long handle, or griddles (large, flat, cast-iron pieces) usually suspended like a pot.

Baking was done in ovens, which were first nothing but helmet- or beehive-shaped pottery items outdoors. Later, ovens were incorporated into the fireplace mass but were usually separate from the firebox. A fire of RIVEN (finely split) wood was built inside the oven to heat the oven mass. When it was hot enough, the fire was scraped and the ash swept out. Good bakers could discern the temperature within a few degrees, even if they did not know such a standard, by how long they could hold an arm inside. Professional bakers could be identified by the lack of hair on their arms; it was singed off in work. Items requiring the hottest oven were put in first, then the next slower, and so on, following the natural cooling of the oven. The time was judged sometimes with a sandglass or by the passage of the sun. Baking was done once a week, and the day started early to get the oven hot enough to allow a full day of baking. When finished, items were removed with a wooden peel, such as those used today in pizza making. Dutch ovens were lidded pots with flat tops and bottoms. Coals were placed above and below the pot to bake a pie or the like.

Near the end of the period, reflector ovens came into use. These used tin to reflect heat from the fire back upon the baking or broiling. Although many small house museums proudly show one, such tin oven implements came in only at the very end of the period, and the large amount of tin they required made them rare until much later.

Broiling or roasting was done on a spit, which ran across the top or front of the fire, supported by ANDIRONS (HANDIRONS) or FIREDOGS, or a special tripod or stand. Those across the front allowed greater control, including the ability to recover drippings for basting, LEAR (gravy) being relatively uncommon except in pies. Small skewers or an iron basket secured the meat to the spit so it would turn. The spit had to be turned manually, often a job for the children. Later, some wealthier households would acquire a CLOCK JACK, a mechanical device driven by weights and gears like a clock that turned the spit at a slow pace. They usually had to be wound every twenty minutes or so. Broiling could also be done in a reflector oven, or on a grill or gridiron set over the coals.

Pottery saw its first use in the kitchen and dairy, where it was early specified for milk products. Germs were unknown, but people knew cleanliness was important, especially around dairy products, and the glazed surface of pottery allowed easier cleaning. Colanders, milk pans, bowls and churns were the most common. Rhenish wines came in stoneware JUGS sometimes called bellarmines. After the early period, pottery was more common, and plates, CHARGERS (serving plates), cups, mugs, jars, PORRINGERS (handled bowls), MONTEITH BOWLS (large bowls with indentations on the rim used to rinse wine glasses between courses), tureens, and coffee, tea and chocolate pots were used. Fancier houses might have a porcelain epergne (a multilayered cake plate or one with arms leading to serving plates) for serving sweetmeats and fruit.

Wood was used for dough troughs, churns, dashers, butter paddles and molds, PIGGINS (small buckets with an integral handle), buckets, barrels, bowls, TRENCHERS (early, plates used under dried bread), mugs (early), mortars and pestles, spoons, dough boxes, dry sinks, rolling pins, cheese forms, paddles (for stirring), scoops and BISCUIT (cookie) molds. These items were called TREENWARE or TREEN.

Leather was used for BLACKJACKS or JACKS (mugs), PITCHED URNS, BOM-BARDS (large pitcher jacks) and bottles, all lined with pitch to make them water-resistant. These items could not hold anything hot or highly alcoholic.

Glass was used for bottles (some with wide mouths for syrups and brandied fruits), case bottles (☞ page 288) (straight-sided to fit in a liqueur case), mortars and pestles, drinking glasses, jelly (gelatin) glasses, decanters and epergne. Glass became common only in the middle and late periods. Before then it was very expensive.

Iron and brass were used to make the numerous small cooking implements. These included long forks or meat forks, skimmers, ladles, spoons, spatulas or peels, butchering axes, meat saws, rendering tubs, sugar nippers, mortars and pestles, grinders and bean roasters.

Eating utensils were made of iron, pewter or silver, early often having bone, ivory or wooden handles or grips. Spoons were common, early being about two and a half inches across, with a seal top (like a sealing-wax seal), or an image of an Apostle, or a rattail with no finial, evolving by the later period into the forms familiar to us. Early knives had sharp points to spear food and usually a flat edge to the blade, which was often used like a spoon to pick up food. Forks became known in the early period only at the very top of society, and they moved slowly down. As late as 1770 Virginia Governor Botetourt carried his own fork in a SHAGREEN (sharkskin) case when visiting, so that he had one if his hosts did not (and he was not likely to have visited the lower classes). Forks started with two tines, then went to three, very late to four. The American Army during the Revolution issued forks made out of twisted wire, which may have been the first time many people saw them.

SEASONING AND PRESERVING

Preserving food for the winter or for use during travel was a major concern before canning. The types of preservation described here kept for years, not months.

Food was preserved by drying or parching in several ways. Meats were cut thin and usually salted, then placed over a slow fire for jerky or in the sun or wind. Large chunks of meat were usually impregnated in dry salt or a brine solution and then slowly smoked and dried. Smoking and drying meat required outdoor temperatures below forty degrees to preserve the meat during the extensive early stages, so it was only done late in the year. Berries, fruits and beans were dried in large, flat drying baskets laid in the sun. Sometimes they were mashed into a paste first, like modern fruit leathers. Fish were either dried on racks in the sun or smoked. Herbs for cooking and medicinals were dried by hanging them in bunches from the ceiling in kitchens or special garden houses.

Root crops such as onions, turnips and beets were braided by the stems and hung in a relatively dry area safe from frost, or stored in baskets under similar conditions, often in a root cellar. Apples were packed in straw and stored in a cellar, or made into fermented cider.

Fruits were brandied, producing two products: the flavored brandy and the brandied fruit. Alcohol was also used as a preservative.

Cheese making was the way to preserve dairy products. Hard wheel cheeses kept better on the shelf, providing less surface to gather mold.

Fat was rendered, separating the unusable tissue from the grease that would keep indefinitely, if prone to get moldy and strong with age. POCKET SOUP was like our bouillon cubes, made from meat trimmings and fat, which set to a hard gluelike consistency and would last for years.

PEMMICAN was a traveler's food acquired from the Indians, comprising shredded dried lean meat in rendered fat, with the addition of wild cherries or other fruit, sugar or maple sugar. It was used by frontiersmen and explorers.

Sailors relied on HARDTACK (PILOT BREAD or SHIP'S BISCUIT), a simple flour-and-water bread baked and then dried to incredible hardness so it would last up to fifty years. Weevils made it easier to eat by channeling through it; the weevils also provided some variety from the rest of the fare, dried peas and salt pork or salt beef. Lack of vitamin C caused scurvy, but this was not recognized until the end of the period. This problem was accentuated because voyages started just after the deprivations of winter to miss hurricane season; thus it had already been months since the sailors had any source of vitamin C.

English cooking emphasized two major flavorings, sugar and salt. Honey was used but had largely fallen out of production, and sugar quickly took its place, growing in importance until it and its byproduct, molasses, were the Caribbean's most lucrative products. About 1600 it was discovered that fruit and other foods could be preserved or cured in sugar, and by 1730 jams were made with it. Sugar was shipped in five-, ten- and fifty-pound CONES, LOAVES or HATS. It was broken into lumps and ground with a mortar and pestle. Maple sugar and maple syrup, though much used in New England, were not popular elsewhere, especially England.

Salt was also used for seasoning and preserving. It was used as a brine to pickle various items, including meats and vegetables, and to cure meats for drying, such as salt pork, salt fish (usually cod, shad or halibut) and salt beef. These meats could also be cured in a dry pack of salt. Salt meats were eaten thinly sliced or were simmered to cook out the salt.

Other seasonings were not used in English colonial cooking to any great degree. This is more true earlier, changing with time. Pepper and butter were the next two to show up frequently. Parsley, sage, rosemary and thyme, as the song goes, were among the most popular after them. In the seventeenth century an aversion to vegetables and herbs arose as a matter of style (they were thought fit only for the poor), but this was not universally accepted. The tastes of the court during Tudor times are easily confused with later tastes because many herbalists and cooks today refer back to them for their greater variety.

BEVERAGES

Nonalcoholic Beverages

Tea was introduced as a medicinal in the early period but did not become common until Catherine of Braganza married Charles II and brought the "Indian" trade as her dowry. Tradition has it that when tea was first served at a country party, the cooks threw away the brew and served the boiled leaves, to obvious disapprobation. But it caught on. In the 1770s, the English consumed eighteen million pounds of tea, or about two pounds per capita per year. As beer provided between one thousand and fifteen hundred calories a day when it was the staple, and tea zero, the nutritional loss caused by the advent of tea was considerable. Tea was shipped compressed into dried bricks, much like Chinese ink or modern chocolate, which were then grated for use. It was stored in tea caddies, small metal or wood boxes, usually with a lock. Although a pound of tea was expensive, it yielded some three hundred cups, so the unit cost was moderate.

Coffee was introduced to England about 1650, where it caught on first but did not gain acceptance quickly. It was widely held to cause sterility and insanity, and an edict was issued by a German prince saying, essentially, "The king's subjects were born and bred on beer, they have won many battles on beer, and I'll be damned if I'm going to allow them to be turned into a bunch of women by coffee." By 1720, however, the Dutch and English were growing coffee in the West Indies. COFFEEHOUSES were private clubs in England during the middle to late periods and were known in larger cities in the colonies. They were especially popular with those wealthy young men who had made the grand tour and who were known as MACARONIS because they affected new continental (Italian) styles. The primary factors in coffee's acceptance in the colonies were the taxes on tea and the resulting boycott leading to the Revolution. Coffee became patriotic.

Chocolate was a drink in the period, generally not a candy until the nineteenth century. Many American-made chocolate pots attest to its popularity among those who could afford it. It was imported from South America via Spain and England.

The high fat and carbohydrate content of the diet required substantial quantities of drink. Aside from hot drinks like tea, coffee and chocolate, most colonists avoided water, which could be fatal, what with cholera, typhoid, amebic dysentery and other waterborne diseases. As a result, most drinks were alcoholic, because no bacteria known to be harmful to man can survive in them.

Alcoholic Beverages

Beer was the staple beverage for the Anglo-Saxon world below the aristocracy. When used in the colonial period, the term usually meant small beer, or a brew watered down to about ½–1 percent alcoholic content. This was enough to kill the bacteria that might infest the water, but was readily potable to all, including children and infants. Beer was so important that a major reason the Pilgrims put in at Massachusetts instead of continuing on to the latitude of their charter was a shortage of beer. Pennsylvania proved good barley and hop country, and the Germanics who settled there became good brewers. Before that, many others discovered it was possible to ferment pumpkins, maple sugar and persimmons. Ale was also well known.

Wine was more important at upper-class tables and to immigrants from France, Italy and the Rhineland. Like beer, most wines were low in alcoholic content. People favored those more like our dessert wines of today, sweet and heavy. Madeira, malmsey, Port, Sherry (Sack) and malvasia were all popular. Mead passed out of fashion with the decline in use of honey.

Native scuppernong, a plum-sized grape, yields a similar wine, which was cultivated early on. It was unable, however, to compete with imported products. The "mother vineyard" near Roanoke was a single scuppernong vine covering four acres. Concord grapes, another native, were tried with similar success. Even Thomas Jefferson could not create an American wine industry, although he tried about the time of the Revolution. Still, both grapes had local usage.

Other styles were drunk, although the young Bordeaux and Chablis wines did not travel well. The heavy ones did, Madeira especially so. The Rhine wines were famous, including those made from the traminer grape. They were shipped in locally made stoneware jugs.

Most wines were shipped in wooden casks and bottled upon arrival. Later, many wealthy houses and taverns had bottles made with their own seal on them. Those who could not afford a custom die settled for their initials. The rest used plain bottles. Wine bottles comprise the largest body of artifacts at most eighteenth-century archaeological sites, often numbering in the hundreds.

Brandy was a popular drink with high potency made by distilling wine. Locally, it was made from apples and other fruits. Apples were further distilled to make applejack or ESSENCE OF LOCKJAW.

Liquors included whiskey (which was later distilled in Pennsylvania), gin (common among the lower class and Dutch) and cognac. The most common was rum, made with molasses from the sugar islands and relatively cheap. Rum figured heavily in the triangle trade and was a major product of New England, with an estimated 3.75 gallons per capita annual consumption. It was used to make BUMBO, a punch made of rum, sugar and water, and SYLLABUB, considered best when the cream was added by milking the cow into the combined rum and sugar.

A few of the wealthy had ice houses, in which winter lake ice cut into blocks was stored in hay, to allow for shaved ice to cool drinks in the summer. These structures went deep into the ground with mounds built over top to provide insulation.

BIBLIOGRAPHY

Many cookbooks are available, including Thomas Jefferson's and Martha Washington's. Contact appropriate museums for specifics or check your library.

Bradley, Richard. *The Country Housewife and Lady's Director.* 1736. Reprint, London: Prospect Books, 1980. Includes much about husbandry and gardening.

Carlo, Joyce W. *Trammels, Trenchers and Tartlets: A Definitive Tour of the Colonial Kitchen.* Old Saybrook, Conn.: Peregrine Press, 1982.

Carter, Susannah. *The Frugal Colonial Housewife.* 1772. Reprint, edited and illustrated by Jean McKibben. Garden City, N.Y.: Dolphin Books, 1976.

Pullar, Philippa. *Consuming Passions: Being an Historic Inquiry Into Certain English Appetites.* Boston: Little, Brown, 1970. A highly entertaining if somewhat superficial view of English tastes in food and sex. Only partially applicable; use in the context I have set.

Root, Waverley, and Richard de Rochemont. *Eating in America: A History.* New York: Ecco Press, 1981.

Rose, Peter G., tran. and ed. *The Sensible Cook: Dutch Foodways in the Old and New World.* Syracuse, N.Y.: Syracuse University Press, 1989.

Tannahill, Reay. *Food in History.* Rev. ed. New York: Crown Publishers, 1989. This volume complements *Eating in America* nicely. *Eating* is problematic in its general history. Where the information contained there differs from mine, use mine. *Food* often is short in American material, but provides better and more reliable sources for international trends such as food migration.

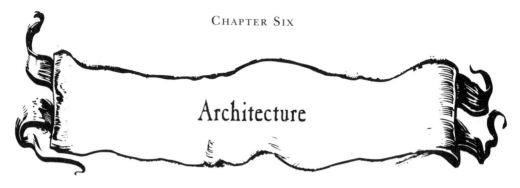

CHAPTER SIX

Architecture

COMMON SHELTER DESIGNS

The earliest forms of shelter were strictly temporary. Tents, pit houses, sod houses and tented pits were all common for short periods of time. As soon as time permitted, more substantial structures were put up. In many cases these were not big improvements. The common one-room houses had dirt floors and were often constructed of posts set in the ground. The more finely finished houses might have sills and timber frames. Walls were often wattle and daub, although settlers who came from an area of England that still had lots of wood might have had riven siding, which could be built about as fast.

The forms had direct antecedents in English halls and yeomans' cottages and the baernes of Scotland. The one-room HALL was a common sleeping, eating and working space. Privacy, even for sex, was not common at this early date, nor was it expected. When these forms expanded, they became the manor house, with one wing growing off an added kitchen and another off the added PARLOR (from the French for speaking room), which functioned as both private office and master bedroom. Regional variants developed as the settlers expanded from one room.

Regional Variations

In the North, where the major concern was heat retention in winter, ceilings were no higher than necessary. Windows were very small, and rooms were arranged around a massive central chimney stack that acted as a heat sink. Kitchens were integrated with the house.

In the South, where the major concern was cooling in the hot, humid summers, ceilings were high, up to fourteen feet, and chimneys were moved to the outside walls to dissipate heat and allow for

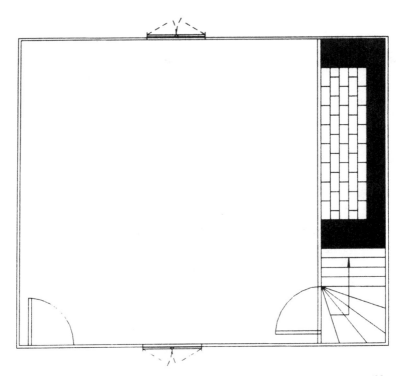

Typical 16' × 20' one-room house. Casement windows optional. Door possibly also on end.

cross-ventilation. Kitchens were later removed because of their heat. Windows became larger earlier, and houses were lighter, more open and airy.

In the middle colonies architecture included a bit of both styles but tended toward the Southern model because of its similarity to the Renaissance designs already common in the low countries from which many colonists had come.

Ultimately, both regions adopted a style inspired by the Italian Renaissance designs of Andrea Palladio, made popular in England by Inigo Jones in the seventeenth century. The essence of this style was symmetry, and the hall-and-parlor style was modernized with a central PASSAGE and symmetrical facade. Some homes combined both common floor plans, one behind the other.

Another common form was the town house, built deep and narrow to conserve expensive street frontage. Distinctive styles were developed in Philadelphia and other big cities.

Interior decor reflected regional variants. One historian has pointed out that most of the famous silversmiths were in New England,

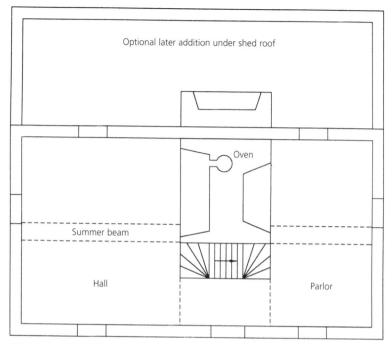

Optional later addition under shed roof

Oven

Summer beam

Hall

Parlor

Plan for typical New England hall-and-parlor house.

and silver displayed in its dark rooms would glow and attract attention better than a dark painting.

General Terms

Buildings are described with specific architectural terms, which were increasingly used in the middle and late period when most wealthy people dabbled in architecture. On the facade of a building, a BAY is the vertical space occupied by a window or door. A PILE is a depth of one room, so DOUBLE PILE is two rooms deep. The GABLE is the end wall of the roof as well as a protrusion for a window. A TOWER might be just a small vertical structure appended to a building—for example, a STAIR TOWER—and is not to be confused with the fanciful Victorian tower.

ROOMS AND OUTBUILDINGS

HALLS were not PASSAGES. Our modern usage of the term for a passage-way is a corruption derived from STAIR HALL, an evolutionary develop-ment of the fact that stairs often rose in the hall and later in the passage.

Rooms could be arranged in ENFILADE, so they ran in a row along

John Adams's birthplace, Quincy, Massachusetts. This house, with riven siding and double-hung sash windows, was enlarged from one room to a typical New England hall-and-parlor home about the same time that its windows were enlarged and the neoclassic pediment was added. Note the massive central chimney stack that held heat from the fire and warmed the whole house. Not shown is a shed roof or "saltbox" extension on the rear.

the main axis of the building. Usually, when so arranged, there was a series of doors in a row making a passage down one side of the room (▢ *page 287*). This style was reserved for large buildings and was not common here, but examples did exist, as at Greensprings, Governor Berkeley's house near Jamestown.

CLOSETS (▢ *page 287*) were small, private spaces, much like a study or dressing room. It was a sign of high respect for a visitor to be shown into a closet, because closets were the most private spaces in a house, assuming it was large enough to have one. From this comes the term to closet one's self away. Also, if you have heard that closets were taxed as separate rooms back then, this explains why: They were separate rooms. For confusion, they were sometimes called CABINETS, because a cabinet of curiosities might expand to take a whole room, usually a closet. CLOSET OF CURIOSITIES was a small private museum room.

A large room, particularly in taverns and other public buildings, might be called a Great Room. Any room might be called a chamber, and rooms above stairs usually carried that descriptor. Thus there might be a "chamber above stairs." Some rooms carried descriptors such as upper middle room. Offices could be separate buildings or

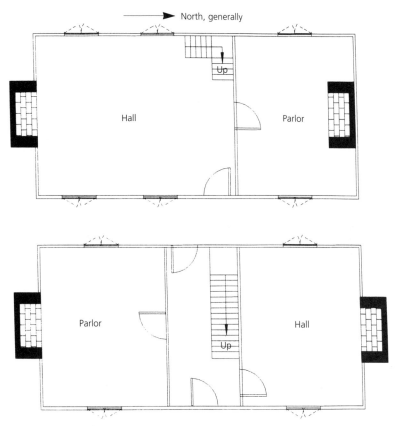

North, generally

Top: Typical 20' × 40' Southern style hall-and-parlor house. Bottom: Typical 20' × 40' Southern style center passage house.

one of the rooms at the rear of a double-pile structure. Front rooms were considered public spaces, the rear ones private spaces. The designation of one space for one function was an advanced part of the new Renaissance-inspired world view and just becoming common near the end of the period. All rooms might be multifunctional, and furniture was put against the walls when not in use to allow flexibility. The room was then said to be AT REST.

Outbuildings were functional appendages. Kitchens could be inside or outside, as could offices. Often in New England, outbuildings were connected because of the winter weather. Most forms are self-explanatory: springhouse (used like a refrigerator is today), dairy (with lots of ventilation and maybe a spring to keep cheeses and other dairy products), scullery (where laundry, soap making, and other dirty work was carried out), stable, coach house, barn, wood shed, garden house,

Lynnhaven House (1726 by dendrochronology), Virginia Beach, Virginia. A good example of a Southern hall-and-parlor house with a yard fenced with riven pales. This is a relatively late date for this type of house, and Lynnhaven House is interesting for containing rare internal evidence that the traditional uses of its spaces were not being followed: The larger room appears to have been used as a parlor, while the smaller was the hall evolving into a mere kitchen. The kitchen end is visible, with a service door.

corncrib, ice house (rare), granary, bathhouse (a shower house; it was rare) and privies or NECESSARIES (the sanitary facilities). During the night and in inclement or cold weather, chamber pots were used in the house, then emptied, either into the necessary or out the window (more common early).

WALL CONSTRUCTION

Frame houses could be made of CRUCKS (massive timbers cut just from the tree, retaining the natural shapes and incorporated into the structure to utilize those shapes); POSTS (straight trunks) set in holes in the ground or on wooden SILLS or stone foundations; or frame, meaning the timbers had been dressed, far more time-consuming. Timber construction required two main components, often visible in the finished house: the SILL or beam laid flat on the ground to which all others were attached, and the SUMMER BEAM, a heavy load-bearing beam that spanned the room and carried the floor above, more common in New

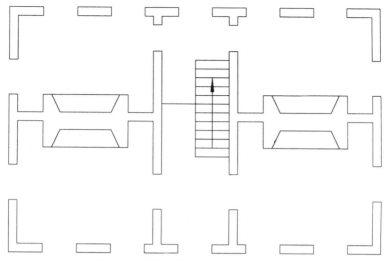

Typical Georgian floor plan. This side (bottom) is the front.

England houses than in southern. The summer beams usually ran parallel to the length of the house, carried by a chimney girth, and were often finished off with edge moldings. Even in homes with plastered ceilings, the summer beam protruded into the room.

Siding could be of any material available. Early, many colonists used a basket weave of split wood or vines called wattles between timbers, over which clay, lime and a binder such as hair or straw was DAUBED. This is really a variant on the half-timber framing of old England. The common riven siding was made of short (about four feet—the height a man could swing a maul) lengths of straight-grained wood, such as oak, split out with a froe, and was quick to make and functional. Weatherboards were sawn out and planed, a process that added significantly to their cost. They could, however, be longer than riven siding. If a bead or three-quarter-round molding were cut along the bottom edge, they required yet another operation, further increasing cost. At the extreme was rustication (fashioning wood to look like dressed stone), a technique George Washington used on the facade of Mount Vernon.

If walls were not wattle and daub, they sometimes contained NOGGING, (filler), made of bricks, straw, mud or other available materials.

Brick walls were at least twice as expensive to erect as frame. The bricks were made on site, usually from clay derived from the basement hole, if suitable. Brick walls started out thick and lost one brick's thickness at each floor. At the first floor, the loss was visible from the outside and was known as a water table, and capped with decorative molded

The Lowd House (left) was built a bit after the colonial period (ca. 1810) but in the style of the late colonial, Georgian-influenced New England house. The Sherburne House (right) is an example of an early (built ca. 1695, expanded ca. 1703) New England hall-and-parlor house that evolved from a one-room house. The gable ends and casement windows can be fully documented by the evidence left in the frame when the building was later renovated. Although it appears symmetrical, close inspection will reveal it is not. Strawbery Banke Museum in Portsmouth, New Hampshire, provides this wonderful chance to compare the early and late side by side. Sherburne house today contains detailed exhibits on its evolution.

brick. Often subsequent floors were marked with a string course on the outside. Rubbed brick was used around doors and windows to achieve a contrasting fine texture. The long part of a brick was called a stretcher and the short end, a header.

Brick was laid in BONDS (patterns). COMMON BOND was comprised of alternating rows of stretchers. Far more popular, especially above the water table and on the facade of buildings, was FLEMISH BOND, in which headers and stretchers alternated in each course (row) of brick. The alternations between each course produced a highly decorative diamond pattern, especially when glazed headers (bricks with a glass-covered end from being exposed in the firing tunnel of the kiln) were used. ENGLISH BOND was used most everywhere Flemish was not, and was comprised of alternating courses of headers and stretchers. To finish a wall square to a corner, window or door, it was usually necessary to cut a brick short to fit. If longer than a header, they were called KING'S CLOSERS; if shorter, QUEEN'S CLOSERS. Sometimes brick was laid in

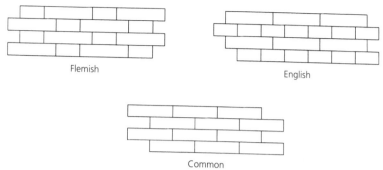

Bonds, or patterns, used in bricklaying: Flemish bond, English bond and common bond.

herringbone patterns or with the owner's initials and a date visible, usually in the gable end.

Stone walls were laid either wet (mortared) or dry (without mortar). Most common was a combination, with interior and exterior surfaces mortared and dry rubble filling in. It was not uncommon to hear snakes and their prey moving inside the walls. Obviously, stone walls were not built where stone was not available.

One final note: Despite a traditional association with the colonial period, the log cabin seems to have existed only in a limited area around Philadelphia where the Swedes, for whom it was a traditional style, settled. Later it would spread west and south to the frontier, primarily via the Great Wagon Road and Forbe's Road from this area.

ROOFING

Roof designs varied greatly during the period. In general, the pitch (slope) of a roof varied with the interior design and the region of the country. In northern, snow-heavy areas, roofs were pitched steeply to shed the extra snow. In homes designed with a story and a half, in which the attic under the roof was used as part of the living space, roofs were steeply pitched to give more usable space. Starting around 1760 the gambrel roof appeared, in which the roof has a double pitch, the outermost nearly vertical, the inner part flatter, to allow yet more room in story-and-a-half designs. If the normal roof was clipped at the outer edges of the ridgepole, so as to have a roofline similar in plan to the cross section of a gambrel roof, it was called a hip roof.

Roofs were made of many materials. Early, many were thatch, either crudely layered or thickly done as in traditional English work today. Bark slabs also were used early. With settlement, shingles were probably the most common, riven with a froe out of red oak (not dressed), cedar or cypress. Weatherboards like those used for siding could also be used in poorer construction. Slate was known but required much more substantial construction to support it and imported stone, so it was not common, except perhaps on certain military structures such as magazines.

Along the gable end and just under the roof were protective barge-boards. Gutters were not commonly affixed to the building, although some box gutters were known, but were usually brick, stone, gravel or oyster-shell troughs on the ground to break the fall of the water and divert it from the structure.

INTERIOR TRIM

Most interior trim was nothing more than painted or whitewashed plaster over lath. Many common homes did not even have this level of finish. In the early and middle period, in wealthy homes the plaster was called SEELED and might be carved into ornate shapes typical of seventeenth-century England and the low countries.

In the middle to late period, wealthy homes might have chair rails, a molded horizontal wooden strip about the height of the backs of chairs which divided the wall. Wooden molding was attached directly to the frame and plaster applied up to the edges.

Most expensive yet was wainscoting (wooden paneling) applied on the interior walls. Some full wainscoting was used, but more common was half wainscoting, which rose only to the height of the chair rails. Wainscoting was most commonly joined, or constructed of floating panels in frames to allow expansion and contraction with the weather. After the period the much cheaper but more unstable method of appliqué was adopted.

At the junction of the wall and ceiling, decorative moldings known as cornice or crown moldings were sometimes used, but only in otherwise substantially finished rooms. Along the floor line, baseboards were always used in any finished work.

Fireplaces were one of the dominant features in the room, both physically and socially, and they received extra attention. The full mantel was comprised of the OVERMANTEL and the FIREPLACE SURROUND, the latter being the more common. The lintel carried the weight of the brickwork over the opening and was either a massive timber (early and in kitchens), a brickwork arch or an iron band. The molding types used around the fireplace varied greatly through the period as styles changed. Study some regional examples. In general, early moldings were nonexistent. Later, bolection (convex half-round moldings) became popular only to be supplanted by more ornate and often classically inspired forms comprised of columns, pediments, broken pediments and the like. The inclusion of a mantelshelf was not only not mandatory, it was often not even common, even in kitchen fireplaces. Some surrounds were made of decorated tiles.

Mirrors (often with candlesticks), paintings or other decorative accents conceived in an architectural style were often placed on the overmantel and the PIER, or wall area between two windows.

INTERIOR FINISH

Most interior surfaces were whitewashed or painted, including almost all pine woodwork. Whitewash was a thin, white surface treatment made of lime in water and was inexpensive. Paint was made of pigments combined with milk, whose casein produced a good and permanent bond with wood and plaster. Oil paints were available but not commonly used for architectural work. Colors were much brighter when new than those we associate with "Williamsburg" paint colors, to the point of being shocking to us today. Painted surfaces and clothing were the only real sources of color in most people's lives other than nature's earth tones and greens. Color also did much to brighten dark spaces, important because of the lack of interior lighting. Even the Puritans of New England used riotous color, despite our Victorian tradition that they allowed only black and white. Only in a small school of Dutch craftsmen was the old decorative style of grisaille (shades of gray) utilized.

DECEITWORK was painted work designed to look like fancy wood grain or marble while in fact costing much less. It was common in finer homes and public buildings. Later, some stenciling became common, and a few examples exist of extensive wall decoration in paint, including overmantel paintings, paintings along stairwalls and the like, but they are very rare.

More common were wallpapers made either of paper, applied in one-foot-square sheets, or leather. Paper was often a single color, or it could be block printed or flocked (decorated with short wool cuttings to have a texture and pattern like cut velvet damask). Leather wallpaper was used in the early to middle period and was very rare. It was worked by repoussé, in relief from behind, and then gilt with gold. It was known as GILT-LEATHER wallcovering.

Floors were usually dirt for common homes and local heart of pine for the more affluent. The wider the boards the cheaper it was to make them, so large homes often had the public spaces downstairs (front) with narrow boards, as a form of show, while the private spaces upstairs and sometimes in the rear downstairs were made with cheaper wide boards. Floorboards were quarter sawn, making them stable and tough. The better floors were of tongue and groove or lapped to prevent dirt from making its way through the floor. Floors were commonly patched around fireplaces to repair fire damage. A very few floors were marble. The Governor's Palace in Williamsburg was notable as the only structure in Virginia with marble floors. Mann Page, who went bankrupt trying to compete with the Palace, may have tried to put in a marble floor. A marble floor was worthy of notice and comment.

Early in the period, sand or rushes were spread on the floors and changed periodically much as we would use cedar shavings in a hamster cage today. Later, floor coverings included carpets (although in the early to middle period they were more used on tables than on the floor); FLOOR CLOTHES (canvasses covered with built-up layers of paint and with a decorative pattern painted on them); and painted stenciled borders, particularly around fireplace hearths. Carpets were expensive, so a U-shaped bed round would be used around a bed to not waste money covering the floor under the bed.

WINDOWS

Windows or LIGHTS were generally glazed from a fairly early date. Before this time, the openings were covered with hinged or sliding shutters and may have been covered with bars or a grill of wood to keep larger animals out (gaps in the cruder structures allowed birds, mice and other small animals in). Window glass, in the form of crown glass (blown into a cylinder, cut and rolled, or spun out flat), was available from England in various sized panes. Smaller panes shipped better and were the style in the earlier periods. Bull's-eye glass (cut around the pontil mark in the center of the cylinder from which crown glass was made and having a distorted, lenslike appearance) was used in doors and other isolated locations as an accent light and with other panes to form a pattern.

Window Types

Until about 1710 to 1720 the prevailing form of window was the casement or CASEMATE, which is the familiar window in modern illustrations of early New England. It opened on vertical hinges like a door or occasionally horizontally like a transom window. The window itself was made in an iron frame, with multiple panes set in with double-sided lead channels known as CAMES. Diamond panes appear to have been the most common shape, but square panes are shown in numerous paintings of the period. Casement windows were relatively small for the wall area of the room, giving less light than we are accustomed to today.

Sometime after 1710, larger sash windows began to replace casements on earlier structures and were incorporated in the newer,

Casement window in wall with riven siding of the Sherburne House, Strawbery Banke Museum, Portsmouth, New Hampshire.

Renaissance-inspired designs. These double-hung windows were similar to modern ones, but the moving lower frame was supported by a rope (sash cord) and a pulley connected to a cast-iron counterweight (sash weight) within the wall. Local styles determined the number of panes mounted individually in mullions in both the fixed top and movable bottom part of the window, but the panes were usually mounted in multiples of at least three in a row. As with other aspects of architecture, the scale of the construction required a greater or lesser number of panes to cover a proportionate area. Some places of special importance were given Palladian windows (page 287), which are taller and have semicircular tops, like church windows. Often, a Palladian window was flanked by two thinner windows rising to within one pane below the base of the arcade.

Shutters and Window Treatments

Windows were shuttered at night and during bad weather. On frame structures shutters were normally placed on the outside of the building and held open with iron SHUTTER DOGS. On brick structures they were normally built into the interior wainscoting framing the window and held closed with latches and pegs or deadbolts. Sometimes small circular viewing holes were cut into shutters.

Cloth was expensive, so window treatments were a great measure of wealth. In many of the plainer homes, no treatment might be used, and in earlier homes the quality of glass made them unnecessary. Slightly more affluent homes might hang simple tab curtains. In the finest homes opulent displays with swags, drapes and wooden valances to which fabric was glued displayed the owner's wealth. Balloon curtains (page 287) were popular for controlling light. A common, cheaper treatment allowing privacy, light control and circulation were venetian blinds, made of wood, usually painted green. Roller blinds were new in the 1760s.

LIGHTING

Artificial lighting was not nearly as common as Hollywood would have us think. Most people lived by the sun, rising at dawn and going to bed at dusk.

Candles were expensive, and a typical family might have only one hundred for a year. Still, one candle throws a lot of light. Most candles were used to light the way from hearth to bed and similar short-term uses. Philip Vickers Fithian was a tutor living in the home of Councillor Robert Carter, one of the richest men in Virginia. Fithian described a dinner at Peyton Randolph's house as extravagant because they had ten candles burning for dinner.

Candle wax was derived from two main sources. Beeswax was considered the best and for Catholic services was the only allowable material. Spermaceti was finer than beeswax but much rarer. The cheapest was made from a thin coating found on the pinhead-sized bayberry, and it took a quart of berries to yield enough wax for an inch of candle that burned about one hour. The labor and cost involved is evident, but labor was cheaper than the other materials.

Because of the expense, large chandeliers were uncommon except . in public buildings. Those in taverns were often made of turned wood with iron arms. Those in public spaces were brass, silver or glass, which enhanced the light. Fine candlesticks were made of metals such as brass, silver or pewter, but more common ones were made of iron. Many had slide features to allow the candle to be totally used. Candle stands could be either a wooden stand on which candlesticks were placed (sometimes called a torchère by those literate in French) or an iron stand with a sliding arm holding candlesticks. The higher the arm was set, the more room illumination it provided; the lower it was set, the stronger the light on a specific work area.

Most people, especially poor families, used tallow (fat), which could be made into candles or used in fat lamps (sometimes called Betty lamps today), or in which rushes could be impregnated before being burned. Tallow was undesirable because it produced a stench when burned. RUSHLIGHTS were inverted pliers-like devices that held the rushes upright so they burned like candles. They do not appear to have been common in the colonies.

Some proper oil lamps were in use from an early date, but the most frequent use was late in the period, when whale oil became common. Before that, where whaling was a local industry, as on Cape Cod, oil lamps were more common. Such lamps were mere globes, usually glass, with a narrow aperture to hold the wick.

Shoemakers' and lacemakers' lamps were glass globes filled with water placed between the light source and the work to magnify the light on the work area. The larger the globe, the greater the intensification, but most were about three inches in diameter. Some were fitted on stands, others on articulated arms. Mirrors or bright metal reflectors were placed behind candles to double the effective output of light.

The importance of the fireplace as a source of light cannot be overstated. Once a person's eyes adjusted to its light, it was adequate for a fair amount of work.

HEATING

Fireplaces were the most common source of heat. Fireplaces heat by radiant heat, so fires were kept blazing and as much heat as possible was reflected into the room. FIREBACKS (cast-iron plates) behind the fire reflected the heat, absorbed some to radiate later, and protected the soft bricks from destruction.

In one-room homes where the fireplace doubled for heating and cooking, fireplaces were large enough to walk into. A blazing fire was kept burning in one area for boiling, and coals were raked out as needed to bake or broil on specific spots on the hearth. Early, almost all fireplaces were like this. With time, and especially in those fireplaces used exclusively for heat (parlors, bedrooms, etc.), they reduced in size as it became apparent that larger fireboxes increased draft and decreased efficiency. A fireboard might be placed across the opening of unused fireplaces to keep vermin and dirt out of the room.

Stoves were just becoming available late in the period in most areas. Most used wood and were fireplaces extended into the room to improve radiation. Some used charcoal or coal, but none were common, with the possible exception of Germanic tile stoves designed somewhat like modern Russian fireplaces with convoluted smoke channels to maximize heat extraction. If coal was used (locally mined or sea coal from England), it was usually in a coal grate in a fireplace (☞ *page 288*).

At night fires were banked and could be fanned again in the morning. If there were servants, one of their jobs would be to have this done before the master got up, so the room would be warm.

Fire Safety

For safety no fires (or candles) were kept burning in rooms that were not in use, except possibly the kitchen. Winter social patterns revolved around those rooms that were heated, such as the kitchen. If servants were present, they slept where they were assigned to work, so workshops, kitchens and offices might be monitored and kept warm.

Most homes had one fire bucket (☞ *page 289*) for every two fireplaces, although some areas required other proportions by law. These buckets were leather, lined with pitch (the refined sap of the pine tree) and kept full of water to douse any sparks that jumped from the fireplace before they could become a major fire. In kitchens, where grease was present, an unlined bucket might hold sand (never wet sand, even though many museums will tell you so). Fire buckets often had the owner's name or design painted on them. During a fire everyone brought their buckets and formed a bucket brigade. Leather was used so the buckets could survive being thrown off the roof of a building without coming apart or cracking at the seams (avoiding the need for two brigade lines—one up, one down) and also so if someone was hit by a buket, they could survive.

Roof fires were common but could be fought successfully, because fire burns upward and it already was at the top of the structure. Ladders were often left on roofs to provide a footing for fighting such fires. Inside, the most common problem was a downdraft blowing sparks out into the room. Woolen carpets or, in rural areas, bearskin rugs were used as smoke detectors. The smell of burning hair would awaken the occupants in time to deal with the problem.

Many old homes show patches repairing fire damage in the overmantel, and larger ones in the floor. Overmantel fires would be put out first, because they could burn up and take out the whole structure, while floor fires were contained.

Late in the period a number of localities obtained fire engines or hand pumps, which were fed from a reservoir and threw water under pressure. Some insurance companies or associations were organized which created the first fire companies and identified members' structures with FIRE MARKS (iron markers) placed on the outside walls. If a structure wasn't owned by a customer, no attempt was made to save it, unless the fire threatened a neighboring customer.

GARDENS

Gardens were grouped by type. Formal or PLEASURE GARDENS were for entertaining, KITCHEN GARDENS grew vegetables and culinary herbs, medicinal or PHYSIC GARDENS grew medical herbs and FRUIT GARDENS contained fruit trees. The more functional gardens were utilitarian in layout, with simple beds. The formal gardens, on the other hand, were developed only during the middle period and required a considerable amount of labor to maintain. Prior to about 1730, formal gardens were highly stylized, with beds laid out in ornate geometric parterres, which sometimes included intricate knotwork borders. Topiary, or the cropping and pruning of trees and bushes into geometric shapes or the forms of mythical beasts, was common at this time, then became passé. These were a holdover of the Renaissance styles and reflected the imposing of order on nature. Later, new philosophies took root, requiring the gardener to spend hours landscaping so it did not look like landscaping but resembled a well-tended natural area. The formal parts of gardens were considered extensions of formal buildings and included in the social use of the building.

BIBLIOGRAPHY

Bailey, Rosalie Fellows. *Pre-Revolutionary Dutch Houses and Families in Northern New Jersey and Southern New York*. New York: Dover Publications, 1968. Also a companion volume on the houses of New Jersey.

Cummings, Abbott Lowell. *Rural Household Inventories: Establishing the Names, Uses and Furnishings of Rooms in the Colonial New England Home, 1675–1775*. Boston: Society for the Preservation of New England Antiquities, 1964. Much good information on furnishings and "things" other than simply room names.

Historic American Buildings Survey. *Virginia Catalog: A List of Measured Drawings, Photographs and Written Documentation in the Survey*. Charlottesville: University Press of Virginia, 1976.

Kelly, John Frederick. *The Early Domestic Architecture of Connecticut*. New York: Dover Publications, 1963.

Kimball, Fiske. *Domestic Architecture of the American Colonies and of the*

Early Republic. New York: Dover Publications, 1966. An excellent survey of architecture, with many plans and illustrations.

Manucy, Albert C. *The Houses of St. Augustine, 1565–1821.* Gainesville: University Press of Florida, 1992. A study of the houses of the town, with information about British changes and many illustrations.

Reynolds, Helen Wilkinson. *Dutch Houses in the Hudson Valley Before 1776.* New York: Dover Publications, 1965.

Whiffen, Marcus. *The Eighteenth-century Houses of Williamsburg: A Study of Architecture and Building in the Colonial Capital of Virginia.* Rev. ed. Williamsburg, Va.: Colonial Williamsburg Foundation, 1984.

————. *The Public Buildings of Williamsburg.* Williamsburg, Va: Colonial Williamsburg Foundation, 1960.

Whitehead, Russell F., and Frank Chouteau Brown, eds. *Architectural Treasures of Early America: An Early American Society Book.* New York: Arno Press, 1977. A series of volumes on each colony's architecture, including drawings and photos based on the Historic American Buildings Survey (HABS) drawings.

CHAPTER SEVEN

Clothing & Accessories

Clothing was extremely expensive due to the high cost of cloth. As a result, most people could afford only one or two complete outfits. Aprons protected clothing from the rigors of work. Worn-out clothes were cut up for patches, used to make CHAR-CLOTH for lighting fires or, if linen or cotton, sold to papermakers.

The colonial period had a number of stylistic periods. Clothing of the upper classes changed the most. Working men's clothing style was influenced but changed relatively slowly while the style of working women's clothes saw virtually no change.

Clothing is an area fraught with pitfalls. Spain, Italy, the low countries, Germany, France and England all had differing styles at the same time. People who traveled (including merchants, sailors, dignitaries and people on the grand tour) would see and describe different styles. In the American colonies the Dutch, Germans, Swedes, English, French and Spanish all interacted in one way or another. Late in the period the macaronis would adopt Italianate styles even in England. A description of a single item may not apply to everyone's experience. The best I can do here is chart the norm of English practice. The referenced movies are useful resources, although remember that most depict upper-class Europe, and the clothing may be finer than that owned by all but the wealthiest in the colonies. Scenes involving court life may show finer clothing than even the wealthiest in the colonies owned; one court gown was reckoned at £100,000. Historical portraiture is another good reference.

FEMININE DRESS

A SHIFT, also called a CHEMISE among the upper class, was an ankle-length linen nightdress with drawstrings at the neck and wrists, or between wrists and elbows, that was the standard undergarment. It was worn day and night and was the most common article to be owned in multiples. It might have RUCHING (ruffles) beyond the drawstring, or none at all. The shift changed very little as it could be adapted to each new style in turn.

A woman was considered naked in her shift alone. Throughout the period showing an ankle or elbow was considered inappropriate, although breasts might be shown during nursing or in certain European fashions (Holland, mid-seventeenth century). In part these ideas came from the physical functionality of ankles and elbows, which were not considered attractive. In the eighteenth century a handkerchief or LINEN might be worn to cover the décolletage, most particularly in cold weather.

Working Women's Clothing

Lower-class women wore much the same style clothes throughout the colonial period. These were simple and functional. Over the shift was worn a straight, ankle-length skirt under which POCKETS, or egg-shaped bags worn on a string around the waist, could be reached through holes in the skirt. The torso was covered with a JUMPS or BODICE, a laced-up vestlike garment with some boning to provide support and shape. A bodice in the early period was a PAIR OF BODIES (⌨ *page 288*) and was sometimes called CORSETS in the plural. Excessive boning was not found among the lower class because it prevented them from working. Some bodices were made of leather, giving shape and support without being too stiff to work in.

The exact cut of the bodice changed a bit during the period. The tabs below the waist level were sometimes rounded, sometimes squared, and the bustline was sometimes cut above the nipple to flatten breasts, other times below the breast for support. During the early period, the waist was long, with the bodice coming to a point well below the waist. During the early middle period, the neckline came off the shoulder, with a shorter waist and puffier sleeves.

To protect this basic outfit, a short apron was added or a longer version called a pinner or PINAFORE was pinned to the gown or bodice.

A hat was a necessary addition, not just for religious reasons (early) but for warmth and fashion. The most common were MOBCAPS, circles of material with a drawstring around the edge that drew them up into a bowl-shaped cap. The wealthy wore mobcaps mostly at home. Lappet (eared) caps were similar to mobcaps with LAPPETS or LATCHETS extending down like a scarf along the throat. PINNERS were small, yarmulkelike coverings for ladies. Straw hats, often decorated with sewn-on ribbons, flowers or other trims, were common and functional in the summer. The finer straw was braided. Women also wore felted beaver hats. As with men's hats, straw and felt hats could be cocked into bicorn or tricorn forms, becoming more common in the last period.

Cold weather required heavy clothing, and this was most easily and practically accomplished with a hooded cape or cloak made of wool, which could be drawn close or used as a blanket. Much clothing was made of wool for warmth.

Aristocratic Ladies' Clothing

A wealth of variety occurred in the dress of aristocracy. While some ladies in the earliest period may have dressed as (lower-class) women did, such dress did not last long. The aristocracy showed its wealth in its clothes, and the merchants emulated them as much as they could.

The pairs of bodies (bodices) were an integral part of ladies' clothing in the earliest years. In the 1460s they were shortened to a blouse-like top, with a low boat neckline, short tabs and puffed sleeves, and then would resume the long form. Later, they became an undergarment worn under the coat (from the French *côte*, rib) or gown, and redesignated stays in the eighteenth century. Near the end of the period they disappeared altogether.

STAYS (⌨ *page 288*) were worn all the time, including during sleep, although NIGHT or SLEEP STAYS had less boning, mostly in the back for support. Children were placed in stays between seventeen months and three years of age, with the intent of forming the desirable shape of an inverted cone. Special adjustable stays were made for pregnant women. The influence of stays on miscarriages cannot be calculated. Prolonged use of stays weakened back muscles to the point that stays were required for support, which accounts in part why older women kept earlier styles after stays went out of fashion. The lack of mobility allowed by stays resulted in a female courtesy (curtsy) known as the SINK. The heels were placed together in first ballet position, at a right angle, and the hands were clasped at about navel height. The knees were slightly bent and then straightened as the eyes were dropped and the back kept straight. In addition to the restrictions on mobility imposed by the stays, aristocratic clothing was cut so the arm could not be raised higher than shoulder height.

Like lower-class clothing, the line of the front of the bodice (even when incorporated into a gown) changed, first long, then shortening, and finally lengthening again.

In the eighteenth century the gown was often short, open in the front below the waist, and ending at about the knees. It was derived from the coat and the bodice and served as the top garment over the petticoats or skirt, which it was cut away to reveal. Near the end of the period, as part of the philosophy that nature should reign triumphant, gowns became nothing but chemises, with a high waist just under the bust, and no stays. Sometimes a fabric wrap was used as a binding

Lady's caraco dress of about 1760 to 1770, showing the profile derived from hoops and stays, with a lappet cap and period fan. Hair is worn up, as was appropriate. Earrings are of the period. Although seemingly plain compared to satins and brocades, the cotton material makes this gown expensive.

under the bust, other times just the gather sewn into the material. White and pale blue became the most common colors. In some European centers the gowns were partially see-through, a source of shock to visiting Americans.

There were many types of gowns. The SACK or SACQUE, with a square-cut neckline and long trains hanging from the shoulders of the gown, was originally a court gown that became very popular in the 1740s and lasted until the Revolution. In the late period it had an integral bodice reminiscent of the seventeenth-century style of long, pointed stays.

The CARACO had a midlength overgown that could flare widely over panniers. The MANTUA evolved from its first introduction about 1680 throughout the period. At first a reaction to the overly stiff boned styles of the 1680s, the mantua was never boned, but later would be worn over stays. At first it had a long overgown folded back around the hips and tied with a sash or belt. The remaining material was worn as a long train. The POLONAISE GOWN was generally straight with drawstrings that could be looped over buttons on the back of the gown to give a draped effect similar to a mantua.

If the gown closed in the front, either with clasps or laces, a STOM-ACHER covered the functional part. The stomacher provided further opportunity for decoration or contrast and often included a BUSK—a flat wooden, whalebone or metal piece shaped like a long leaf—to stiffen the face (*page 287*).

The petticoat, (earlier, PARTICOAT) might be made of the same material as the gown or a contrasting material. It may even have belonged to another gown. Under the petticoat might be found underpetticoats or a FARTHINGALE. In some early styles the petticoats might be layered to reveal the underpetticoats as well.

The farthingale (VARDINGAL, FARDYNGALE, VERTHINGALE) arrived from Spain in the early period. It it was usually a wood or metal frame, essentially cone-shaped, over which the petticoat hung. The English adopted the French farthingale (*page 288*) or HAUSSE-CUL (a doughnut-shaped roll set on the hips), which gave a more bell-like shape to the petticoats. In the early period the long busk pushed the front of the farthingale down, tipping it up in the back as can be seen in many late-Elizabethan portraits. It passed from fashion by about the 1640s, although some use was made a bit later.

In the eighteenth century the farthingale was replaced by the PANNIER, a cloth-covered basket frame that rode on the hips and projected out to the sides only. Panniers served to accentuate the narrow waist derived from the stays but were collapsible by folding and could be used as pockets to carry items. They reached their widest forms about 1750, then quickly narrowed and disappeared.

BED GOWNS were short jackets worn over the shift when sitting up in bed, and occasionally as informal wear, especially among the working women. Women's riding habits were based on men's clothing, although they had full skirts.

Hair and Wigs

Hair was generally worn up, off the face. Letting hair down was considered risqué. Neck-length side curls were allowed, and special locks of ringlets to be worn under hats were available in the later periods. In the early period hair might be dressed on pie-shaped forms seen in Elizabethan portraits. In the mid-seventeenth century ringlets were fashionable.

Although ladies wore high, cylindrical wigs in the 1770s in Europe, they were a rare occurrence in the colonies, occurring mostly in the larger, more cosmopolitan cities such as Philadelphia and Charles Town. They were almost always cause for comment. Such wigs were rarely taken off, even at night, and setting mouse and louse traps in them was not unheard of. Calash bonnets, worn in the very late period and made popular by the high wig styles, were made with a collapsing wire framework extending the sides in front of the face.

MASCULINE DRESS

Clothing for men falls into two distinct eras during the colonial period, the first roughly corresponding with our early period, the latter with our middle and late periods. In the earlier style, clothing was still Elizabethan in basic concept, with a suit of clothes comprised of a DOUBLET, breeches and cape or CASAQUE. After about 1680 the coat, waistcoat, breeches and shirt became the basic form.

Working Men's Clothing

Working men's clothing followed the fashion more than working women's did, but ostentation had no place here. The leather doublet or jerkin of the early styles gave way to a leather vest, jacket or apron in the later ones. As armor, the relatively cheap and durable leather protected the shirt underneath from the hazards of daily labor. Better craftsmen might wear waistcoats and simpler versions of higher-class clothing.

Frontiersmen wore buckskin only if they were far from civilization for a long period of time, although they might wear buckskin breeches. The rest of the time they wore shirts and linen hunting (rifle) shirts or hunting jackets, the difference being whether or not they opened in the front. These long, T-shaped frocks had extensive fringe to wick water away and allow it to drop off. Hats were felted round hats, often turned up on one side with feathers or an animal tail stuck in for decoration. Coonskin hats were not worn.

Gentlemen's Clothing

In the early style, the doublet was a heavy, sometimes leather, short jacket, often extending forward at the front seam like a suit of jousting armor. One costume historian has suggested this style is coincident with a need for body armor, and the doublet may well have met this need. Some were SLASHED (cut in the sleeves or body) to allow puffs of the shirt to protrude. The slashings were often PICKED OUT in contrasting thread, including gold or silver wire. POINTS (small inverted cones of metal) were sometimes used to trim doublets. The cape was relatively short and sometimes weighted at the lower corners. (Fighting with a sword and a weighted cape was an effective multiweapon technique.) The breeches were fairly tight and had a separate codpiece, a sheath or pouch for the penis. At times the codpiece was quite overt, but increasingly it was incorporated into the breeches.

For a good part of the period, the coat reached to below the knees, de-emphasizing the mostly hidden breeches. As first introduced around 1660, the coat was a rather straight, formless sack, but in a short time it developed into a full-skirted, almost kiltlike form, with pleats around the back to provide adequate flair and fullness. Around 1700 this style was replaced with a more straight cut down the tails, but it still extended fully around to the front of the body. These coats were heavy, with increasingly massive TURNBACKS making large, often ornate, cuffs. This style reached maximum fullness around 1740–1745. The coat then began a gradual narrowing toward the tails of the nineteenth century, as the front portions of the tail were first turned back and fastened with hooks called FROGS (turnbacks were still found on regimental uniform coats in the Revolution), then the tails were slowly cut away into increasingly narrow forms. The coat continued to flow from the body to the tails through the colonial period, the abrupt cutaway of modern formal wear coming later. In the 1760s a standing collar appeared. Earlier there were occasional broad, flat collars.

In the earliest days breeches were called SLOPS and were loose and balloonlike. As coats cut away in the front, breeches were increasingly exposed and assumed more importance in the style. Near the end of the period, the breeches were exposed from the rear, and they became much more tightly fitted. Men were known to pad their legs to enhance their appearance; at least one man is known to have lost his leg during a dance, to the merriment of the crowd. The male courtesy involved MAKING A LEG (⌨ *page 288*)—flexing the leg muscle into good form while tipping the hat. About 1750 the fly front was replaced by a square-cut FALL buttoned at the top. In the middle period, breeches were cut full in the seat and laced up over a gusset in the back, allowing considerable weight change without need for a new pair.

Waistcoats were long vests, shortening in length as the period progressed, but at first as long as the coat. The waistcoat was often worn with several buttons undone to allow the stock (a neck tie) to be gathered inside through the gap, or to allow a ruffle to protrude from within. Some, called sleeved waistcoats, had holes which allowed sleeves to be tied on with TAPE (ribbon).

Garters held up the hose and at times were displayed outside the clothing. Later, garters were incorporated into the breeches as tabs, with the hose rolled above the knee and girded in place. Small garter

Portrait of John Carter (son of Robert "King" Carter) painted by Sir Godfrey Kneller (portrait painter to the crown from 1688 through his death in 1723) during a visit to London in the first quarter of the eighteenth century. The portrait shows the full-cut coat of the period and the stock. This is one of many family portraits on display at Shirley Plantation, Charles City, Virginia, and shows the value both of portraiture to show costuming and of visiting sites near your work to obtain firsthand knowledge of local tastes.

buckles were used to fasten garters in place. Suspenders were generally not used.

When worn without the coat, the shirt, breeches and waistcoat were known as SMALLCLOTHES. Capes were common until about 1740, when they passed out of fashion. Like ladies' clothes, gentlemen's coats were at first cut in the sleeve to prevent raising the arm high. The modern extend and lunge of fencing, for example, were not part of the fencing style because they could not be physically performed in the clothing. Gentlemen might wear a BANYON (long, straight, Turkish-inspired robe) with a negligee cap for undress.

Hair

PERIWIGS or PERUKES came into England from France in the late 1630s, although Charles II and the court did not wear them until 1663. Wigs were at first highly curled and shoulder length. Over time they became larger, reaching midback length between 1680 and 1700, then again reduced in size after about 1710.

When wigs became smaller, they also became simpler, losing the curls except the two at the sides. The straight hair was drawn back into a short, dressed ponytail, which was usually folded back into itself or contained in a small bag for neatness. At this time if a man could not afford a whole wig, he could purchase just the tail to add to his own hair. During this period, wigs were dressed with fat mixed with cinnamon and cloves and powdered with perfumed flour, which was sometimes colored (☞ *page 288*). Special powder rooms were provided in finer homes for this purpose.

The size, style and material of the wig were badges of rank. The finest wigs were made of human hair, then, in descending order, yak, goat and horse mane. Some men even left their hair showing at the front of the wig to emphasize that they were indeed wearing a wig.

Heads were shaved at breeching (see page 131) and once a fortnight (two weeks) after that. At night the bald head was covered with a negligee cap. Wearing a wig required straight and upright posture, for lowering the head risked FLIPPING THE WIG, a most embarrassing event.

Facial Hair

Styles in men's facial hair changed much in the colonial period. In the early days, beards were either similar to Vandyke beards or they were full but closely trimmed along the jawbone and cut square, as in the portraits of John Smith. After 1630, when Louis XIII personally trimmed his officers' beards to a mere tuft of hair on their chins and mustaches, this style became common throughout France, which largely set the styles for Europe. After the beginning of the eighteenth century, facial hair disappeared among civilized men (pirates, trappers and the like continued to wear beards) and remained out of fashion until after the colonial period. At no time were mutton chops common.

Men's Hats

Men wore hats of several forms. FLOP HATS, worn during the eighteenth century, had round crowns and round brims, with one side turned up and pinned, often with a button so it could be let down in bad weather. Similar hats had been worn earlier, although most had squared crowns and wider brims. Some of these had iron frames inside the crown to protect the head from sword blows. The stereotypical tricorn was popular in the later period, but the bicorn, turned up in only two places, was also becoming popular at this time, particularly for military wear. Lightweight, fitted, fabric negligee caps were worn at night to cover the shaved head. Light infantry and dragoons wore tall helmets made of hardened leather, while grenadiers wore tall, bearskin-covered hats to make them appear more imposing.

Servants' Clothing

African immigrants wore the clothing in which they traveled until they were sold in the New World. After that, they were generally given clothes befitting their tasks and rank. As most new immigrants were bought for field work, they were usually given shirts, breeches, hats and possibly hose and shoes. Later, as they or their children learned the language and possibly skills, they might move up in rank. House servants might be finely dressed in LIVERY (house uniforms) to reflect well upon the owner. Craftsmen and kitchen staff would be somewhere between, dressed comparably to freemen in similar postions.

SHOES

Shoes were essential to people who walked as much as the colonials did. Most shoes of the colonial period were straight-lasted, or symmetrical, made to fit either foot. They actually matched the bone structure of the foot better than shoes made to fit only the left or right foot and allowed longer life by switching the shoes to equalize wear. Some, like the moccasins adapted from the Indians, were made to the shape of each foot. English shoes were constructed much more heavily than these.

Most shoes were fully welted, containing an outersole, innersole and shank made of thick, heavy sole leather, which provided real support for the foot. Lighter, more flexible dancing (turned) shoes were made inside out and pulled through themselves so the stitching was hidden inside. The finest dancing shoes were made of strong, supple and expensive dog skin and could be worn out by one night's dancing, so PUTTING ON THE DOG meant something then. MULES (STITCHED-DOWNS) were the equivalent of slippers, a simple top stitched to a single layer of sole leather. Some mules were made with back straps, others with stitching on the soles for traction for tennis and fencing.

In the early period shoes were fastened with laces and covered with ornate leather or fabric decorative rosettes. About 1700 the use of buckles began, which were small at first, then grew to their largest size about 1750, then reduced in size again to the end of the period. The buckles attached to one of two latchets and caught the other, allowing the shoe to be reversed, as the buckling latchet was always worn to the outside of the foot. Buckles were only for the wealthy and for dress shoes. Common and work shoes dispensed with the latchets and used laces. Dress shoes could have the latchets cut off and be converted to work shoes as they aged. Toe styles could be square (early and work), rounded or pointed. Heel height could vary a bit, with men's shoes high about 1660, but most shoes looked much like modern ones.

PATTENS were wooden soles with straps raised up on iron supports to keep a person out of the mud. Boots were for two purposes: Riding boots were tightly fitted to the calf so the rider could feel the animal and control it better, and jackboots were made of hardened heavy leather and worn by postilions and cavalrymen for protection. Neither were designed for walking, which could be quite painful with boots on, as the dragoons captured at Bennington could attest.

COSMETICS

Cosmetics were commonly worn during the eighteenth century. Flour, white lead, orrisroot and cornstarch were common bases to produce the esthetic of a pure white face. The best were in a fairly greasy base, for they stayed in place. Over these a true red rouge was used to highlight cheekbones, in a manner that would be considered overdone today. Lip color and rouge were made from crushed cochineal beetles. Cochineal was an expensive imported commodity; country women substituted berry stains. Lampblack (carbon) was used to highlight eyebrows and lashes, which were groomed with fine combs. BEAUTY PATCHES were small black patches (usually circular but often shaped like the suits of cards or fleur-de-lis) used on the face and body, originally to hide the sores of venereal disease but then becoming de rigueur. It is worthy of comment here that few European faces were unscathed by smallpox, but a handsomely pocked face was not considered unattractive, only an excessively pocked one.

As a white skin tone was desirable, upper-class women sometimes wore masks (often clenched in the teeth when horseback riding), gloves and veils when outdoors to protect themselves from the sun and keep their skin white.

ACCESSORIES

A variety of accessories were worn or carried in the colonial period. Garters, fastened with small garter buckles, were used to hold up stockings, which were heavy, long socks. A GIRDLE was a belt used to carry tools, not to hold up the clothing. In the very earliest days expensive clothing was decorated with brass or gold POINTS, small decorative pendants worn like fringe. Hooks and eyes were used to clasp pieces together. Gloves were worn in the early period for protection from swords and during work, as well as to keep warm. SNUFF HANDKERCHIEFS were large (about two feet square) and used in the highly stylized ritual of taking snuff (☞ *page 288*). Etuis and chatelaines were worn on girdles to carry sewing equipment, writing equipment, calendars or other daily necessities in a small, usually ornate, metal or tortoiseshell capsule. Wallets could be large and were used to carry papers and paper money. Purses were for coins. Suspenders were only worn late in the period, invisibly, and then usually for heavy work. After the early years, swords were not commonly worn except for ceremonial purposes. Jewelry was minimal except at formal events, where small pendants, earrings and an occasional brooch were worn. Rings were the most common.

Fans were carried by both ladies and gentlemen, and some (lower-class) women. The simpler ones were made of paper over wooden sticks, while the more elaborate were glazed paper, silk, lace or chicken skin over bone or ivory sticks. The fancier ones were double-sided and often printed with designs on both sides. Although many museums make much of fan language, the one used in the later eighteenth century was not the complex nineteenth-century Spanish language popular among interpreters, but rather a simple and subtle language of flutters, beats and gestures or an almost semaphore-like spelling code. See the sidebar on page 119 for some examples.

STORAGE

Clothing was not hung up as is done today. Instead, it was folded and laid flat in chests, on shelves in CLOTHES PRESSES (not actually a press, but a case piece with drawers or shelves behind the top doors) or in drawers. For travel it was either packed flat or rolled much like a soldier does in a duffel bag today. Trunks and portmanteaus were the most common luggage.

LEVEE

Related to dress was the LEVEE, a social custom among upper-class women during dressing. In the colonial period it was not improper for

BASIC EIGHTEENTH-CENTURY FAN LANGUAGE

Meaning	Action
Anger	Strike palm of hand with closed fan
Jealousy	Flutter open fan before face
Concern	Fan very quickly
Coquetry	Fan slowly and languidly
Can't talk	Tip of closed fan placed to lips

a lady to entertain visitors in her bedroom, but rather common, as her bedroom was often her sitting room. The levee was a formal entertainment while completing dressing, including making up and setting the hair. Surviving guest lists indicate that men were entertained as often or more so than women.

BIBLIOGRAPHY

Arnold, Janet. *Patterns of Fashion: Englishwomen's Dresses and Their Construction.* New York: Drama Book Specialists, 1972.

Buck, Anne. *Dress in Eighteenth-Century England.* New York: Holmes and Meier, 1979.

Klinger, Robert L. *Distaff Sketch Book.* Union City, Tenn.: Pioneer Press, 1974. Sketches and patterns for women's clothing, shoes and accessories of the Revolutionary period.

———. *Sketch Book 76.* Union City, Tenn.: Pioneer Press, 1974. Sketches and patterns for men's clothing, shoes and military accoutrements of the Revolutionary period.

Ribeiro, Aileen, ed. *The Visual History of Costume.* New York: Drama Book Publishers, 1989.

Spring, Ted. *Sketchbook 56.* St. Louis Mo.: Pioneer Press, 1983. Men's clothing and military gear for the French and Indian War, Rogers' Rangers.

Waugh, Norah. *Corsets and Crinolines.* New York: Theatre Arts Books, 1970.

———. *The Cut of Men's Clothes, 1600–1900.* New York: Theatre Arts Books, 1968.

———. *The Cut of Women's Clothes, 1600–1930.* New York: Theatre Arts Books, 1968.

CHAPTER EIGHT

Marriage & Family

SEX ROLES AND
THE DIVISION OF LABOR

I t has often been said that women in the colonial period had no power. This was true in regards to property ownership (when married), the franchise and other legal distinctions, but not true when it came to sex roles and the division of labor. Women had their own sphere of influence, and a capable practitioner here could exert strong influence outside her sphere. In a broad sense, a man's sphere was outside the home, including politics, war and commercial business, while a woman's sphere was within the home. Men might have the final say in decorating, an extension of building the house, but in many households the woman had as much or more influence in the management of the estate as her husband did. Women were active participants in farming and farm management.

Such a role required education, literacy and an ability to figure and understand basic accounting and management skills, in addition to women's traditional skills such as cooking, sewing and child rearing. On the large plantations the mistress would relegate performance of many basic tasks to servants, while she concerned herself with management. At the lower-class levels, women did all the domestic work, and extra labor in the fields as available.

Because the sexes had distinct roles without duplication of effort, loss of one partner required speedy remarriage to keep the system working smoothly. Surviving spouses would often remarry within a month of their loss, regardless of gender. The Victorian ideal of mourning had not yet arisen. In time a few sects would come to require a "seemly" period of mourning, for example, the Quakers (one year). Marriage was still largely a business arrangement; love was considered unimportant until after life expectancies and overall wealth rose. With the shorter life expectancies of the early years, children in the seventeenth-century Chesapeake were often unrelated to the adults raising them by the time they were teenagers. First one natural parent would die and the survivor would remarry, then the survivor would die and the stepparent would remarry. What is interesting is that such children were raised for the corporate good, even when there was no genetic investment.

MARRIAGE

The best place to begin to understand the differences between then and now is marriage. Marriage had always served one of three purposes: to produce legitimate heirs, to obtain money or property, or to obtain title. As such marriage was a business contract having nothing to do with love. That was what affairs were for. Marriages for love, or with love an important factor, were just becoming common during the early period, and then only for the middle classes. Sanctified marriage, as distinct from a contract, had been established for only about 150 years. The newer Protestants adopted a view of sanctified marriage in which procreation and the allegory of marital love could justify sex within the religious framework, whereas sex outside of marriage was considered immoral and criminal.

Many traditions describe marriage at a young age. For certain low classes established here, it was possible; however, early marriage was impractical for most. Immigrants could not enter into indentures until age twenty-one, and then were further bound to celibacy for five to seven years. This drove the marriage age up to between twenty-five and thirty and had the effect of removing many people from the reproductive pool until they became infertile or died, limiting the ability of the population to grow dynamically. Through the period aristocratic marriages were conducted with twelve-year-old brides, but it is questionable whether they were consummated until later. Statistics for the South commonly show ages between fourteen and sixteen for women, but men generally were in their majority before marriage.

Marriage customs varied with religions and regions, but a few things pertained to all. Because of the high cost of clothing, wedding attire was not special, except at the very highest court levels. Instead, the celebrants wore the finest clothes they already owned. White was not an obligatory color. Most such customs come from after the period, although in the very late period customs gradually shifted toward the more modern ones. Even here it is wise to be cautious. White was then becoming a common color for dresses, so when one hears about a white dress for the bride, it may not imply a special bridal dress symbolic of virginal purity. It is better to see the marriage ceremony merely as a symbolic rite of passage into a period of acknowledged sexual activity, with a few religious overtones.

In the Anglican church, marriage required the POSTING or PUBLICA-TION OF THE BANNS a fortnight before the wedding, so that any person with reason to object to the marriage had opportunity to do so. The ceremony was to be performed by a minister within a church, before noon, and only during certain seasons of the year. On the South's plantations this broke down and most services were held in the bride's home, with noon the nominal assembly time, but actually starting about two o'clock to allow travel time. Twelfth Night (January 6) was a favorite date for weddings.

In lower-class Virginia, the party assembled at the groom's house, then passed to the bride's house in a riotous footrace, with the winner getting a bottle of liquor. Next came a heavy wedding breakfast with beef, venison, chicken, pork and possibly bear, during which the bridesmaids protected the bride's slipper. If a male guest stole it, the bride was forced to redeem it with another bottle of liquor before the ceremony. A minister said a short service, little more than an exchange of "will you take's" and a blessing. The festivities then began with a dinner, followed by drinking and dancing until about sunrise. Before midnight the bride and bridesmaids stole off to her room, shortly fol-lowed by the groom and groomsmen. There, with the couple in bed, a variant on our modern garter and bouquet rituals was performed. Taking turns, the bridesmaids stood at the foot of the bed with their back to the couple and threw a rolled-up stocking at the bride. The groomsmen then repeated the performance, aiming for the groom's head. The first to connect were the next to be married, not necessarily to each other. In the morning the couple was disturbed again and toasted by the party.

COURTING

Among the aristocracy of the Southern colonies, marriages were still largely arranged. Restrictions on the inheritance of couples who mar-ried without parental approval, and laws requiring the approval of parents in marriages involving minors, acted as a strong brake on the heart. Courtship could be a protracted business negotiation. A young man, interested in a young woman, would first interest his father in the union. His father would then write a letter of introduction to her father, including financial settlements the young man would have upon marriage. The recipient, if interested, would reply with a letter setting forth his approval and his own financial gifts. The young couple were then free to see if they had anything in common. Falling in love before this point was considered a brash breach of etiquette.

The corporate interactions of New England society created more apparent spontaneity, but in fact the process of evaluation had been going on all the young people's lives.

BUNDLING, in which courting couples were allowed to spend the night together in bed fully dressed, is a much-discussed and difficult-to-interpret custom. The presence or absence of a chaperone, or of a BUNDLING BOARD to separate the couple, is hotly debated and seems difficult to accommodate with modern views. In general sexual activity was not endorsed, but if a child were conceived, a marriage would almost certainly take place and the conception ignored in accordance with other attitudes toward premarital sex. Bundling became controversial after 1750, leading to a popular debate over mores and personal responsibility.

Outside those areas where bundling was practiced (generally the Germanic areas and some in New England), courting took place at organized functions such as dances, horse races and church and by calling on the lady at home during the day.

ATTITUDES ABOUT SEXUALITY

One of the most misunderstood aspects of colonial life is sexuality. Our modern view, essentially post-1850, heavily colors our thinking, leading to many misconceptions about earlier times. The chaste, virtuous woman on a pedestal was a product of urban middle-class society and was largely an attempt by women to break the natural reproductive cycle that was their number-one cause of death. Prior to that time, if women had a sexual image, it was as the insatiable and uncontrollable biblical Eve. Men, on the other hand, were seen as rational and capable of controlling themselves.

Class Influences

Class had much to do with how one viewed sexual matters. The gentry always operated under nearly absolute power, and with it came an open prerogative that was virtually impossible to deny. Fondling or sexual possession of servants was widely accepted. Marriage was still considered a business arrangement. The areas of the country with well-established populations of aristocracy continued in this style, with some moderation.

The lower classes had little or no opportunity to advance through marriage, but they were particularly concerned to select healthy and strong mates to help ensure survival, and whose children would be able to care for them in their old age. Farmers—who bred, birthed and slaughtered animals and were rather earthy themselves—viewed sex without shame and sex roles as division of labor.

The middle class took some unpredictable turns as they rose in the cities of England and transported themselves here to farms in the colonies (they managed to industrialize significantly only after our period). Looking for a way to distance themselves from both the earthy farmers and the wastefully profligate gentry, this group of thrifty businesspeople, for many reasons, became identified by their sexual views. Dangers exist in drawing with overly broad strokes, or ignoring the non-Puritan middle class in other locations, for "puritanical" ideals are artifically carried back from urban Victorian or contemporary England to agricultural America.

Regional Influences

The Virginia Colony, settled by many younger sons of landed and titled Englishmen, and the rest of the South, with similar colonists, tended to carry on many upper-class ideals. Land being the English basis of wealth, it was common to decentralize onto large estates where the master was virtually undisputed, and at the same time to make political unions joining land-holding families. Throughout the South, the very few women available for much of the early years meant they had ample opportunities for extramarital relationships and could expect to survive discovery because they would surely be welcomed by the new man if rejected by the old.

New England, on the other hand, was more urban, with the population settled in small towns around the church. The population came from urban centers in England and vigorously espoused the newer ideas of Protestantism. In this view the role of the family was central. The family became a miniature commonwealth, headed by the husband, and responsible for bringing up godly souls. On a larger scale the community had the same responsibility to police individual and corporate behavior. Solitary living was forbidden in many areas, forcing all members of society into close quarters where they were subject to scrutiny by their peers. Privacy as we know it was not held important, especially if its violation discovered some moral hazard to the community. Witnesses in court repeatedly recount peeping through walls, listening at doors, and even tearing boards up and doors off hinges to afford a better view of illicit behavior.

Most New Englanders during the early period made their living by farming, which accounts for some dichotomy between the theoretic ideals of the urban centers of England and the reality of New England life, which accepted sex openly, if within prescribed bounds. At least one man was prosecuted for publicly masturbating outside a church on Sunday. The prosecution was for masturbation, not violation of the Sabbath or public display.

Miscellaneous Matters

Throughout the colonies, the bed and bedstead were the most expensive possessions, so many homes did not have them. Children were often present in bed with a copulating couple, or all were present in a common room on mattresses on the floor. Later, with the advent of modern ideals of privacy, this would change.

Beginning about 1700, new philosophies began to pervade European thinking, including ideas about sex. As part of the swing in thought from pure man imposing order on the chaos of nature to corrupt man emulating divine nature, the purpose of sex was seen to change from procreation within marriage to pleasure within (and, for some, without) marriage. Changes in social and economic life as the world became more commercial, industrial and mercantile brought large segments of the population into areas where their habits were difficult to police, especially as the influence of the churches moderated.

The language of sex has not changed much. The biggest change is that words now considered obscene were in common use early and only gradually passed into the obscene. "Hump," "roger" and "fuck," especially the latter, were commonly found in early court records as slang terms for the sex act and had no negative connotations until sometime during the later periods. The penis was referred to by slang terms such as "rod" and "yard" (as in yardarm).

Northern Europeans generally wore their shirts and shifts or more during sex. Full nudity was uncommon until much after the colonial period. Full nudity was described as "from nature," while a person wearing a shift was "naked in [his, her] shift." "Undressed" was a state between nakedness and dress.

The natives presented another factor. It is difficult to believe all that the records tell us of their sexual habits; facts were likely distorted to make a case to seize land. According to the records, various tribes practiced polygamy, institutionalized (mostly religious) male homosexuality, promiscuity (especially as a courtesy to travelers) and abortion and infanticide, as well as regulating family size by late weaning. If homosexuality were as characteristic of Indian culture as some early records would suggest, the Indians would not have scorned the early all-male settlements because of the lack of families as strongly as they did. Their criticism of a society that, by absence of women, was at least suggestive of a state of homosexuality similar to that under which the Indians were alleged to have lived indicates the allegations were largely unfounded. Despite problems of veracity in the records, it is clear that some traditions were different enough to cause discomfort for the Europeans, and at least one community emulated "free love" Indian practices, to the disgust of its Plymouth neighbors.

PREMARITAL SEX AND BASTARDY

Premarital sex seems to have been tolerated as long as it was, indeed, premarital, but couples who delivered before term after marriage were still punished, did penance and made public confession for their premarital lusts. Late in the period a marked rise occurred in premarital conception rates, and this has been seen as a rebellion by the young to acquire say in spousal selection on the basis of affection. Surveys of premarital sex have compared marriage dates and birth dates. In England, during the colonial period, between 10 percent and 30 percent of children were born within eight months of marriage. In the early Chesapeake the rate was about 30 percent, but then dropped over time. In early New England it was about 10 percent, but rose to near 33 percent in the late period.

Bastardy was problematic in many colonies. Because bastards (WHORESONS) became a social burden, most colonies proscribed bastardy with severe penalties. As a result, the rate was kept down to under about 3 percent, with some segments, such as Quaker congregations, not recording a single case until 1780, and others running under one per one thousand live births. Opposing this, however, was the economic value derived from impregnating slaves in the Chesapeake region, where rates ran as high as twenty-six per one thousand despite similar statutory penalties.

Punishments for bastardy included whipping (ten to forty lashes) and fines as high as five pounds. Men, owning property, were often fined, while women, without property to pay a fine, could only accept whipping. Mothers of bastards occasionally engaged in infanticide to avoid both costs and stigma. Because these women usually claimed stillbirth, hiding a stillborn bastard was a capital offense, and by the later period real stillbirths required witnesses so as to prevent conviction for murder. Preachers sermonized at the executions of such convicts on the theme of the ultimate destructiveness of illicit sex. Prosecutions, however, were uncommon.

UNORTHODOX SEXUAL BEHAVIOR

Bastardy rose, as did prostitution. While some areas always had prostitutes, most self-contained communities prevented it. But mercantile centers such as Boston, New York, Newport, Charles Town and others developed fairly extensive businesses. Philadelphia had an area known as Hell Town. As today, there were a wide range of professionals, from the streetwalker through the brothels of various prices to the kept woman or mistress, who was less common in the colonies than in England. Prostitutes were known as DOES, PUNKS, NIGHTWALKERS, LADIES

OF PLEASURE, WHORES, STRUMPETS, MOLLS, DOXIES, NUNS or BAWDS. Taverns and millinery shops were popular fronts for brothels, called BAWDY HOUSES, NUNNERIES, PLEASURE HOUSES, DISORDERLY HOUSES or HOUSES OF ILL REPUTE. The madam might be called a (REVEREND) MOTHER. Enough prostitution was present for New York to order raids in 1753 and Philadelphia in 1772, and riots occurred in which brothels were burned or the women chased out. Despite this, prostitution in colonial America was not as extensive as in England, where directories of the women were published.

Adultery was defined as sex between a married woman and a man not her husband. Sex between a single woman and a married or single man was fornication. Adultery brought the death penalty in most colonies, although it was rarely imposed. Fines of five to thirty pounds, whipping, banishment or posting a bond forfeitable on a repeated violation were more commonly used. Adultery was cause for divorce and accounted for half the divorce cases in seventeenth-century New England. Fornication, as a lesser charge, still carried heavy penalties, for it could lead to production of bastard children. Fines of up to five hundred pounds of tobacco (about a third of one man's yearly product) or ten pounds (reduced to fifty shillings if the couple were betrothed) or whipping were common. Behavior that could lead to these crimes was also punishable. One man in Virginia paid a twenty-pound fine for profanely drinking and dancing with a married woman, while a father who allowed his son to live with an unmarried woman in New England was convicted as an accessory to fornication.

Sodomy was a male crime and required evidence of "unnatural" penetration, including two witnesses, for the death penalty. It included male/male and male/female anal sex and buggery (sex with an animal), but it did not include female homosexuality. We know of a small number of buggery executions in the seventeenth century, none in the eighteenth. Because buggery was believed to result in monstrous offspring, a man convicted was required to point out his partners, who were then killed before him as a prelude to his own execution. With proper punishment and confession, a male homosexual could be reintegrated into society without stigma.

The status of boys in English society changed over the period. Until they were breeched, boys were considered women. After adolescence they were men. In the intervening years they were neither during the early period. With time, breeching came to signify acceptance as men. This change occurred in England about 1680, but until then, boys were a perfectly acceptable outlet for male sexuality. Since the prevailing English view of sexuality was based in power and the submission to power, no man would willingly submit to another man. A boy, however, who was less than a man and may have been considered a woman, was under no stigma at all in providing sex, and no male lost any standing by taking it. This places special relevance on the boys sent to Virginia in 1607 and other early settlements, but would surely have run afoul of the New England strictures against nonprocreative sex, although the aristocratic nature of Chesapeake society almost assuredly meant English aristocratic practices were continued without comment. Needless to say, the records contain little about pederasty.

Lesbianism (referred to as LEWD BEHAVIOR, ACTS AGAINST NATURE or UNSEEMLY PRACTICES BETWIXT WOMEN) was more tolerated, since women were at first seen as sexually irrepressible. Also, no seed was wasted as in male deviant sexual practice. Whipping or fines were the two most common punishments, although some colonies had a death penalty on the books. The repentant were accepted back into the church and society without permanent stigma.

Rape was a crime against married or engaged women or girls under the age of ten. Rape of a man's spouse or child was an attack on his property. In all other cases, the woman was considered to have given in to her inherent lustfulness and consented, reducing the crime to mere fornication. Witnesses were essential to prove rape, for if a woman did not cry out for help, she consented by not resisting.

One area in which this attitude did not quite hold was in impregnating a female servant. Most indentures prohibited pregnancy (which had the negative effect of removing her from the available pool for most of her reproductive years in the limited life expectancy of the early period). If a servant violated this condition, however, not only was she punished, but a year was added to her term of service to compensate her master for lost time. Masters began to demand sex from female servants, gaining both personal pleasure and an extension on her term of service. Often, a servant so abused could not prove the master's actions. Consequently, the courts began to remove servants from masters who allowed them to become pregnant.

Clearly enforcement of penalties had a lot to do with who and where a person was. The most severe punishments were meted out to blacks, servants and the poor in grossly disproportionate numbers. Apparently a person who could avoid placing the results on the public tab could do as they pleased. As a result, viewing the laws to gain an understanding about the real character of life is difficult, because almost all colonies had similar laws, but most were quite selective in enforcement. In seventeenth-century New England some seventy-two rape cases are recorded; more than half resulted in convictions, but only six ended with executions. Otherwise whipping was common. In eighteenth-century Massachusetts, though only 14 percent of those accused of rape were nonwhite, three of the five executed were, while the remainder were laborers. Blacks who raped white women received the harshest penalties, including burning alive (New York) or castration (Pennsylvania, New Jersey, Virginia).

Some contraception was practiced, with gut condoms, known as ARMOR, used rarely and coitus interruptus the most common form. Results were sporadic, but attempted birth control was nonprocreative and grounds for divorce. Abortion with herbs was known but rare. Female orgasm was believed to be required for conception.

Venereal disease was a hazard that could render its victims insane and then kill them. This insidious disease had no cure, although treatments included ingesting QUICKSILVER (mercury). Women particularly might not show symptoms, making them believe they had been cured, and thus spread the disease further. Syphilis and gonorrhea were both known by those names, although "French pox" or "the French disease" were the most common appellations, and some said Signor Gonorrhea had paid a visit. Face patches were worn to cover the scars left by syphilis. The first documented case of syphilis in the colonies was in 1647, in Boston.

BIRTH RATES AND LIFE EXPECTANCY

With the exception of the limitations upon indentures mentioned earlier, birth rates were apparently intentionally kept high throughout the colonies, with women weaning fairly early. In general, a woman would bear a child every two to three years between marriage and menopause, with as many as twenty-five pregnancies not uncommon.

Survival rates were a different matter. Between 25 and 50 percent of all women died in childbirth or from childbed disease, and the infant mortality rate was comparable. For children eleven was a magic age; survival past it gave a reasonable chance of long life, although many diaries even at eighteen reflect the joy and thankfulness of another year still alive. To some degree survival depended on genetics. Those with strong natural resistance to disease survived. Those who were inbred or weak did not. Thus families might run from two to twenty-five people, and the "average" is difficult to determine.

Statistics for life expectancy are varied and difficult to interpret. A large percentage of the population died in infancy, and another large segment died in their early childbearing years. Mortality in the seventeenth century was high, and people in their forties and fifties were ancient, while later in the period old age would come to be what we know today. Some statistics for the eighteenth century indicate an average life expectancy of forty-five, which required a large number to live into their nineties to counteract the downward influence of early deaths.

FAMILY STRUCTURES

The early period saw high mortality among parents as well as children, and a population unable to enlarge itself. Children might find themselves in families unrelated to them, either by successive marriage and death (one parent dies, the other remarries, then dies, the stepparent then remarries) or, particularly in New England, by placement in another home in accordance with New Englanders' views on the communal welfare and, at the extreme, solitary living. Outside of New England, the isolated nature of the single-family plantation created just as strong a family unit.

Later, stable and extended families would develop. By the end of the period it was not uncommon, if requested (and sometimes without a request), for a relative to carry on the work of building a house or educating the children of a widowed family. Among the wealthy in each colony (and sometimes across borders), an extended family developed not unlike today's Fortune 500 owners (some twenty-six families) or the Hollywood dynasties. The reasons were similar: Each group interacted socially among themselves, allowing young people the best opportunity to meet within the group, and it was good business to ally different businesses and families.

At the lower social levels, things did not change much except mortality dropped somewhat and stability increased proportionately. The family was still a mutually dependent group, parents seeing children as the means of support in their old age, and each individual helping the others to survive in a difficult economic climate.

CHILDREN

Pregnant women looked forward to birth with a mixture of joy and fear because of the risks entailed. After the colonial period women created the "virtuous woman" who loathed sex, as a way of breaking the natural reproductive cycle and reducing their risk.

Most women delivered at home, sometimes with the assistance of a MIDWIFE. Because of the high natural mortality associated with childbirth, midwives were especially susceptible to complaints of negligence or witchcraft. More often than not, after the first couple of children (after the second or third child, the birth canal is often enlarged enough that normal birth is quick and relatively painless), the working-class woman worked (often in the fields) until she went into labor, stopped long enough to give birth and secure the baby, and then went back to work. The more fragile lady of leisure often took more time to recover, but not in every case. Some were remarkably strong and strong willed.

In the early days special BIRTHING, NURSING or CRICKET STOOLS were used to position the body vertically for birth. This practice continued along with the traditional manner of LYING IN in bed. Despite New England traditions of borning rooms, I am not familiar with any documentation for such a specific room use in the period.

Most women made pads of dried grass, fuzzed barks, linen, tow or rags for postpartum and menstrual discharges, as well as swaddling clothes for infants. Rags were too valuable to dispose of, so they were washed and reused.

About six weeks after giving birth, women were CHURCHED, or presented in the church in a purification ceremony descended from the old presentation in the Temple of the ancient Jews.

Children were not considered special throughout most of the period. Infants of both genders belonged to the woman's sphere, as they were dependent on her for their care. Both boys and girls wore dresses, some a simple T-shaped tunic tied in the back for ease of changing and expansion as they grew. At about sixteen to eighteen months girls were placed in their first stays and would remain in them virtually all their lives. Boys were also placed in stays at an early age, to force them into correct posture. Unlike the girls' stays, a boy's stays would be removed before he became dependent on them for support.

The potential for damage to a child's soft head was known, and PUDDINGHEAD CAPS were made of leather with padded rims and top to protect the head. Walkers were used, although not commonly, usually made of turned sticks in a pyramidal form with space for the child to stand in the middle.

At about six years of age boys were BREECHED. This involved removing them from their dresses and stays, shaving their heads and fitting wigs, giving them clothing befitting an adult male of their station and expecting them to act like young adults. The social implications of breeching changed with time. In the early years, boys were not yet men until they passed through adolescence. In the middle and later periods, breeching fully initiated them into the world of men.

Families maintained a distance from children, loving them but expecting them to die. In part, this was manifested in the manner in which children were brought up. In general, after infancy children were not brought up as children but as young adults, contributing to the general welfare as soon as capable. Playtime was over, although to see play as strictly ended would be shortsighted, as even adults played many games we associate with children today. Education and games were mainly designed to ready the child for the practical needs of life and were focused in two areas: skill development and mental faculties. The higher the class of the child, and the later in the period, the better the opportunity that a life of leisure and privilege allowed a real childhood, while the working-class child was simply another mouth to feed and a laborer to help the family community.

EDUCATION

Educational opportunities were limited. While almost all Protestant religions shared a belief that it was necessary to be able to read the Scriptures for oneself (to avoid being sent to damnation by a priest who, maliciously or unintentionally, misled the soul—the so-called Devil Deceiver doctrine), there was little organized education to make that possible.

Boys often learned to read, figure and perform other necessary basic functions as part of their apprenticeship at a trade. Any person involved in a trade or in selling a marketable product needed to know enough math to keep books and not be cheated. To some degree the skills taught depended on the trade, but some, such as bookkeeping, reading and measuring were fairly common to all. Some trades, such as surveying, required advanced knowledge.

Girls were generally taught at home. Basic letters and numbers were taught early, and samplers—embroidery pieces with letters, numbers, phrases and designs—were produced as early as age six. Advanced reading skills were acquired by reading aloud at night, often from the Bible, literature, letters or, later, from newspapers. Many girls began to compile a RECEIPT (recipe) book, which included not just food recipes, but formulae for medicine and for many household processes including stain removal and dyeing. Upper-class girls might become fluent in Greek and Latin as well as English.

Many students learned their letters from battledores or hornbooks, which were sheets printed with letters, numbers and a few basic sentences protected behind sheets of flattened transparent horn bound in leather.

Some sects, such as the Quakers, did sponsor public grammar schools, but these were limited in geographic distribution. A few scattered public or sponsored schools existed, including some aimed at training blacks.

Most upper-class children were taught by private tutors hired by one family or by a consortium of gentlemen. Sometimes promising children from poorer families in the area were allowed to take basic classes from these tutors. Rarely, these consortiums amounted to private academies. Such tutors taught Latin, Greek, rhetoric, geometry, logic and advanced mathematics, in addition to often serving as dancing masters and disciplinarians of their young charges.

American colleges were expensive, a year's tuition running about one to two years' income for a small farmer (ten to fifty pounds).

Loans could be obtained from outside sources, but only Dartmouth had a work-study program.

Degrees were conferred in defiance of the English monopolies of Oxford and Cambridge, making colonial colleges technically UNIVERSITIES. By the Revolution at least nine colonial institutions were granting degrees, as opposed to still only two in England. Between 1717 and 1747 some fourteen hundred men graduated from colonial colleges; in the next thirty years about twice that number of degrees were awarded.

The colonial college was more interested in disseminating knowledge than in research or self-perpetuation. Thus, it tended to provide strictly undergraduate work. Students interested in careers in law or divinity apprenticed or went to study at the Inns of Court in London or one of the Scottish institutions. The decentralized colonial population prevented any real think tanks from forming.

PLAY AND RECREATION

Both children and adults played games of skill and chance. Many games we would consider children's games today were popular with adults, particularly if a gambling element could be introduced. The amount of time a person could devote to recreation depended on whether they were rich or poor, the time of the year, and, if rich enough to allow leisure time, the burden of social and governmental obligations carried by the individual. In addition to the recreations listed here, please refer to the sections on dance, theater, music and literature.

GAMES, TOYS AND AMUSEMENTS

Games of Skill

archery: Still practiced in the early period (the tradition of Agincourt and Crecy), but not used militarily because the Indians were more afraid of guns.

badminton or shuttle-cock: Played with wooden racquets called battledores. It was more common in England.

bat-fives: Fives played with wooden paddles.

billiards: (☞ *page 287*) Popular at taverns, which often had tables. More like today's snooker than pocket billiards. At one end was a wicket of ivory, at the other a post called the KING. Pockets were HAZARDS. Scoring was for putting one's ball through the wicket, brushing the king without knocking it over, or sending an opponent's ball into the king or a hazard. The end of the shovel-shaped stick was held with the fingers to thrust the ball.

bowls: Oval balls bowled toward a small jack, similar to boccie.

boxing: An old English sport. Common in the colonies among the lower classes. Considered uncivilized by the French.

cricket: Bowler bowled underhanded; bat was J-shaped. Otherwise like today's game, requiring much strategy, skill, quick thinking. Catching the fast-moving, hard, leather-covered, thread-wrapped cork ball with a bare hand is a typically English pastime.

cudgeling: A popular game at fairs with professionals taking on all comers. With an oak stick for a saber and a heavy rope wrapped around the left arm for a shield, the objective was to break the skin on the opponent's pate first. Contemporary descriptions report the sound as that of a boy running with a stick along a picket fence.

fencing: Required discipline, poise, footwork, grace, small movements, eye/hand coordination and necessary military skill. Used foils with a leather mask with slits for eyes. Also called SMALL SWORDPLAY.

fives: Handball, played off a wall. May have been limited to the late period.

hoop and stick: Wooden hoop about two and a half feet across, nine-inch sticks. Boys ran, driving hoop with stick. Girls threw hoop from stick to stick between two girls, learning balance and movement within restrictive clothing.

ninepins: A bowling game with nine pins and one ball, with the object to bowl exactly thirty-one pins. Overages required exactly nine to score; less than thirty-one lost. Rarely mentioned, but the nature of the references indicate it was a popular game throughout the period.

quoits: Wooden or rope circlets thrown over a post. Horseshoes was a common man's version. Very common.

riding: The upper classes learned balance, necessary social grace and military skill from riding.

skating: Ice skating was particularly popular among the Dutch, but also common among the English. One story tells of a man, captured by Indians, who escaped by skating away on stolen skates over frozen lakes after duping his captors into thinking he could not skate.

tennis: (⌨ *page 287*) An indoor game relatively unknown in the colonies due to the need for specialized courts and equipment. Not played like modern tennis.

wrestling: Possibly learned from the Indians, it was most popular with the lower-class frontiersmen. There were three special forms: gouging of eyes, biting and choking. If any were not agreed to, the fighters were scrupulous to avoid them. Otherwise, people lost eyes and ears. Sometimes called boxing.

Board Games and Games Teaching Thinking

backgammon: Very popular in the eighteenth century. IRISH backgammon was played as today; in TRIC-TRAC or TICK-TACK (French) all men started from the ace point; SICE-ACE was for five players each with six men; DUBBLETS used a different placing; and KETCH-DOLT piled all the men in the center of the board.

chess: As the modern game, but without formalized play. Ruy Lopez, one of the first great players to study the game, after whom one of the most famous openings is named, lived just before this time. One bit of contemporary strategy was to place the board so the sun shone in the opponent's eyes. Not popular in the South.

dominoes: Popular in France, but not popular among the English until about 1800.

draughts: As today's game of checkers after 1756; before then, a simpler seventeenth-century French version was played. Not yet played scientifically.

nine-man morris: Each player alternately placed one man of nine on intersections of lines, then first player moved one piece along a line. When a player got three in a row, he could remove one of his opponent's pieces. Winner removed all his opponent's pieces.

the most royal game of goose: Track game with hazards along the way. A great betting game. Dates at least to 1597.

Card and Gambling Games

all-fours (pitch): Today's seven-up or setback. A game of luck, popular with the less intellectual types. Looked down upon by the whist sort.

basset: Similar to faro, not often played in the colonies. Known to those who traveled to England.

cockfighting: Roosters were bred to kill each other with silver or steel spurs attached to their own spurs. Popular in improvised rings outside of taverns. Considered brutal by many; a long-lasting carryover of such Elizabethan games as bear baiting.

cribbage: Like today's game but with five cards and sixty-one holes; invented in the mid-seventeenth century.

cross and pile (toss-up): Ancient gambling game. One person tossed a coin in the air, the other called it before landing. CROSS equals heads, PILE equals tails. Forbidden of American officers by Washington's General Orders of October 3, 1775.

faro: Known but not often played. A casino game for large groups of players playing against the dealer on each card turned up. Made more popular by French soldiers during the Revolution.

hazard: The player first named his "main," then threw his dice. He won immediately if he threw his main, lost on any one of several "crabs." If he survived, his throw was his "chance," and he won by again throwing it, but if he threw his main he now lost. Hoyle's mathematical analysis about 1750 simplified the game into modern craps.

hussle-cap (hustle-cap): Coins were shaken in a cap, then thrown for a heads or tails pattern. Popular with children. Forbidden of American officers by Washington's General Orders of October 3, 1775.

lanterloo (loo): A fast three- or five-card gambling game for any number of players, but best with five or seven. Played with counters called FISH made of ivory or mother-of-pearl. A fast way to lose a lot of money, because the stakes doubled each hand.

lotto: As a private game, today's keno. As a means of selling goods or awarding prizes, a proper lottery, with overall odds of about one in five.

ombre: A Spanish game similar to whist known in the colonies.

put: An early form of poker, played with three cards, as a low-class gambling game. Known as a sharper's game before 1674.

quadrille: A Spanish game similar to whist known in the colonies.

slam: A fast two-handed gambling game played like rummy but scored like cribbage. Gave way to whist in popularity.

whist: The predecessor of bridge, whist was a popular game among intellectuals because it required concentration. It supposedly was named for the silence during play. First scientifically studied by Hoyle in 1742, thence very popular.

Toys

bilbo catcher: A stick with a cup on one end, a spike on the other, and a ball with a hole for the spike on the end of a string. Taught eye/hand coordination, discipline.

dolls: Mostly homemade of many materials; a very few bought; made of wooden pegs jointed together. Always dressed as adults, as were children, even though sold in stores as "babies." Some quite finely dressed.

tops: As today, but also whipped with strings on sticks.

Children's Games

Children's games included hopscotch, leapfrog, blind man's bluff, hide and seek, prisoner's base, flying kites, marbles, lacrosse, knucklebones, swings and jump rope.

PETS

Pets were commonly kept by the colonists. Dogs served as both pets and hunting animals. Cats were companions and kept rodents at bay. After about 1650, when things became settled enough to allow for such frivolity, birds provided music, even being taught to imitate popular tunes played on small flutes (the name "recorder" is believed to come from the term for a bird beginning to repeat its tune, or record). Red birds (cardinals) and mockingbirds were popular exports from the colonies to England, mockingbirds fetching two guineas each. Imported birds were available, including canaries, mynas (the first in England belonged to the Duke of York in 1664), parrots and bullfinches. They were quite expensive, especially if trained in London to sing. Squirrels were popular pets. One was killed by lightning while in its owner's pocket; the young owner survived. Deer were also tamed, and ran in and out of some houses at will.

DEATH AND DYING

During periods of significant change in mortality rates—whether a drop, as in the Victorian era and modern day, or a rise, as in the plague-ridden late Middle Ages—people have typically ascribed great importance to death. By contrast, death in the colonies was an everyday but not overly noticeable part of life, so it was not given undue thought.

Most people died at home. There were no hospitals as we know them. Medical care, including surgery, was provided in the home. The major causes of death for women—cooking burns and childbirth—

occurred in the home. Accidents, including farming mishaps, occurred at or near home. With the exception of the voyage to America, only the occasional person died in travel, in battle or on an expedition. Without widespread industrial manufactories, industrial accidents, although possibly common within a trade such as iron founding, were rare for the society as a whole.

Burying Grounds and Tombs

In the North, where towns were the center of society, the town burying ground was the norm. Coffins were set into the ground, and carved stones were set at the head. In the South, with its dispersed population, small family burying grounds on the plantations were common. Tombs were flat, above-ground vaults, although below-ground interment with headstones was known. There, burial in the churchyard was reserved for travelers, indigents, townsfolk, ministers and others. Tombs set in the floors of church aisles were also common, and these were reserved for the most esteemed and revered members of the community. Obviously, since the place of honor was in the aisle, walking on the grave was not a taboo. A few highly select persons were interred in crypts under public buildings, and large families might have a crypt rather than individual tombs.

New England tombstone decoration provides a highly controlled study medium. There are three principal decorative motifs. The oldest of these is a grinning death's head, often winged. About 1700 this was slowly replaced by a winged cherub. The final form, a willow tree and urn, dates to the very end of the colonial period and into the next century. The transition from death's head to cherub has been seen as the transformation from Puritan severity to the hope of a more deistic, humanistic society. The rate of this change can be strictly documented. It took hold first and fastest in the more literate centers, such as Cambridge, then moved into the countryside at about one mile per year. This suggests some of the other cultural changes discussed in this book occurred at similar rates. Southern tomb decoration is generally less morbid than that found in New England.

Embalming and Shipping

Although embalming was known well before the colonial period, and removal of soft organs, which were separately buried in viscera chests, was known in the seventeenth century, little evidence exists of embalming at any but the highest court levels. By comparison, it seems to have been fairly common to ship bodies from the place of death to home in casks of cheap rum.

A gravestone from the old burying ground in Salem, Massachusetts. Note the double year date; this stone was cut in the time when Europe had adopted the Georgian calendar and England had not, placing January in different years on the different calendars. Also of interest is the collation of three distinct funerary images: Death and the grinning death's head on the same stone with a cherub into which the death's head evolved, and Father Time with his hourglass and scythe. Usually these three images were used individually on a stone. Note also that Father Time, not Death, is given the job of the reaper. The scythe is of the then-new modern form.

Funeral Customs

It is difficult to say with certainty what funeral customs were like in the colonies. The English common funeral was a pompous and expensive rendition of a baronial state funeral, the exact details of which changed significantly during the period. This style of funereal excess was not likely to have enjoyed much vogue among the Puritans, and evidence from Virginia shows the wealthy planters were troubled by its excesses. In the early period such pomp was unavailable because of economic pressures, and during the latter periods it was unlikely to be seen except at certain state funerals like that of Lord Botetourt in 1770, or of Governor and Lady Calvert at St. Mary's City. The following discussion, then, hits certain key features and notes how they changed during the period.

Late Elizabethan customs included the use of expensive black velvet

MOURNING CLOTHES, but about 1600 the practice began to pass. Mourning clothes of a cape, hat, hose and shoes were still occasionally worn into the eighteenth century, but they were worn only for the funeral, were made of lighter materials and were reduced in size and volume. More common were black ribbons or armbands. It is unlikely that Elizabethan practice continued in the colonies, due to the exigencies under which the colonists labored during the early years of the 1600s. Mourners might have mourning rings or mourning gloves bequeathed to them in the deceased's will and would wear them to the funeral.

Coffin shapes changed during the period. Through the 1630s at least, coffins were straight tapers from head to foot and gable roofed, with a ridge made of two boards nailed together running the length of the coffin. This ridge allowed the palls (cloth covers) to be seen in procession. Many palls had armorial devices or other decorative motifs emblazoned on them. After the 1630s, coffins assumed a form with the head narrow, widening to the shoulders, then tapering to the feet, with a flat lid. This style remained common throughout the remainder of the period. With time, many such coffins would be covered in velvet which was nailed in place with decorative brass-headed nails.

Sometimes, particularly early, coffins were made of lead sheet, shaped around the shrouded body and taking an anthropoid shape. Few such coffins were used in the colonies. Another use of lead was in a standard coffin to make it more airtight. A few such coffins have been found in the colonies, related to state funerals. Some coffins had furniture, such as hinges, handles and coffin plates or deposition plates—decorative silver, brass or tin plates engraved with the occupant's name and other information. Many times the body was not interred in the coffin; the coffin belonged to the parish and was used repeatedly for storing and transporting bodies to burial. Personal coffins were made to fit the owner.

The use of a winding sheet or shroud was common in the early period. This could be nothing more than a linen sheet, tied off above the head and below the feet and sewn up along the side. More formally, it was fitted, tied with a knot at the head like a burnoose, then bound around the calves or ankles. Some shrouds were made in advance, and a bride's trousseau might include several, including those for infants. Later in the period, shrouds sometimes left the face exposed. By the early eighteenth century, shrouds were being replaced with shifts or shirts and hoods similar to lappet caps, the hood held in place with a broad chin band. Shrouds were often the only container for the body. An act of Parliament required burial in flannel clothes. Whether it was ever enforced here is questionable, particularly in New England, where local laws required production of linen fabrics.

Bodies were generally not buried with jewelry or other fittings. An

One of two family funerary hatchments at Shirley Plantation in Charles City County, Virginia. Other isolated survivors indicate that although such formalities were rare in the colonies, the wealthier homes fully emulated English aristocratic practice.

occasional wedding ring was worn. Eyes were closed upon death. Hands were traditionally placed with the right upon the left, in one of four ways: arms crossed, hands upon the shoulders; hands in a praying posture at the bottom of the rib cage; arms folded along the bottom of the rib cage; or arms straight with the hands crossed covering the groin.

A hatchment was a diamond-shaped board with the armorial devices of the deceased on it, carried in procession before the body and placed outside the home on poles. Hatchments were very rare and associated with upper-class homes only.

Funerals were distinct from burials. Bodies were laid out on the stretcherlike BIER or on joint stools (low tables fifteen to twenty inches high) in the home for several days if weather permitted. Unless there was reason to delay it, interment took place about three days after death. It was usually a private affair. The funeral could be delayed for as much as several weeks and was a public event.

As with weddings, funerals took place in the church or at home depending on the region. In the Anglican service, the Order for the Burial of the Dead was read. The prayer book of 1559 or 1662 was used. Puritan funerals were simpler, usually involving a sermon and interment. The best indication we have is from English practice during the Commonwealth, when the Book of Common Prayer was forbidden, and services were extremely plain, almost brutally so. No service was used, but family and friends might process to the interment, about the only holdover being the casting of sprigs of rosemary into the grave.

At funerals, hats were removed; a funeral cake or wine sealed in block wax might be served, as might a feast either before or after the funeral; and in the seventeenth century guns might be fired. Muffled drums, clubbed muskets and mourning banners could be used in a procession, particularly in state and military funerals. Some of the local poor (sometimes one for each year the deceased had lived) were often invited to partake of the abundance at this time.

In the colonies the body was laid in state in the home, in part to allow time for a person pronounced dead in error to come to life again if so disposed, then taken to the church in a procession, if the funeral was performed there. The procession involved four to six bearers, usually poor, who carried the casket, and pall bearers who carried only the edges of the pall. At the church gate the minister met the procession and preceded the body into the church, where it was laid feet facing east on the bier or on stools. Relatives followed the body, then guests in pairs. A sermon with eulogy and prayers were said, then the procession departed again for the interment ceremony, where the minister again presided until after sprigs of rosemary were thrown in and the first shovelfuls of earth were cast.

State funerals, especially in the middle period, were ornate affairs modeled on the formalities required by the College of Armourers in England. They were larger, with more members in the procession carrying hatchments and other badges of rank or accomplishment, and had far more opulent use of fabrics and mourning clothes.

After a person died, two VIEWERS appointed by the court took an inventory of his estate for the purpose of valuing and probating the estate. These inventories were filed with the clerk of the court. Some are vague, barely five lines long, while others are quite specific, listing items room by room. The inventory for Lord Botetourt in Virginia lists over sixteen thousand items room by room.

BIBLIOGRAPHY

Cleland, John. *Memoirs of a Woman of Pleasure.* (*Fanny Hill*) A contemporary erotic novel, it is mild by today's standards, and provides much information about aspects of life not otherwise recorded.

Cotton, Charles. *The Compleat Gamester or Instructions How to Play at Billiards, Trucks, Bowls, and Chess.* 1674. Reprinted in *Games and Gamesters of the Restoration.* Edited by Cyril H. Hartmann. London: G. Routledge and Sons, 1930.

D'Emilio, John and Estelle B. Freedman. *Intimate Matters: A History of Sexuality in America.* New York: Harper and Row, 1988.

Geddes, Gordon E. *Welcome Joy: Death in Puritan New England.* Ann Arbor, Mich.: UMI Research Press, 1981.

Litten, Julian. *The English Way of Death: The Common Funeral Since 1450.* London: Robert Hale, 1991.

Spruill, Julia Cherry. *Women's Life and Work in the Southern Colonies.* New York: W.W. Norton, 1972.

Tannahill, Reay. *Sex in History.* Rev. ed. Chelsea, Mich.: Scarborough House, 1992.

Bay

Plymouth Bay

ay is very
ill of Flatts
n the Sea
ngerous
nk and
nt
ck
w
for a
d We
letts in
a place of
l Vessells and
ar here .

Plymouth

Cedar P. XI

Marks I.

Rocky ground

Gurnet head

channel to way

Browns Sunken Islands

Monement high Land

Barnstable
reason of
Run a Shoe

Note that t
Bars are bu
are set dow
Water, and
there is the

Barnst
C.

rds Bay is very dangerous
ng and Flowing is but small

Sandwich

XI

ds Bay

Barnstable

Tucgguiset
Woods Pt.

hole

North Chan
3 Coarse Sand 3
Southacks Cha
Horseshoe sant

arpolin Cove

foot

Tucgguiset Point

PART THREE

Government & War

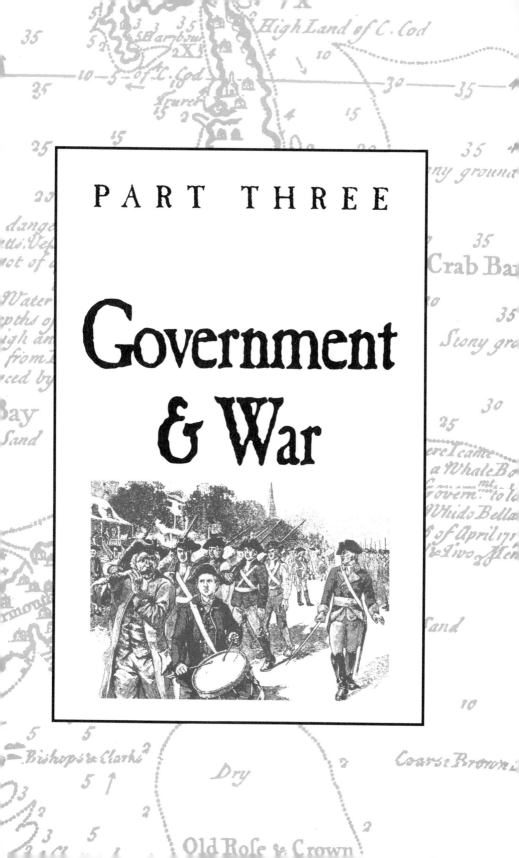

CHAPTER NINE

Government, Law & Politics

GOVERNMENT

One of the most chaotic structures of everyday life in the colonies was the political framework. Some colonies were founded as virtual autocracies, under the sole rule of a proprietor, like William Penn in Pennsylvania and Lord Baltimore in Maryland. Some, like Virginia, were first organized as businesses, funded and ruled by a for-profit corporation. Others, like New Jersey and New York, fell somewhere between proprietorships and royal colonies. And all, with time, would have their original charters revoked, their original governments repudiated, and new royal governments imposed with more or less success.

Many irritants of the Revolutionary era were the result of this process. As colonists were not willing to have their original rights revoked, and George III attempted to regain a large amount of royal prerogative, friction was inevitable.

Certain elements can be commonly ascribed to the various colonies' governments.

Most early charters granted the colonists the sole right to tax themselves. Even when royal status supplanted earlier forms, this was one right the colonists refused to give up, ultimately fighting for it. The right to tax was conferred on the lower house of the government, representing the landowning colonists, although the governor could introduce an act for consideration.

Most colonies had some form of representative assembly, even if the colony was a proprietary one. This was necessary to allow the immigrants enough say in matters of government that they would be willing to immigrate and make the colony profitable for the proprietors. These legislative assemblies were modeled on England's Parliamentary system, with the governor or proprietor standing for the King, an appointed upper house or council, usually about a dozen men, for the House of Lords, and an elected lower house, usually two from each county, for the House of Commons. The lower house was often called a House of Burgesses or a (General) Assembly.

In most colonies, councillors served three distinct duties: as members of the governor's privy council (modern cabinet secretaries), as justices on the high court of appeal (modern Supreme Court justices), and as members of the upper legislative house (Senate). These men were carefully selected and appointed by the king through the governor (or some similar arrangement), often for life on good behavior. They represented the most highly placed, visible and influential men in the colony and were often heavily intermarried. These were the strings the governor, often newly arrived from outside, could pull to get his policies enacted in the colony.

By comparison, the members of the lower house were elected in what can be called representative government, not a true democracy.

The Franchise

Officeholding requirements usually were the same as those for the franchise and varied among colonies. Again, some generalizations can be drawn. Women were excluded, as were nonwhites. Persons bound by indentures, court order, apprenticeship or other obligation were not entitled, and those in their minority were excluded. Most had to be landowners (the yeoman was the lowest class of English landholder, and thus the lowest class entitled to vote), with the exact amount of land required, developed or not, depending on the colony and even the year. There was a customary comparable value clause for holdings in towns.

Finally, most royal colonies made membership in the Church of England a requirement for franchise, because the king was the titular head of it, and total allegiance to the king was required. In New England, congregational membership was substituted. In practice, the religious requirements got bogged down in the political problems described in chapter sixteen. New England could refuse to grant the franchise to Anglicans even when the New England colonies became royal colonies. The Dutch churches in conquered New Netherlands got special exemptions. Any colony with established toleration was wide open on constitutional grounds.

Even allowing for the head of household to "represent" his entire family, male and female, less than 15 percent and more likely under 10 percent of the population in most colonies was "represented." The actual voting populace was probably under 5 percent, and elected the socially highest bracket from within their own ranks.

147

Government in New England, with organized towns, town meetings and churches, may have appeared somewhat more democratic than elsewhere, but church membership, as opposed to church attendance, was the franchise criterion, and the proportion of the population thus represented was small.

Processes

Under company charters individual governance procedures were implemented, while most proprietary colonies utilized a combination of autocratic means and a representative assembly. In royal colonies after 1700, most bills were introduced in the lower house, although they could be introduced by the council. They were then sent to committee for detailed work and debate, then back to the floor, where they were read again and voted on after yet another reading.

Differences between the upper and lower houses could be worked out in conference committees, and the governor could sign or veto the bill. Technically the assembly could not override a veto, but in practice compromises were often worked out. All bills approved by the colonial establishment were bound in red tape (ribbon) and forwarded to London, where they were reviewed by the Boards of Plantations and Trade and any other applicable agencies before being submitted to the King for final approval. If the King approved, the bill finally became law. If not, it was stricken down. The colonists might wait as long as six years to hear back.

A problem existed in differentiating between persons sent on official missions and frauds. In the early period small brass tokens of identification were issued to officials coming to the colonies, upon presentation of which the colonists could be assured the person was authentic. Likewise, large seals of state were kept by the governors of each state to impress in wax affixed to official documents. Documents requiring a number of these seals, from different agencies, would be adorned with ribbons holding on their ends the four- to six-inch-diameter seals.

Elections

The process of attaining elected office varied in details throughout the colonial years, but many things were common. A WRIT OF ELECTION was an official document issued by the governor or other authority calling for an election and setting its date. Writs were generally read in the churches and might be posted. The actual process of campaigning often began before the writ was issued, as the necessity for elections was generally predictable, and certain activities were constrained by law after the issuance of the writ.

Elections could be occasioned by any of several events: passage of a legal interval since the last election, death or malfeasance of an office-holder, arrival of a new governor, dissolution of an assembly by the governor, or at the governor's prerogative.

In most areas, nomination was attained automatically by incumbents unless they specifically certified they were not running, while new candidates could announce their candidacy or be asked to run and agree. An important part of running was obtaining INTEREST, which was used both in the sense of obtaining someone's interest or support, and carrying someone's interests or issues. Often, a prudent candidate would first determine whether he could obtain any interest before declaring, and if support was not forthcoming, he would wait until an incumbent was stepping down, when he might gain interest for himself.

Once nominated, the candidate had several courses of action. If the election were uncontested or his interest were great enough, he needed to do very little. He might travel about his county or other district, meeting voters at races, church, balls, picnics and other events. If the election were close, he might engage in TREATING, although this was often made unlawful between the issuance of a writ and the close of an election. Still, many would promise to treat their supporters at the polls after the election. Treating entailed the liberal dispersion of bumbo, toddy, punch or cider and possibly food. Occasionally balls were given after the election.

Election day was different in different parts of the country. In the dispersed South, eligible voters gathered at the polling place, generally the courthouse, about noon. The sheriff, responsible for the conduct of the election, read the writ and declared the polls open. In a simple election, he could ask the supporters of the incumbent(s) to form a group on one side and the supporters of other candidates on the other side. If all parties were satisfied with this DIVISION, the election was concluded. If not, a party could ask for a formal POLL, in which individual votes were recorded.

In New England, with a centralized town structure and more levels of government including the town and the colonial government, elections took a slightly different form. Most local officials were elected in town meetings, and colonial officials were elected by the freeholders at the general court. With time, DEPUTIES were elected at the local levels, who went and elected the colonial officials. Later deputies would carry the proxies of their fellow freeholders.

CRIME AND PUNISHMENT

Like many other aspects, crime and punishment changed significantly during the period and from region to region. Moreover, it is difficult to determine exactly which laws were meant to be literally enforced and which were reserved for worst-case situations.

Generally, misdemeanors and any offenses committed by slaves were tried in the local county courts. Felonies (those crimes involving loss of life or limb), and large civil suits (greater than approximately ten pounds) were tried at the general courts, or courts of oyer and terminer, at which the governor's council generally presided, after being reviewed by the county court as a grand jury. Matters pertaining to the high seas, including the condemnation of plunder taken during privateering, were heard in admiralty courts.

In the later, royal period, most free colonists were afforded the rights of English common law, including trial by jury of their peers, confronting their accusers, calling witnesses, presumption of innocence and the use of counsel if they chose and could afford it. In practice, most people defended themselves. Earlier, many of the proprietary colonies' courts followed the same traditions based on the old manorial courts of the English countryside. Most of the early charters guaranteed the colonists the rights to English common law.

In general, the colonies needed labor and colonists and were not prone to strictly enforce capital laws for minor offenses as would contemporary London or Paris, both of which had a surplus unemployed population. Leniency was often granted on the first offense in the hope that the criminal would reform and reenter the work force. With repeat offenses death was ordered to remove a confirmed malefactor from the community. Likewise, debtors here were more likely to be freed, as the courts recognized they could not pay their debts if they could not work.

Persons convicted of felonies who would be executed could beg the mercy of the court, which might listen if the crime were not too heinous and it were a first offense. They could also plead BENEFIT OF CLERGY if they could read and (before about 1700) were male, or plead BENEFIT OF BELLY (pregnancy), which would not save the malefactor but would buy time for the child to be born. A husband was generally held liable for his wife's felonious actions, unless he could prove he was neither materially present nor culpable. A woman who committed crimes with or at the order of her husband might be let off and the husband prosecuted; sometimes they might be sentenced together.

In the event a nonfatal sentence were given, most courts ordered the crime BURNED AT THE HAND (branded into the base of the thumb on the right hand) from which comes the custom of raising one's right hand when sworn in, so the court could see the criminal record.

Officially, a verdict could be appealed to the king in London, but the appellant was required to pay the expenses to transport the entire establishment, including the prosecutor and witnesses, to London and house them until the King could hear the case. It is doubtful if any appeals were ever made.

In general, enforcement was stricter in the early years, when in effect the colonies lived under martial law, which eased with time. Social, religious and economic pressures were all related to any crime and could effect the severity with which local authorities would act. Any study that presents tabulations of laws implies that there was much more crime than evidence suggests was actually prosecuted. Fragmentary records for the forty-two-year period ending 1778 in Virginia indicate only about 126 executions, or three per year, were carried out in the largest colony.

Hanging at the neck until dead was the most common form of capital punishment throughout the period. At some times and places, and for certain particularly heinous acts, burning at the stake was ordered, but this generally was an earlier punishment. Hangings were major public spectacles. Archaeology at the gallows in Williamsburg found chicken bones, paper and all the other rubbish we associate with a football game. Felons were drawn on a cart (seated on their own coffin) to the gallows (☞ *page 288*), raised, the noose placed and the horse slapped. Sometimes the drop was not enough to break the neck, and then the crowd got a real show as the victim slowly suffocated, turning various colors and dancing on the rope. Anthony Dittond went through three minutes of this, until the sheriff (hangman) pulled on his legs to end his suffering. The rope broke, and, after waking up and talking with the crowd, Dittond climbed back up on the cart unassisted. The second time the rope held.

A person convicted of high treason could be drawn and quartered, and this was possibly ordered in one case related to Bacon's Rebellion in Virginia. Here the criminal was drawn behind a cart to the place of execution, hanged by the neck, but cut down before he died and ritually disemboweled; then the body was cut into four separate pieces and buried in widely separated, unconsecrated ground so the soul could never rest. Cases are known of quartering after a normal hanging.

Misdemeanors received corporal punishments far more often than imprisonment, generally considered cruel and unusual and a waste of taxpayer's money. Fines were imposed more often on men, who presumably had property with which to pay, than on women. Banishment from the colony was also an alternative, more likely to be used in New England, with its strict concerns of ideological pollution, than elsewhere.

The stocks (a pair of boards with holes for the ankles and a "seat" consisting of the sharpened edge of a board) and the pillory (a board with holes for the hands and head at chest height) were both ordered for a variety of petty crimes. Persons sentenced to either might hire someone to wipe their faces, because people were known to suffocate in England from the mass of eggs, tomatoes, rotten fruit and other rubbish thrown at the criminal by the crowd. This deluge was only the prelude, because then ants, wasps and other insects would discover the wonderful mess on the face and torment the prisoner more than the humiliation and pain of standing or sitting for several hours in a designedly uncomfortable manner. Sometimes, particularly earlier, sentences in the pillory included having one or both ears nailed to the pillory and cut off at the conclusion of the punishment. Later, this became an added punishment, although the pillory, and nailing, remained the more strict punishment for first-time felony offenders and others shown leniency from the gallows, such as second-offense hog stealing, perjury, first-offense forgery and petit witchcraft.

Convicts might also be sentenced to stripes or lashes on the bare back, or whipping. Sentences varied from twenty to one hundred lashes or more, but thirty to fifty seems to have been most common. Death could result from forty to fifty lashes. Lashes were laid on with a cat-o'-nine-tails, a short leather whip with multiple tails, each knotted at the end. Often, in extensive sentences, a surgeon stood by to douse the criminal's back with buckets of salt water during the whipping. A person receiving an extensive number of lashes for a lesser crime might be allowed an interval for the back to heal before the remaining lashes were administered, but for more heinous crimes lashing might continue until all skin was removed and the organs fell out.

In the early and middle period, women who slandered were ducked, or tied to the end of a long lever and immersed in water repeatedly for thirty seconds at a time, sometimes until they begged for mercy and apologized.

A strong public component was in all punishment. Stocks, pillories, whipping posts and other punishment devices were located in the town center or at the local courthouse or church, and execution of sentences was cause for a public gathering. The crowds appear to have enjoyed the spectacle, participating with gusto.

SOCIAL STRUCTURES

Colonial society was highly class based, though to a lesser degree than contemporary England was. As detailed throughout this book, many factors contributed to the breakdown of the old system, particularly in the early and middle years. Canada, established much later when a more intact English society could be transported, was much stricter in class distinctions, apparent on visits to early sites in Upper Canada. Likewise, Florida, another late addition, experienced a fairly rigid class structure, even though many of its founders came from the gentry of

South Carolina. Although class consciousness was great in the early years, its early breakdown in the face of necessity can be seen when the Virginia colony named John Smith, a mere yeoman's son, as governor, meaning he outranked titled gentlemen.

Historians of some schools have portrayed a lack of class consciousness in colonial society as a way to distinguish the American experience and explain the reality of a later day. I have emphasized the process of transformation from the rigid structures of England to the modern society, which must have taken place at different rates in different places. The household, town and township structure of New England can be seen as a strong leveling force, but caution must be used. Only about 10 percent of the New England population were church members, and thus able to vote, a statistic not unlike the landholding elite of Virginia. In Virginia, the wealthy planter's obligations to his tenants, slaves and poorer neighbors could be (and were) construed as comparable to his affections for his immediate family, but that did not prevent the FFV, or First Families of Virginia, from establishing a headlock on the power of government through intermarriage, not unlike the twenty or so families who today own the majority of the Fortune 500 companies.

The colonial upper class was comprised of the GENTRY or ARISTOCRACY. In England this would have been the lower, untitled nobility and the wealthier landowners, a blurred line even then. The king could grant title to members of the aristocracy, thus elevating them to the PEERAGE, and heraldic emblems could be purchased. Under the laws of PRIMOGENITURE, estates (land being the basis of wealth in England) could be passed only to the oldest son, so as to keep the estates cohesive and large enough to support that family in style.

Younger sons, raised in the manor, were turned loose with annual allowances equivalent to a journeyman's wages and expected to make livings in law, the military (fathers would often purchase the commission) or the ministry. Many of these younger sons emmigrated to the colonies and sought land there to enable them to live in their accustomed style. The terms "lady" and "gentleman" pertained to this class only. Later, in the Victorian era, it became courtesy among the middling sort to use these titles as compliments to members of their own group. Here in the colonies "aristocracy" or "gentry" might not have quite the meaning they did in England or France, but they still denoted a group of people distinguishable by their wealth and attitudes.

Common people comprised the rest of the population, although distinctions existed within this group. The terms "men" and "women" related broadly to commoners. The commoners who counted were those with land or property. A small percentage of these were the merchants and craftsmen, who might make good to excellent livings. These, and some of the large planters, were the middling sort, or middle class. Far more people lived as yeoman farmers, poor planters who comprised the bulk of the population and lived a lifestyle virtually indistinguishable from the slaves and other servants beneath them in social standing.

Any planter with good manners, good management and more than a fair share of luck could rise up into the middling sort and from there into the lower gentry. Acquisition of land or other wealth, courtly graces acceptable to one's betters and a slow rise in public esteem comprised the path. After a person was established well enough in his community, the natural path was to seek membership in the church vestry. Here, they learned dirty courthouse politics as well as gained a local following. A reputation was built through good management, and the next steps might be to stand for sheriff, a militia officership and finally for election to the colonial assembly. By this time, the person was well established as a member of the lower gentry. Whether they could continue to rise depended on their social graces, for with the increase in rank came a wider geographic area and an ever narrowing and more critical circle of aristocratic people who exercised power. Increasingly a gentleman was one who acted like a gentleman.

Freemasons

The Free and Accepted Masons, or Freemasons, were perfectly suited to the temperament of the eighteenth-century gentleman, judging from the large number of members it enjoyed during the late period. Virtually everyone in the circle that ran the Revolution was a Freemason. The Freemasons provided a network beyond the scale of the individual colonies and may have been a major factor in the organization of the separate colonies into a nation. Not organized formally until 1717 in England, Freemasonry quickly spread to the colonies, and by 1731, when Franklin joined, there were several lodges here. Masonic ideals may have influenced the separation of church and state.

LOCAL TAXATION AND BLUE LAWS

Among small historic house interpreters more confusion exists about local taxation and the presence or absence of blue laws than about anything else. As taxation was a local or colonial prerogative, the rules changed in each colony. For example, many places claim closets did not exist in most early homes because they were taxed as additional rooms. (The closet was in fact another small room, not, as we know it today, a place to hang clothing—which was folded and stored on shelves or in drawers.) In some such places taxation was not even on a room basis, but in others it was. Other interpreters point to the gambrel roof in the same manner. Whether gambrels developed from existing story-and-a-half houses to allow more room in the half story and avoid the extra cost of more wall construction, sills, plates and the like (the most likely reason) or to avoid paying taxes on an extra floor is a chicken-or-egg question. If your work requires detailed knowledge of local taxes, please do careful research on your specific area and date of interest.

Blue laws, such as the oft quoted ones ascribed to New England about dress (more properly known as sumptuary laws) or kissing one's wife on the Sabbath, are as troublesome as taxation is. Please refer to the sections on crime and punishment and sex for information on laws on the books not commonly enforced, then ask questions like: If the Puritan religion openly recognized sex within marriage as symbolic of the divine union, what point would there be in criminalizing a kiss on a Sunday? Other blue laws fall to similar scrutiny. Although many such laws were actually placed on the books at one time or another, collecting them and ascribing the attitudes suggested by the laws en masse to the entire period, even within one region, is dangerous. For example, drab dress in New England was not common in the early period but became so by the middle one. Many such laws are still on our books today but not generally enforced. Again, please do detailed local research, in this case avoiding sources that are too old or that avoid the question altogether.

BIBLIOGRAPHY

Bishop, Cortlandt Field. *History of Elections in the American Colonies.* 1893. Reprint, New York: AMS Press, 1970.

Greenberg, Douglas. *Crime and Law Enforcement in the Colony of New York, 1691–1776.* Ithaca, N.Y.: Cornell University Press, 1976.

Jones, Alice Hanson. *Wealth of a Nation to Be: The American Colonies on the Eve of the Revolution.* New York: Columbia University Press, 1980.

Semmes, Raphael. *Crime and Punishment in Early Maryland.* 1938. Reprint. Baltimore: Johns Hopkins University Press, 1996.

Weiss, Henry B. and Grace M. *An Introduction to Crime and Punishment in Colonial New Jersey.* Trenton, New Jersey: Past Times Press, 1960.

CHAPTER TEN

Warfare & the Military

GENERAL CLIMATE

Today a wide gulf exists between the military professions and the remainder of society. In the colonial period this was not the case. Most males between the ages of sixteen and sixty (except those practicing strategic trades, such as gunsmiths, iron founders and paper makers) were in the militia (local defense force), and leading citizens of whatever class assumed the roles of officers and studied the military arts to attain basic competence. Some went far beyond. Even women learned to handle weapons, some as a survival skill, others just through association with their militia spouses. When militia were called out for service, it was usually within the borders of the colony and for a limited period of time such as thirty or sixty days.

In the European armies, officers were gentlemen who purchased their commissions. A wide social gulf existed between them and the common men, who were sometimes enlisted by putting money in their hands (TAKING THE KING'S SHILLING) while drunk, which was held legally binding, other times by forced conscription. Desertion was punished by hanging.

In many ways the colonies were far ahead of Europe in the development of arms and tactics. The colonists fought two wars, that against the Indians, fought at a distance almost solely with firearms, and one against European armies, fought hand to hand with pole arms (see page 158). The newer tactics influenced colonial conduct in the situations involving the older, as skirmishing tactics came more to the fore between Europeans.

UNIFORMS AND CEREMONIES

Uniforms evolved only around the turn of the eighteenth century and distinguished the individual unit. The coat color tended to be uniform for the infantry throughout an army. Most British units wore red; French, white; and (later) American, blue. The color of the facings or turnbacks (lapels, the inside of coattails turned out, cuffs, etc.) indicated the unit. Musicians and the artillery wore reversed colors, with the coats the color of the unit facings, and the facings the color of the coats, to distinguish them on the battlefield. Hats were often decorated with cockades or rosettes denoting allegiance or alliances. Officers wore gold-braid epaulets on their shoulders and gorgets (necklaces) derived from early throat armor. Decorations were large and gaudy. In general, because most combat took place in the open between one hundred yards and six feet, camouflage was not needed, but easy identification of friends and foes was greatly needed.

Ceremonies provided the formal structure of the soldier's day. Reveille awoke him. Orders were read and other necessary business dispatched at assemblies. Trooping the colors taught the troops to recognize the unit's flags by parading them slowly before an assembly. Work details or fatigue parties were detailed off at morning assembly. Retreat ended the official day, lowered the flag, and detailed the night watches. Tattoo marked the end of the day, after which a soldier needed the password to be about.

INFANTRY

The infantry (foot soldier) was the mainstay of the army. Although the basic tactics remained constant throughout the period, significant changes occurred through the period. Many of these changes polarized around 1700, when most European armies reorganized and became professional.

Early, the main weapon was the pike. Pikemen deployed in massed lines two or three deep and protected each other like the quills on a porcupine. Holes in the line were places where one man could be double-teamed, leading to tactics that moved the mass of men together and kept them compact. A charge was conducted slowly, at cadenced pace, to keep the lines together. Pikemen were effective in stopping cavalry and fighting other pikemen. Later, the bayonet and musket replaced the pike. Tactics remained essentially the same.

Musketeers were (early) those infantry equipped with muskets. These men provided covering fire from the flanks (sides) and, while the armies were far enough apart, in front of the pikemen. Two to three volleys (rounds) at a time were standard. Musketeers' job was to disrupt the opponent's masses of pikemen, creating holes to exploit. When a charge began, they dropped back behind the cover of the pikemen. Later, all infantry carried muskets.

Targeteers were gentlemen and wealthier commoners, who owned swords and targets (small circular shields) used with them. These were the skirmishers, small, mobile, light troops that could move within and around the edges of the masses of pikemen, attacking them while they were preoccupied. Later, with more versatile, professional armies, these disappeared.

After the reorganization, three new types of infantry appeared: LINE INFANTRY, the main group, equipped with musket, bayonet and hanger; GRENADIERS, or large, strong men (English minimum six feet tall) given the jobs of storming fortified positions, forming the reserve and holding the difficult places; and LIGHT INFANTRY, or small men well suited for scouting and skirmishing. The grenadiers and light infantry were the elite troops, and usually each regiment (around eight hundred to one thousand men) had a company (eighty to one hundred men) of each. The local, part-time militia were often of necessity used by the Americans as line infantry, but they were not reliable as they were prone to break and run. The British used them as light infantry.

CUTTING WEAPONS

A pike was a handheld twelve-foot (half-pike) to sixteen-foot pole arm (mounted on a pole) with a steel spearlike head on the end. A halberd was a shorter pole arm with a vestigial ax head and was often carried by sergeants as a badge of rank. A bayonet was a long steel blade. To about 1740 a plug bayonet was stuck in the barrel of the musket. Later a socket was used to attach to the end of the musket barrel. The bayonet caused about 80 percent of all casualties, so the great liability of the rifle was that it could not hold a bayonet.

Swords varied greatly with time and place and generally were reserved for gentlemen. Rapiers were early, long, thin thrusting swords, the kind favored in movies, developed to pierce joints in armor. In Elizabethan England they had become so long that special laws were passed limiting their length, and guards at city gates would break off those found longer. Later, the gentleman's smallsword was a rapier blade with the base (forte) thickened to allow them to parry saber blows. Broadswords were heavy cutting weapons, usually used by the cavalry, from which the saber evolved, which was only slightly lighter. Hangers were short, lighter sabers issued to infantry in the eighteenth century. Thrusting weapons relied on precision, speed and skill, while cutting weapons relied on power derived from heavy swings. The guard (the portion protecting the hand) might be nothing more than quillons (cross bars) in a cross hilt, or the grip might be enclosed with a knuckle bow (a bar connecting the quillons with the pommel, or counterweight) and other parts making cup hilts (🎥 *page 288*) (round, bowl-like guards), basket hilts and swept hilts (🎥 *page 287*), which were different by degrees. Some blades had notches or guard parts designed to break an opponent's blade (⚑ *page 288*).

Knives were (early) the main gauche (parrying) knives, used by the left hand to parry sword thrusts. Later, a frontiersman might carry a hunting knife to use in close or for throwing. Many frontiersmen carried tomahawks (or hawks), also used close or thrown. Axes could also be thrown.

FIREARMS

Locks

The early military used matchlocks, (⚑ *page 288*) which were fired with a burning piece of slow match (rope soaked in saltpeter). The colonials found slow match unsuitable for fighting with Indians and ambushing because the glow or smell revealed it, and they had supply problems in keeping enough match. To keep one man on guard duty for one year required a mile of match. The colonists adopted snaphaunces (early flintlocks) about one hundred years before Europe did. With these, soldiers could snap shoot, and no consumables were used unless the weapon was fired. A few of the first flintlocks were wheel locks (⚑ *page 288*), in which a flint was scraped against a spring-driven wheel to ignite the charge, but most were doglocks, in which the half-cocked (safety) position was held by a dog that was manually removed. The true flintlock had an integrated half-cock position; a pan in which the priming powder was placed; a pan cover integrated with a frizzen, which the flint struck to create the spark and which opened the pan to accept it; and a touch hole by which the fire entered the barrel. Flintlocks were prone to more misfires than matchlocks. Some Spanish troops used a miquelet lock.

Musket drills (manual exercise) were complex, involving as many as twenty-five separate steps, but could be executed in as little as twelve seconds by crack troops, fifteen by the average. Each army has its own. They became simpler with time: matchlocks required more steps for safety. The American Army used the simplest.

Tools

Gunpowder, made of saltpeter (potassium nitrate derived from bat guano), charcoal and sulfur, was carried in horns or cartridges. Powder horns were flattened (more common early) or round and might be engraved or carved. Some early ones had built-in powder measures, but later a separate measure was adopted because of the tendency for the whole horn to go off if a spark was left in the barrel when the measure was emptied into it. A bandolier (⚑ *page 287*) was a shoulder

SAMPLE COMMAND SEQUENCES

Matchlock Commands (page 288)	*British Flintlock Commands, 1764*
Recover!	*Recover!
Secure your match!	*Half-cock your firelocks!
Pick!	
Shake out your pan!	
Handle your primers!	*Handle your cartridge!
Prime your pan!	*Prime!
Close your pan!	*Shut your pans!
Blow off your pan!	
Cast about your piece!	
Charge your piece!	*Charge with cartridge!
Draw out your scouring stick!	*Draw your rammers!
Shorten your scouring stick!	
Put them in the barrels!	
Ram down your charge!	*Ram down your charge!
Withdraw your scouring sticks!	
Shorten your scouring sticks!	
Put up your scouring sticks!	
Return your scouring stick!	*Return your rammers!
Take up your piece!	
Blow off your match!	
Cock your match!	
Poise!	*Poise your firelocks!
Try your match!	Cock your firelock!
Present your piece!	Present!
Open your pan!	
Fire!	(Give!) Fire!

*"Prime and Load!" or "Quick-time load!" replaced these steps for drilled troops.

strap with twelve little wooden bottles, each of which held one charge, but they were abandoned because they also had a tendency to blow up. Hunters and early soldiers carried a small priming horn with fine-grain priming powder and a larger horn with coarser charging powder. Powder was always scarce in the colonies, and the amount a frontiersman could obtain and carry was a determining factor in how long he could stay out. Cartridges were paper bottles holding one charge of powder and ball; they were carried in a leather cartridge box or cartouche box, holding up to thirty-five cartridges and worn on the right hip on a shoulder strap or a belt.

If cartridges were not used, bullets were carried in a bullet bag or pouch. Early musketeers took them out of the pouch and put them in their mouths before action, using saliva to clot the powder and avoid the need for wadding, which was crumpled paper (often the cartridge) or grass used to keep the ball and powder from falling out. Bullets were balls of lead cast in a bullet mold, which belonged to either the hunter or the army, for which a ladle was carried. A hunter could recover lead from a tree or his victim. Goose shot was made by dripping liquid lead into cold water; its teardrop shape caused more damage than round shot.

A ramrod (earlier called a scouring stick) was used to push the charge to the bottom of the barrel or to hold a worm (a corkscrew attached to the end to clean soft debris from the barrel) or cleaning patches. Riflemen used other patches, made of grease-coated fabric, to bind the ball tightly to the rifling and give the ball a spin. They were carried in a patch box in the stock of the rifle. The tight fit required a ball starter, to get it in the bore without breaking a ramrod, and a patch knife, to trim the patch around the ball. These tools, and others such as a screwdriver for repairs, pick and whisk for cleaning the touch hole and pan, a loading block with the balls prepatched and set in a hole in the block for fast loading, a lock cover to keep the lock dry in wet weather, skinning knives, ball and shot pouches, fire kits and the like, might be carried in a possibles pouch or hunting pouch worn on a shoulder strap on the right hip. One tool not likely to go into the field except with a military unit was a powder tester (eprouvette), a small pistol-like device in which powder was fired and its power measured. For matchlock weapons spare match was carried, sometimes in a matchcase, and flint and steel were necessary to light the match.

Firearm Types

Muskets were long, smooth-bored military weapons with (later) a receiver for a bayonet. Muskets with a military load, loosely fitted to the barrel to allow loading when the barrel was clogged with black powder residue, were accurate at first to about one hundred yards but later about 10 percent accuracy at 70 yards. Used by a trapper or hunter with a patched round and cleaned after every few shots, accuracy improved greatly. British muskets were known as the Brown Bess, because the barrel was browned (acid colored) on the early models. Three Brown

Bess models were made, each a bit shorter than the previous one. The barrel was held to the stock with pins. The French used the Charlesville, with the barrel held in with bands of metal. American muskets were either Committee of Safety patterned after the Brown Bess or Charlesvilles supplied by the French. Many Americans had hunting arms, some one hundred years old by the time of the Revolution. By law a member of the militia had to provide his own firearm. Such arms were often fowlers or were trade guns made for the Indians.

Rifles were specialized weapons used on the frontier by professionals. Despite tradition, New England did not have any rifles. They mostly came from western Pennsylvania, Maryland, Virginia and North Carolina where German gunsmiths married the short-barreled jaeger (hunter's) rifle with the long-barreled English smoothbore fowler sometime about 1730. Rifles had spiral grooves (rifling) in the barrel which imparted a spin to the ball, allowing greater accuracy at longer ranges with less powder and smaller balls. A very few English used the Ferguson rifle, which was breech-loading. Rifles were 90 percent accurate to two hundred yards, 50 percent up to four hundred yards.

The blunderbuss was a specialized riot gun used as a sawed-off shotgun in towns and shipboard warfare, with a wide, expanding bore. The Pilgrims did not hunt with them.

Pistols were not common except among the wealthy. Usually carried in pairs, they were often worn in front of a saddle in leather pistol buckets, hung like saddlebags. They followed English or French designs but were not very accurate, so were limited to personal defense. An attempt to arm cavalry with them proved disastrous.

ARMOR

Body armor was still in common use to about 1700. Obsolete armor was shipped from Europe to the colonies, where it worked well against arrows. Mail (woven steel rings) breathed well, was flexible during work and stopped arrows. Quilted armor, made of canvas with batting between, stopped most arrows. A combination of mail and quilted armor was scale, in which a canvas backing supported individual metal plates sewn on like shingles, covered with more canvas. Against Spaniards, full plate armor including breastplates (⌦ *page 287*), backplates and upper thigh armor might be used. Such plate armor was convex to deflect musket balls. Later on sappers (combat engineers) still used such armor to protect them from close-in fire during work on siege trenches.

Helmets, such as the cabosset helmet (⌦ *page 288*), were designed to deflect sword blows and were generally high and rounded, coming to a seam. A few closed helms providing complete protection including

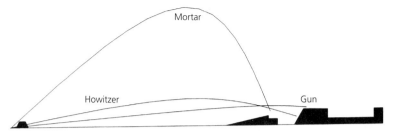

Uses of guns, howitzers and mortars in a siege.

a visor were used in the colonies, but they proved unwieldy in the woods and were abandoned. Later all helmets were abandoned, except for hardened hats for light infantry and cavalry, who might fight with sabers.

ARTILLERY

The seventeenth century saw artillery (cannon) go from employment only in sieges, serviced by mercenary professionals working for whichever side owned them at the moment, to a highly effective battlefield tool. Prior to 1588 no major naval battle was fought with guns, and both sides in the Armada battle experimented to see what was the best way to use them. The English favored lighter, longer guns that could reach a distance. The Spanish used shorter, heavier crushing weapons. As it turned out, the Spanish method was more effective, but they did not get a chance to prove it. Over time ship's cannon became shorter and heavier, designed to smash a ship's heavy timbers.

In field artillery (which supported the infantry), exactly the opposite was happening. Cannon had been large, heavy and immobile, designed for smashing the walls of fortifications. This function continued as siege artillery, but during the Thirty Years' War (1618–48) the Swedish King Gustavus Adolphus developed a gun made of bars and hoops of iron reinforced with shrunken leather, which could be moved rapidly about the battlefield by horse and deployed quickly. He used cavalry to threaten the enemy into forming squares (walking forts of pikemen formed in a square), the standard response to cavalry, then brought up his cannon to destroy the massed infantry. His success using this method almost made him a Protestant Emperor. From this time on both field and siege artillery were used.

Artillery appealed to the educated, as it required skills which could be mathematically expressed as ballistics. It was also, in part because of its early tradition as a mercenary arm, the first truly professional arm. In the colonies, during the Revolutionary period, the same was true. Henry Knox, a Boston bookseller who carried books on artillery, formed the Boston Independent Artillery Company and later, as Chief of the Artillery, used them as the cadre for the American Army, setting a standard still held high.

Siege artillery was often moved by ship wherever possible. When on land it moved slowly, by oxen, without carriages (see page 165). Garrison guns were used inside forts. They were similar to siege guns, to which they had to respond, and naval artillery since they often were given the task of stopping ships.

Classification of Artillery

"Cannon" was both a generic term loosely meaning artillery and a specific term meaning a type of long-barreled, heavy weapon. Generally, there were three subclasses: guns, mortars and howitzers. Guns were long, high-velocity, flat-trajectory weapons used for sharpshooting like a rifle. They were employed to dismount other cannon, batter holes in the walls of a defensive position, attack ships and surgically destroy obstacles. Mortars were short, low-velocity, high-trajectory weapons used to lob bombs (powder-filled shells) high into the air over obstacles and search out "safe spots" hidden from guns. Bombs could be set to explode either in the air to create shrapnel or after impact to dig holes or batter through the roof of a fort with hopes of breaking into a magazine, exploding among the powder and destroying that whole corner of the fort. A hermaphrodite weapon was the howitzer, moderately short barreled with an in-between trajectory to do a bit of both.

Names of Artillery

Carronades were shorter, heavy guns used aboard ships. Murderers, murtherers or (later) swivel guns were small, often breech-loading, guns mounted on swivels on the side of ships and in forts, used to fire scattershot against personnel. With a bore of three to four inches, they could cut quite a swath, hence the name. Later came battalion guns (also called grasshoppers), light (three-pound) cannon used as infantry support weapons. There were usually two to three guns per one thousand men, and they were used in leapfrog fashion, advancing in front of the infantry, firing, then reloading while the infantry advanced, then advancing again and firing. They were light enough to be pushed by two to three men and could be carried by a crew of eight to twelve. They were no match for heavy siege guns.

Gun parts were expressed in calibers, the diameter of the ball. Cannon size was denoted by the number of pounds the round weighed. Light guns ran three to six pounds; heavy, twenty-four to thirty-six pounds.

The American Grand Battery in the second siege line at Yorktown, with (front to back) two batteries of siege mortars on heavy mortar beds, a light gun on field carriage, a battery of howitzers on field carriages and three batteries of siege guns on garrison carriages.

Tools, Carriages and Equipment

Carriages were the chassis on which the cannons were mounted. They were of essentially two types: field, with large wheels designed to roll easily across terrain and a joined double trail reaching to the ground, and ship or garrison, with four small wheels and a low, boxy, stable structure, designed for use on wooden or stone decks. The trail of field carriages was longer for guns and shorter for howitzers, allowing both better elevation of the latter and an angle designed for the recoil, which drove the entire unit backward. Ship and garrison carriages were tethered to the hull or rampart with ropes in pulleys and mounted on an upward sloping platform to handle the recoil. Mortars were mounted at fixed elevation on flat timber beds. Trajectory was controlled by the amount of powder used.

Field carriages were supported by caissons, iron-bound wooden trunks about twelve feet long slung across two sets of axles and in which tools and ammunition were transported. Smaller guns had a small ammunition chest mounted in the trail but removed before action and placed behind the cannon. On ship and in forts small boys called powder monkeys carried the powder from the magazines to the guns

165

ARTILLERY COMMAND SEQUENCE

Attention!

Tend the vent!

Advance the worm!

Worm out the piece!

Advance the sponge!

Sponge out the piece!

Handle the charge! — The gunner might call out a powder amount or range and specify ammunition type.

Charge the piece!

Ram down the charge!

Run out the piece! — On garrison and ship carriages.

Take aim!

Pick!

Prime!

Make ready! — The gunner stood off to the upwind side to observe the fall of shot.

Give! Fire! — The sequence was repeated.

in brass-hooped, wooden powder tubs or buckets.

Cannon needed several tools to service them properly, and many a woman proved her knowledge of them when a spouse was stricken and she took his place. A gun required roughly six men to fire: a gunner; one man each for the worm, sponge/rammer, vent and ammunition; and one to fire it.

Worms were corkscrews used between rounds to remove from the bore old wadding that might hold a spark. A rammer and sponge were usually mounted on opposite ends of the same shaft, allowing the bore to be swabbed out with water to put out any residual sparks and to be loaded with the same tool. A linstock was a long pole that held a piece of slow match and was used to set off the cannon, while the cannoneer stood safely off to the side, away from the recoil. A brass wire pick was used to open the cartridge bag, and a powder horn was used to prime the vent (touch hole) through which the cannon was fired. If cartridges were not used, a brass ladle was used to measure and insert the loose powder into the bore. An artilleryman might use calipers to check the size of the balls and tangents to measure the elevation of the gun. If firing at a flammable target like a ship or a town, hot shot (solid shot heated red-hot in a shot oven) might be used to ignite it.

Projectiles

Projectiles fired by cannon included solid-shot or round-shot cast-iron balls; hot shot; bombs; bar shot, with a half ball at each end connected by an iron bar about eight inches long; chain shot, two round shot connected by a length of chain; grapeshot, made of a disk of wood with a shaft coming up the middle, on which were placed a number of approximately one-and-a-half-inch round shot, the whole being bound with cloth and twine, which traveled some distance before scattering; and canister, a tin can filled with scraps of metal, rocks, or whatever else might be lethal, which scattered at short range. Bar shot and chain shot were used against the rigging of ships. Grapeshot and canister were used against personnel, acting like giant shotguns. In an emergency, double canister might be called for.

CAVALRY

Cavalry, troops that fought mounted on horseback, usually with lances or swords, were not used much in the New World. Later in its place were dragoons, light infantry mounted for rapid movement but who fought mostly dismounted, although they could occasionally fight from horseback. They were particularly favored in the South, where horses were common and distances relatively large.

STONE FORTIFICATIONS

Stone fortifications were expensive and time-consuming to build and relatively uncommon in the New World. Those that existed were at key points such as Fort Ticonderoga on Lake Champlain covering the Hudson route from Canada; the Castillo de San Marcos in St. Augustine protecting the northern bounds of the Spanish empire and the treasure fleets in the Bahama Channel; the Citadel at Halifax, Nova Scotia; Fortress Louisbourg covering the St. Lawrence waterway; and Fort Niagara defending the Great Lakes portages. Most date from around the turn of the eighteenth century or later.

In construction, stone forts brought to the New World the latest in European engineering and technology incorporating elements designed to deflect cannon shot. The basic structure, usually square but not always, was made of nearly vertical curtain walls which were protected at the corners by bastions designed to allow defenders to fire along (enfilade) the curtain walls, catching attackers in a close-range cross fire. All lines were angled to prevent any dead zones that fire

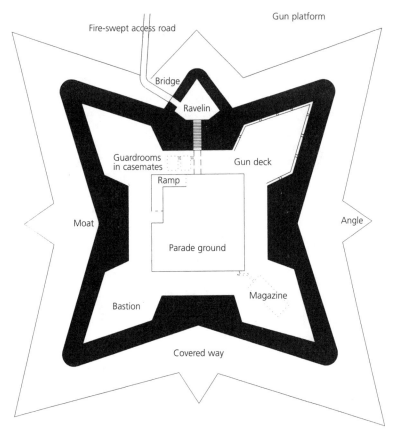

Typical stone fortress. This side (bottom) faced the enemy.

could not cover and to provide an all-around killing zone. Within the walls was the parade ground. An earthen hill called a glacis surrounded the fort, designed to deflect cannon fire, protect the lower walls of the fort and provide a covered way for infantry to surround the fort and fire out from a protected position. Inside this, a dry or wet moat might surround the inner fort.

The gate and bridge were protected from direct fire by a small, triangular ravelin placed directly in front within the moat. Often a sally port and small footbridge led out of the fort on a side away from the main gate (and usually nearer the enemy) to allow infantry to counterattack or sortie from within the fort. Inside the fort walls and opening onto the parade ground were vaulted casemates in which supplies were stored and people quartered. An especially heavily constructed casemate, usually in a bastion, might hold the powder magazine. Food and ammunition supplies, wells and cisterns were all critical

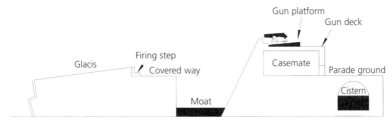

Cross section of typical stone fortress. Not to scale.

to endure a siege. The flat roof of the walls, above the casemates, was the gun deck where the fort's artillery was mounted. Here, and in the covered way, a parapet protected the defenders. If it was too high for infantry to shoot over, a firing step was included.

FIELD FORTIFICATIONS

Field fortifications (earthworks) assumed far greater importance in America at the time of the Revolution than elsewhere simply because colonial soldiers were farmers who knew how to dig and felt safer in earthworks than in the open. This is one of the ways in which the Revolution foreshadowed the Napoleonic and later wars and presented challenges to the British who were not yet accustomed to the new tactics. Many varieties existed, each with its own French name, but a few are worth noting. A redoubt was a small, enclosed earth fort used outside a main line of defense to double (split) the attacker's lines and buy time by providing another objective for the attackers to assault before the main position. A fleche was an open-backed trench, usually in the shape of an arrowhead (hence its name), often an infantry position covering an artillery position. In defensive positions the dirt was piled on the inside of the ditch from which it was removed, creating a high wall and dry moat.

Fraise (sharpened logs about eight feet long, thrust nearly horizontally out from the ground) were often placed above a man's height to form an obstacle. The ditch was often filled with loose, sharp branches to make footing hazardous, and the ground beyond the ditch might be treated the same way. Abatis (trees thrown down with their butts facing the enemy) and cheval-de-frise (logs with crosswise sharpened stakes, greenbriar and other thorny plants) were used as we would barbed wire.

Any obstacle set up to protect a position must be covered with fire to be effective. The inside of the position had firing steps. The MAIN DEFENSE LINE or INNER DEFENSE LINE of a fortified position was the main line of defense. Changes in the direction of the works created a

Siege plan of the siege of Yorktown, September and October 1781. Based on French maps and archeological evidence.

hornwork, shaped like a horn or an angle, which might also protrude from the lines to allow fire along the lines or in enfilade.

SIEGES

A siege is the process of systematically reducing and capturing a forti-fied position. The French developed the science of siege warfare during the late seventeenth century. In general, a first siege line (a parallel) was opened parallel to the defender's position and far enough away to allow cannon fire to reach but not to be too effective, so as to protect your own men. Sappers (combat engineers) dug the trenches using structures on wheels to protect themselves from incoming fire. The trench was on the attacker's side of the wall being built, providing cover.

After the first parallel was built and cannon provided covering fire, APPROACH TRENCHES or ZIGZAGS were built toward the enemy's position.

They were shaped so as to never allow the defender to fire along (enfilade) the trench, approaching much the way a small boat beats into the wind. A second parallel was built into which cannon were moved, allowing more effective fire. The process continued as many times as necessary until the parallels were close to the defender's walls. From there mines might be shafted under the walls and a chamber built to hold powder detonated to cause a breach in the wall. Breaches might be cut by artillery, which fired at the lower part of the wall, piercing it and collapsing the part above. The total of all these trenches was known as THE WORKS.

Once a siege began (and given equal odds) nothing could prevent the fall of the position unless a relief force attacked the attackers and lifted the siege, or unless the defenders could be evacuated, usually by sea. Consequently, a practice arose that we find strange today. A convention called the Honors of War was offered to a garrison that had valiantly defended its position, that had engaged in at least one sortie (counterattack), which usually sought to spike (or render inoperative by driving a spike into the touch hole) one of the attacker's guns, and that could march in parade formation through the breach in its walls. If the defenders accepted the Honors, they were allowed to march out with flags flying and music playing a tune of the victors', surrender their post and arms and march to the nearest friendly post where they rejoined the service. If they refused the Honors, no quarter was given when the position was finally taken. The breach in the walls proved to all, including the kings, that the position was no longer tenable, and the honors preserved the expensive professional troops to fight again. At Charles Town, the British refused to offer Honors to the rebels, who reciprocated at Yorktown.

Certain tools were used in a siege, some by both sides. Gabions (🔲 *page 288*) were large baskets of branches or vines filled with dirt and used as we would sandbags. Fascines were bundles of sticks used to fill in obstacles. Caltrops were four-pronged iron implements designed to always have one shaft facing up to cripple a horse or a man.

MILITARY MUSIC AND SIGNALING

Musicians were the signal corps of the early army. An order was passed by the drums, using beatings to identify the wing, division or unit to whom the signal was addressed and then giving the order. As an order was sent, it was repeated at each smaller unit affected. Drums were paired with fifes early on, then with oboes or HAUTBOYES and again with fifes about the middle of the eighteenth century. Trumpets were used only by the cavalry, dragoons and on ships. Bugles were not used.

After about 1760 some units had private BANDS OF MUSIC hired and maintained by one or more of the officers. These were classical wind octets: two oboes, two clarinets, two horns and two bassoons, although the first American manuscripts leave out the clarinets and use four oboes instead. These played for messes, dances, amateur theater and the troops' morale.

Other signaling methods were used, including fires and flags from hilltops and messenger riders or couriers. Messages sent by courier, even by ship, were usually sent three ways to ensure receipt.

INDIANS

Warfare with the Indians emphasized the differences in weaponry available to the Europeans. At first, the colonists used firearms because the Indians used both archery and close-quarters combat and did not fear them as they did firearms. Later, as firearms became more common among the Indians, frontiersmen from Pennsylvania, Maryland, Virginia and North Carolina became so adept at irregular tactics (hiding behind rocks and trees, etc.) that a small number could defeat or dissuade large numbers of Indians. When regular British officers ran the show, however, they refused to be advised of the dangers of a few "savages," and disastrous defeats like the destruction of Braddock's army ensued when the French and Indians ambushed them. These defeats were due more to the arrogance of the leadership than failings among the colonists.

The major problem the native cultures had in meeting the colonists was a different concept of warfare. A war with more than a handful of casualties was considered unthinkable to the Indians. Touching or striking an enemy was often more important than killing him. The European concept of a virtually total war for conquest or eradication was inconceivable.

When tactics with large-scale economic repercussions were used, including the burning of villages and fields, the Indians could be defeated relatively quickly (although not always without excessive losses), as was demonstrated repeatedly in seventeenth-century Virginia, King Phillip's War in Massachusetts, South Carolina and the Revolution in New York State.

Indians were frequently used by both sides in colonial wars as scouts, trackers and skirmishers, although during the Revolution their place in the American army was often taken by frontiersmen.

BATTLE

For the individual engaged in battle during the period, combat was an intense, personal experience. While this is true for all times, most soldiers today fire vast quantities of ammunition at targets they cannot see. In the colonial period, not only could they see their enemy, most of the time the sides were about as far apart as football teams at the scrimmage line. Cromwell spoke proudly of standing "at thrust of pike" for three to six hours, during which time a second's inattention on the part of a solider would result in painful and fatal disemboweling. If fear overtook a soldier, his own officers stood behind, ready to kill him for his cowardice as he ran. The individual lived totally in the moment, and details were difficult to remember later. They might recall their neighbors, defeated or victorious, but that was about all.

Officers had it a little better. Field officers commanded the units on the overall field and, in theory, could see the larger picture. In reality, they could see little. The "fog of war" was very great in the days of the musket and bayonet, as black powder created great clouds of white smoke that obscured the lines, the origin of the phrase "the smoke of battle." Then there was spatial separation. In the early days of the colonial period, small units of men fought in relatively compact groups, but they often operated as small detachments engaged in flanking or diversionary moves. Later, the armies would become larger and spread out over too much terrain for any one officer to be able to see everything. Once troops were out of sight, the only way to know what was happening was to hear the fight and signals and to guess what the sounds meant. Couriers carried status reports and orders but might arrive too late to affect the outcome. Once a fight became general (hand-to-hand) it was out of the control of any but the line officers.

Line officers got their title from commanding the troops lined up in direct contact with the enemy. They were only slightly less involved than the men, ensuring that immediate needs were taken care of and using individual initiative to take advantage of opportunities or solve problems. They usually knew what their own objectives were and had an idea of the overall plan of battle, but they could not know if any but their immediate neighbors were succeeding or failing. If their immediate neighbors were failing, a natural tendency was to fall back to protect their own flanks, turning a setback into a defeat.

In such circumstances men relied on leaders who they knew and trusted to get them through. A competent officer could snatch victory from certain defeat. Good examples are Anthony Wayne at Morristown and Saratoga and Daniel Morgan at Cowpens. A mediocre one could lose a sure thing.

The individual tactics used varied widely throughout the period and from situation to situation, although most were based on the principles described above. The military art in the period practiced complex evolutions or drills for moving men in specific ways, all of which was preparatory to the real battle. Refer to the bibliography at the end of this chapter for more information.

THE FRENCH AND INDIAN WAR

The French and Indian War (1754–63) was the American version of the Seven Years' War in Europe, which saw England and her Hanoverian allies arrayed on one side with Frederick the Great of Prussia against France, Spain, the low countries and Russia. In the New World the fight was over the Caribbean Islands and the portions of English claims between the Alleghenies and the Mississippi, especially the Forks of the Ohio where Pittsburgh stands today and where the French were attempting to build Fort Duquesne. Forbe's Road was cut across the mountains of Pennsylvania to support the British attack. Ultimately, the English won, taking Havana from the Spanish, which was traded for Florida, and Canada and the territory east of the Mississippi from the French.

The French had fortified a chain of trade routes from Fortress Louisbourg through Quebec, Niagara, the Forks of the Ohio and down the Mississippi to New Orleans. This cut the British off from the interior and in the Ohio and Detroit area invaded Virginian claims. France's Indian allies raided English frontier settlements. England concentrated on breaking the northern end of the chain, taking Montreal, Quebec, Niagara and Fort Duquesne.

In the long run the war was significant in several ways. It gave a generation of Americans real combat experience that paid off in the Revolution. It created the huge debt that England attempted to pay with the soon-to-be-hated stamp taxes and others. In the aftermath, English troops were permanently quartered in the colonies, not only creating tensions which contributed to the Revolution, but also providing much cultural exchange. Forbe's Road became the major emigration route over the mountains until the Erie Canal was built.

THE REVOLUTION

The Revolution has many explanations. Many concentrate on simple answers, but the issues were complex and often involved the economic view of colonies combined with George III's attempts to reassert the authority of the monarch. How the average person viewed it depended on his own circumstances. Many in Parliament were sympathetic to the Americans, as were some of the officers sent to America.

The population was fairly evenly divided into Patriots, Loyalists and undecided. Many of the Loyalists were found in the South, particularly in the backcountry where the Scots and Irish had settled after the Clearings as punishment for their rebellion in 1745, an act they were not hasty to repeat. Many specialized in trade with the Indians which gave the British good ties to the Indians, already concerned about colonial expansion. New York also had a large contingent of Loyalists. Elsewhere the highest-placed colonists could be expected to remain loyal, as they had the most to lose. The Patriots were ultimately smaller farmers who needed land and could not get it on the coast. The British Proclamation of 1763 was seen as a breach of contract to the Patriots as the British had promised them land in the Ohio if they won the French and Indian War. Many enlisted in the Revolution on the promise of free land, which, upon successful completion of hostilities, was ultimately granted in the Ohio valley. The nonaligned had many reasons, from religious (Quakers) to fence-sitting. In the end, the insensitivity of the British and an inability to restrain Indian allies often decided them as Patriots.

Patriots were not angels. Known or suspected Loyalists were often stripped, treated to a bath of hot tar, a coating of feathers and a ride out of town on a fence rail. Scalps were often lifted while the Loyalist was still alive. The burns and scars sustained, if one did survive, were proof enough to encourage others to leave and find refuge in Florida or Canada. Property of those who fled was seized, and emotions ran high.

Like many guerrilla wars, the Americans could not lose the Revolution, but they would have a hard time winning it. The British needed all the merchant shipping available to them to supply their troops in North America (365 ships per year) without adding reinforcements or accounting for attrition, while also fighting another war with France, Spain and Holland in the Caribbean and India. This fact kept the Americans from being overrun. But to win, America had to be able to meet the British in open field using European tactics near colonial population centers, something that required trained, regular troops that did not exist at first.

There is a myth about the patriots using guerrilla tactics and rifles, neither of which made a major contribution. Once Washington found out how much the British troops feared riflemen, however, and without funds for proper uniforms, he dressed the army as riflemen for psychological effect. Later, Baron von Stueben taught the patriots to fight like regulars at Valley Forge, and they were able to stand up to the British for the first time at Monmouth the following summer. From then on America had a regular army.

To win, the Americans needed a powerful ally in Europe. To gain one, they needed to beat the British to prove they were capable of doing so. They did this first at Saratoga, by capturing an army of some five thousand, then at Monmouth. France formally recognized the United States on February 6, 1778. Spain and Holland entered the war and sent ministers but did not at first diplomatically recognize the new country.

Finally, the new country could count on great popular disenchantment with the war in England, which further hampered English recruiting and financing. Ultimately, after the loss of a second major army of seventy-five hundred at Yorktown, this sentiment led to peace.

The Revolution itself took place in a series of geographically distinct campaigns. The first was fought around Boston in 1775 and 1776. The next was around New York City in 1776 and included battles at Trenton and Princeton. The 1777 campaigns were fought in the Hudson Valley (where Saratoga was a turning point for the colonials) and around Philadelphia. Philadelphia was abandoned by the British in 1778 to return to New York, during which movement the Battle of Monmouth was fought. The same year the British seized Savannah; in 1779 stalemate reigned. In 1780 the British took Charles Town and began a campaign that raced through the South and ended in the loss of a second British army at Yorktown the next year, with the help of the French navy. A period of phony war ensued in 1782 while a peace was negotiated (see the Time Line, which starts on page 6).

BIBLIOGRAPHY

Bailyn, Bernard. *The Ideological Origins of the American Revolution.* Cambridge, Mass.: Belknap Press of Harvard University Press, 1967. A thorough study of the political and philosophical basis of the Revolution.

Boatner, Mark Mayo. *Encyclopedia of the American Revolution.* Third ed. Mechanicsburg, Pa.: Stackpole Books, 1994. A massive reference of people, events, places and things.

Dunnigan, Brian Leigh. *Glorious Old Relic: The French Castle and Old Fort Niagara.* Youngstown, N.Y.: Old Fort Niagara Association, 1987. An overview of the history of one of the keystones of the war for empire, guarding the Niagara portage.

Jenson, Merrill. *Tracts of the American Revolution, 1763–76.* Indianapolis: The Bobbs-Merrill Co., 1967.

Kent, Donald H. *The French Invasion of Western Pennsylvania.* Harrisburg, Pa.: Historical and Museum Commission, 1981.

Larrabee, Harold Atkins. *Decision at the Chesapeake.* New York: C.N. Potter, 1964. Covers the southern campaign that led to Yorktown, and the Battle off the Capes which sealed Cornwallis's fate, but most interesting for details of life and battle aboard ship.

Marshall, Douglas W. and Howard H. Peckham. *Campaigns of the American Revolution: An Atlas of Manuscript Maps.* Ann Arbor: University of Michigan Press, 1976. Contemporary maps with good overviews of the campaigns and actions of the war.

MacKenzie, Frederick. *The Diary of Frederick MacKenzie.* 2 vols. "Eyewitness Accounts of the American Revolution." New York: New York Times, 1968. The wartime diary of a British officer who served from Lexington to the end of 1781. Wonderful.

Neumann, George C. *Swords and Blades of the American Revolution.* Harrisburg, Pa.: Stackpole Books, 1973. A picture encyclopedia of weapons, this also contains information on tactics.

Neumann, George C. and Frank J. Kravic. *Collector's Illustrated Encyclopedia of the American Revolution.* Harrisburg, Pa.: Stackpole Books, 1975. A reenactor's bible, this picture encyclopedia contains not only arms and military implements but tents, luggage, tools, games and domestic items with short descriptions.

Nofi, Albert A. *The American Revolution. Strategy and Tactics*, no. 34 (September 1972). An excellent short overview that deals with many issues not readily found in other histories, such as statistics and logistical information, but in an accessible manner.

Purcell, Edward L. and David F. Burg, eds. *World Almanac of the American Revolution."* New York: World Almanac, 1992. An almost day-by-day listing of events connected with the Revolution.

Russiello, William R., and Lawrence J. Albert. *The Saratoga Campaign, 1777. Strategy and Tactics*, no. 30 (January 1972). A short, readable discussion of the campaign that brought France into the Revolution as an ally, with discussions of tactics and combatants.

Sobel, Robert. *The American Revolution: A Concise History and Interpretation.* New York: Ardmore Press, 1967. A basic, concise study of the war, not so much from a military viewpoint as from the overall political and social ones. A very readable introduction, but its small size means it skips things.

Thacher, James. *Military Journal During the American Revolutionary War.* "Eyewitness Accounts of the American Revolution." New York: New York Times, 1969. The journal of a doctor who was with the American Army from near the beginning to the very end.

The Uncommon Soldier of the Revolution: Women and Young People Who Fought for American Independence. Eastern Acorn Press (NPS), 1986. A reprint of several magazine articles including journal entries.

Wendel, Thomas. *Thomas Paine's Common Sense: The Call to Independence.* Woodbury, N.Y.: Barron's Educational Series, 1975. One of the most influential pamphlets of the Revolutionary period, with introduction and notes.

CHAPTER ELEVEN

Money, Economy, Trade, Travel & Navigation

THE MYTH OF
SELF-SUFFICIENCY

One way English culture changed significantly during the colonial period was the shift from an agrarian and subsistence lifestyle, characteristic of preindustrial societies, to a more modern society based on manufacturing and trade. Although the farmer could grow his own food anywhere, the manufacturer faced a range of modern logistical problems, including the assemblage of raw materials and the distribution of products, and the ancillary problems of marketing, accounting and insurance. In the process merchants solved a wide range of trade and communication problems.

The farmer cut down the trees to clear his land and thus obtained most of what he needed for heat and to build his house, barn and fences. In contrast, the best place for a manufacturer to make a product might not be where all the raw materials could be found. Even for products like iron where materials and manufactory were close, the customer might not live in the frontier area where the necessary resources existed.

There is a myth about the self-sufficient American farmer, who made his own shoes, mended his own tools, grew his own food, wove his own cloth and fought with the rest of the world when it got involved in his business. This probably applied to no more than 2 percent of the population on the frontier and, although they might fight an occasional bear or Indian, they moved on to more wilderness when the rest of the world appeared.

The colonies were partially self-sufficient on the frontier fringe. In the early days, when the frontier ran along the coast, most settlements might qualify for this distinction, but as time passed these areas would represent a smaller proportion of the population as the frontier moved farther and farther inland and the settled areas became larger. The citizens who espoused such ideals were seen by the rest as less than cultured, less than wealthy, less than equals and often less than civilized, regardless of their true personal circumstances.

The average citizen bought most manufactured goods from firms in England that were already highly industrialized and specialized. Local artisans, by and large, were thus confined to repairs, although in every colony there were outstanding examples of different crafts. At the highest market level much local variation in style was sought, and the local craftsmen could best meet these individual demands. For more information, see chapter fourteen.

Many planters and merchants dealt with large merchant houses in England, or more often Scotland, which were known as FACTORS. Traditionally the term applied to the overseas offices or agents of the European merchant's house, and often the offices were given to a son as he assumed responsibility within the family company. In the colonies, it was used as a contractual agreement between the American firm and its European agent, although some factors sent other factors to deal directly with the American market. Some factor relationships lasted generations, and the factor acted for the colonist in many ways including marketing his products or crops, purchasing goods, lobbying, and corresponding to help the colonist stay abreast of the latest styles and trends.

Most citizens of the New World kept a keen eye on the Old for leadership in tastes and products. This solved one of the problems for the manufacturer. If the locals in New York or Savannah already looked down their noses at the colony-made product and instead desired European goods, there was little need for advertising campaigns to convince them to buy. As previously mentioned, even Thomas Jefferson, who attempted to push an American wine industry, couldn't compete with the European product. Beginning about 1650 and growing more formalized, a theory of the economic function of the colonies grew and was codified into law reflecting this view of the material world.

THE NAVIGATION ACTS

The laws known generically as the Navigation Acts served the mother country by providing that few goods could enter or leave the colonies without being transshipped, via English hulls (colonial included) manned by not less than 75 percent Englishmen through middlemen in England, who collected tariffs.

In general, the colonies were not permitted to manufacture in those industries where England had well-developed businesses, and the colonies were expected to provide the raw materials and products scarce in England. In this way English and colonial shipwrights and sailors were protected, both for their own benefit and that of the Royal Navy, and English pottery, textile and merchants businesses were protected. In the colonies, production of tobacco, iron, sugar, fish, coopers' products, lumber, furs, wheat and rice were likewise protected.

A summary follows of the major Navigation Acts and their effects. Changes in the rules could make or break a merchant or town.

1650   Forbids all foreign ships "to come to, or Trade in, or Traffique with" any of the American colonies.

1651   Clarifies some issues, allows commerce between England and Asia, Africa or the Americas only in ships that belong to "the people of this Commonwealth or the Plantations thereof, and whereof the masters and mariners are also for the most part of them of the people of this Commonwealth." Goods destined for America, England or Ireland must be shipped in English hulls or those belonging to the place of manufacture or its principal port.

1660   Sets the 75 percent English limit for the crew. Some question exists whether colonial seamen were English for crew calculations. Establishes the English hull monopoly in both directions. Also ENUMERATES certain products that must be shipped only to England, Ireland, Wales, Berwick-upon-Tweed or the colonial plantations: sugar, tobacco, cotton, ginger and indigo.

1662   Defines "English" as "His Majesties subjects of England, Ireland, and his plantations."

1663   Salt can be imported directly to colonies to help fishermen, along with wines from Portugal and her islands, Madeira and the Azores.

1699   No colonial woolens (yarn or manufactures) exportable from any colony.

1704   Enumerates naval stores and rice, except rice could go to any port south of Cape Finisterre.

1722   Beaver and other skins are added to enumerated list.

1732   Export of hats is banned like woolens, above.

1750   Pig and bar iron duty-free to England, but no facilities to produce finished products are allowed to the colonies.

ca.1763 Enumerated list is expanded to include most products, such as: hides, skins, potash, pearl ash, iron and lumber. Wines from Portugal and her islands are taxed highly if imported directly to the colonies, less if imported via England.

Trade was regulated not only within the structure of the English world, but different colonies at times regulated trade with other colonies. In the early seventeenth century Virginia forbade trade with Maryland except under special permit, and the city of Norfolk existed on a close though illegal relationship as the port of northern North Carolina. So close was this tie that in the nineteenth century Norfolk threatened to secede from Virginia if not given a railroad. Some colonies were more tolerant in this regard, and often this was a reflection of religious and immigration tolerance. Because of the problems caused by such policies, the Interstate Commerce clause of the Constitution was adopted.

MONEY, VALUE AND THE ECONOMY

Forms of Exchange

Money was a problem for the colonists. England refused to allow them to mint currency or print paper money (known as MEDIUM or MEDIUM OF EXCHANGE), much like the United States government today does not allow the states to print money; so cash was in short supply throughout most of the period. The attempts by Parliament to regulate colonial efforts to print paper money were one factor in the dissension leading to the Revolution. The colonists adopted a number of strategies to survive. Barter was used, although probably not as commonly as some would have us think. Its significance probably depended on what commodities were being discussed and where the traders were. Those on the frontier were more likely to engage in barter than those in the cities. The commodities in part depended on the service being purchased. Millers were known to take their fee in a percentage of the ground grain. Then again, grain was an essential food and could always be traded for other goods or sold for cash. Other persons involved in the production of primary materials, such as sawyers, tanners and the like, were more likely to barter. In reality barter is nothing more than the exchange of accounting write-offs in a credit economy.

Fishermen, farmers engaged in producing cash crops (like rice, indigo, tobacco and flax), iron founders and other industrial manufacturers were more likely to sell their products abroad. These people often dealt with factors who extended credit, often as a future (commodity) against the current crop. Smaller producers sold to a local jobber who consolidated product into shippable quantities and acted as a factor, extending credit against purchases. As a result, much of the economy of the colonies existed only on paper, as credit, much as ours does today. Account books were a major product of bookbinders, for even local merchants operated in this manner to some degree.

Many factors offered accounts on which BILLS OF EXCHANGE, like modern checks, could be drawn. Contested bills were those on which payment was refused, and the collection penalty varied from colony to colony, leading to a market in which speculators bought contested bills in colonies where the penalty was lower and took them to colonies where higher penalties allowed a reasonable return. Letters of credit were similar but usually sent by one party to another for the benefit of a third.

Some merchants refused to sell on any basis but READY MONEY (CURRENCY OF THE REALM, CURRY, CASH). Those who could afford to were few and far between, but many advertised better rates to cash customers. It was common to bargain or CHEAPEN the price.

Those merchants who did operate on credit were continually in court to collect on bad debts, but, unlike in England where a debtor could be put in jail until they paid, in the colonies the need for labor and the realization that a debtor had to be free to work to pay off his debt limited this practice.

All transactions were carried out in English money, whether they were conducted in barter, accounting write-offs, credit or cash. The English system was based on a pound (sterling), divided into twenty shillings, each divided into twelve pence. A halfpence (bawbee) was half a pence, a farthing was a quarter of a pence, a guinea was a pound and a shilling, and a groat was about four pence. (Notation: £.s.d, so £1.1.1 was a guinea and a pence.) The problem was that English coin was scarce, and the colonists pressed into service any currency available. In 1704 Queen Anne issued a table of equivalents, known as proclamation money, but it is questionable how effective it was. Approximate equivalent values are included for comparison, but exchange will be discussed below.

Spanish currency included DOLLARS (PILLARS; SPANISH MILLED DOLLARS if minted in Spain with milled edges; SPANISH HEAVY DOLLARS or MEXICANS if made in Mexico; PIECES OF EIGHT; COB MONEY) worth five to six shillings; PESETA (PISTAREEN) worth a quarter of a dollar; BITS (one piece of eight, REAL, RIAL, ROYAL), an eighth of a dollar; DOUBLOONS, sixteen dollars; PISTOLE, eight dollars; and FOURPENCE (half a real), five to six pence. From Peru came the CROSS DOLLAR worth four shillings, four pence and three farthings.

Italian currency included DUCATS and DUCATOONS, worth seven shillings, and VENETIANS or Venetian SEQUINS. The Dutch provided

GUILDERS worth twenty-one pence and LIONS (DOG DOLLARS). The Portuguese provided the HALF JOE, JOES (JOHANNES), STIVERS worth a twentieth of a guilder and MOIDORE worth six pieces of eight. The Germans had RIX DOLLARS worth four shillings and six pence. From France came the LIVRE and the FRENCH CROWN while Scotland sent the MARK (MERK) worth thirteen shillings and four pence.

Many colonies used their local authority of taxation to circumvent restrictions by issuing paper money "good only for payment of taxes" but which circulated before being used for that purpose. Massachusetts was the first to do so, taking up the new Swedish idea of 1660 and printing OLD TENOR (obviously known as such after new tenor was printed in 1737 and 1740 in Rhode Island) in 1690. After 1774 Congress issued CONTINENTALS, both paper money and securities, which quickly became the standard by which to judge the worthlessness of anything. In 1781 Maryland issued paper currency called red money.

Exchange rates were constantly changing as inflationary and deflationary pressures were at work. The world operated, however, on a bullion standard. Although the values quoted above were set by various legislative acts, most businesspeople used a MONEY BALANCE (a small portable scale) to measure the actual bullion content and conducted the transaction on that basis. This measuring was also done because some persons SHAVED or SKIVED the edges of coins to remove some of their real value. This is why the Spanish MILLED the edges of their dollars as our quarters are today, which made this coin a much preferred medium of exchange when it was available.

Wages and Economic Pressures

The wages a person earned varied much over time and with the occupation they followed. Studies show that, in Virginia, the average annual wage for a skilled craftsman was between thirty and one hundred pounds, a gentleman's estate might gross one thousand pounds or more, and a small farmer only ten pounds.

To equate colonial moneys to today's is difficult, but a fairly simple rule can be followed. A person today, purchasing the same product made the same way out of materials made the same way, will pay roughly the same percentage of their wage for the product as a person of equal economic status in the past would have. For comparison, at the present time an average shop rate runs about thirty-five dollars an hour for labor. If you make ten dollars an hour, this costs you three and a half hours of work, and the same ratio applied to a craftsman making thirty pounds a year or two pence per hour.

The economy suffered vicissitudes both locally (to an extent perhaps difficult to understand today) and internationally. Local events included Indian uprisings, hurricanes, cold spells, droughts or

SAMPLE EXCHANGE RATES FOR COLONIAL MONEYS DRAWN ON LONDON: PER £100 LONDON MONEY

Approx. Date	MA	NY	PA	VA	SC	GA
1660	112	-	-	-	-	-
1675	123.89	125	125	-	-	-
1700	139.43	134.96	155	110	146	-
1725	289.11	165	139.34	117.5	672.16	-
1750	137.33	179.33	170.6	125.94	702.28	-
1774	135.3	180.62	169.46	130.3	700	108

SAMPLE ECONOMIC CYCLES: DATES OF TURNS AND DURATIONS

Date of Trough	Date of Peak	Duration (Trough to Trough)	Duration (Peak to Peak)
-	1701	-	-
1705	1708	-	7
1710	1713	5	5
1716	1719	6	6
1721	1725	5	6
1733	1738	12	13
1739	1741	6	3
1745	1749	6	8
1750	1752	5	3
1756	1759	6	7
1764	1766	8	7
1768	1770	4	4
1771	1772	3	2

floods, poor harvests and internal strife such as Bacon's Rebellion in Virginia. An event like the Commonwealth could adversely affect the Southern Loyalist colonies while being a boon to New England. And on the international level, wars could affect the safety of shipping products to markets, as well as the availability of the markets themselves.

Obviously, disruption in the ultimate markets by disease, weather, political shifts or other factors could also affect the colonies. Reference to the Time Line which starts on page 6 will show more factors playing to disruption than to stability. As a result, the colonial economies were on a constant roller coaster. Consult a local history to find out what was happening in your subject area.

One other factor that affected the economy was the view taken by the government in England. What was good for the factors, manufacturers and middlemen was not necessarily healthy for the colonists, and many of the pressures that led to the Revolution were founded in a recognition of a need to establish a more workable system than that allowed under the Navigation Acts. Local production changed during the period in response to these pressures, including the replacement of tobacco with other crops and manufactures in the Chesapeake during the later period and the growth of the merchants in New England.

ILLICIT TRADE

Historians differ on the extent of illicit trade. The long, heavily indented coastline, decentralized population, lack of radar and other surveillance technology, lack of funding for interdiction by colonial governments, colonial interests that differed from national interests and difficulties finding ships at sea all contributed to fairly widespread smuggling and some brief occurrences of piracy throughout the period. The profit motives to citizens of European countries and colonials alike were high enough to allow smuggling in violation of national acts when the perpetrators were far enough from the authorities to act independently. In addition, governments allowed exceptions to their own acts when it was expedient, such as the shipment of rice and fish direct from the colonies to Spain. These amounted to little more than sanctioned smuggling in light of the Navigation Acts' premises.

Piracy

Part of the purpose of the Navigation Acts was to allow the formation of convoys to the colonies to help protect from PIRATES (PICAROONS) and to lower losses. Piracy enjoyed a short but violent life on the American coast, a slightly longer spell in the Caribbean, and longest in more remote corners of the world. Piracy was just one aspect of illicit trade, most of which involved smuggling goods around the Navigation Acts and other countries' similar legislation. Ever good entrepreneurs, Americans were involved in all aspects of it.

Piracy started out with a bang in the 1680s in the Caribbean, then was chased out by the appearance of the British fleet and moved to the island of Madagascar off the east coast of Africa. When chased out of there, it returned to the Atlantic, settling along the gold, ivory and slave coasts of Africa, before being chased out in turn. A brief flare-up in the Caribbean and coastal continental waters died out about 1720.

Pirates were as colorful a lot as their literary portrait depicts, and primary sources show the writers of old knew pirates' speech well. The pirates lived a life of paradoxes: extremely democratic, with elected captains who could not make any decision without a vote of the crew, except in battle where their talents were relied on; living with extreme wealth, yet low ambitions; brutal, yet not willing to take on a fight with the authorities, even when odds greatly favored them and the defense was of their home operating ports.

In part, given the short duration of the golden age of piracy, pirates owe their popularity to an early but keenly developed sense for public relations. Given that no one could enjoy the spoils of piracy if he were dead, pirates would rather intimidate their victims into surrender than fight them. Every once in a while, then, they committed atrocities just so the public would know what it might expect if it chose to fight with a pirate and lost. On one occasion off the coast of Africa, a slave ship was set afire with some seven hundred slaves chained in the hold, and the pirates lay close enough to enjoy the screams of the victims. But by far the best practitioner of the art of intimidation was Blackbeard or Edward Teach, who starred in the last act off the coasts of Virginia and North Carolina. Teach, as his trade name implied, sported a massive black beard in which he would tie ribbons and burning slow match, so that he looked the very demon from hell when he BOARDED A VICTIM, or came aboard his prey's vessel. Carrying six pistols in a sash across his chest, he was powerful enough that, in his final battle, although drunk and wounded with five pistol shots and nearly thirty saber cuts, he broke Lieutenant Maynard's sword with a single blow of his own.

Perhaps the single greatest item of interest in the piracy period was the number of upstanding citizens who were involved in one way or another. Edward Teach enjoyed the patronage of North Carolina governor Charles Eden, who saw the goods brought in by the pirates as a way to balance North Carolina's lack of a seaport and export trade in an economy where existence was based on such trade. Fredericke Philipse, a mid-seventeenth-century immigrant to New Netherlands, became one of the wealthiest men in New York, holding property that stretched for twenty-one miles along the Hudson. His seat can still be visited today at Philipsburg Manor, part of the Sleepy Hollow Restorations. He made much of his money supplying the pirates of Madagascar and laundering captured goods, with the help of the royal customs inspectors. A change in governors forced him off the governor's council and cost him several ships on suspicion of being involved with pirates but did not hurt his long-term wealth or standing.

Smuggling

For every person involved, however remotely, with piracy, many more regularly engaged in smuggling. Some historians discount the extent to which smuggling occurred but then report that, in the area of molasses tariffs, smuggling was so common that royal revenues actually declined after imposing a stricter tariff.

Enough scattered references exist, however, to indicate smuggling had a substantial effect on the local economies. New York and Charles Town merchants supplied Spanish Florida during its course of war with England. A potter in Yorktown, Virginia (whom the governor, in a report on manufacturers to the Board of Trade in London, called so poor as to be unable to support his wife and children) was shipping goods all around the Atlantic basin from Maine to the Azores. After being appointed supervisor of roads for Yorktown, this potter paved the streets with shards from his manufactory.

The two major interests in the smuggling trade were to bring in products from foreign sources more cheaply than through England and to provide goods to foreign markets that could not fulfill their needs through their own approved channels, in part because of imperial decay and revenue problems. A third motive was the development of industries forbidden under the Navigation Acts, such as potteries and iron foundries. In the process of pursuing business the colonies developed a certain disrespect for the establishment, which viewed them theoretically, not as living people but merely an asset on England's ledgers, while they had to solve real problems of living. Even the royal governors could straddle such a fence.

Pirates preferred the fore-and-aft-rigged ships used in coastal shipping to the square-rigged ships preferred by the navy, because of their speed, maneuverability (especially against the wind) and handling. Thus the colonial fleets were ideally suited for smuggling, and the long coastlines were difficult to patrol.

THE TRIANGLE TRADE

Perhaps the best known trade, and one which touched on all aspects of the colonial world, was the Triangle Trade, named because the route had three legs, each of which had a certain type of product interrelated to the others. This trade route ran between New England where grains, textiles and rum were put on board ships, to Africa where these were exchanged for slaves (for more information about slavery see chapter thirteen) and then to the Caribbean where the slaves were sold to sugar planters in exchange for molasses and sugar, which was then shipped back to New England where the molasses was converted to rum to begin the cycle again. There were some spurs off this trade:

Sugar went not only to the colonies but back to England, and some of the slaves wound up in the deep South on indigo and rice plantations and in the Chesapeake on tobacco plantations. These destinations, however, were secondary and tertiary and the slaves sold in the South were generally considered unfit for the Caribbean market. Ironically, the more unfit they were for the Caribbean, the more likely they were to live out a full life. Products from these secondary sources generally went to other destinations (rice to the Iberian peninsula, tobacco to England) on other hulls over other routes.

The triangle trade was, at one stroke, a great unifying force in the colonies and a great source of division. It did not get into full swing until the late seventeenth century, about the same time the religious faction died out in New England to be replaced by a new merchant class. By the mid-eighteenth century many of the leading thinkers in the North and middle South were against the commerce in human beings, but all parties were economically dependent on the trade, New England only slightly less so than the South.

This type of trade had a long tradition into which the European traders connected. Slaves came mainly from the interior of Africa, captured in battle or raids and traded to the coastal tribes. On the coast they were placed in ships for the Middle Passage, the voyage to the New World. Humans of all types were considered cargo in the seventeenth century, and the lower classes (later to be "steerage") were considered cargo into the eighteenth. Cargo was carried in the hold of the ship and not allowed up on deck except when weather permitted.

Slaves were segregated by sex and carried on wooden bunks in two "packings." LOOSE PACKING implied they were able to lie side by side on their backs, nose to toe, and chained in position. In TIGHT PACKING they were chained on their sides, nose to toe. They were fed gruel once a day and allowed on deck occasionally if the weather permitted. The cargo and decks were washed down with buckets of sea water once every two weeks if the ship was English, once a month if Dutch. Meanwhile, vomit (from seasickness) and bodily waste accumulated on the bunks around the "cargo." The Middle Passage deserved its bad reputation. Approximately 15 percent to 25 percent of all slaves embarked died during the average two-month course of the voyage and were dumped into the sea. Slavers did not use the fast, narrow rigs; they preferred the slow, round-hull, full-rigged ships for their greater carrying capacity.

As with the drug trade today, emotions ran high on the issue of the Middle Passage. The planters of the Caribbean and the South held the New England ship owners responsible for the execrable conditions. To the moralists in the North, conditions on board ship were created by the economics of meeting the Southerners' demand for slaves. Obviously, the views of each party on how to end the offense were different, and the New England view was ultimately expanded into the full-blown abolitionist position in the nineteenth century.

OVERLAND TRAVEL

Overland travel was difficult, but that alone did not keep those with a need from engaging in it. Perhaps the greatest cost was in time, which tended to prevent the average farmer and craftsman from traveling much. Travel then was for the gentry, the military and professionals such as sailors, messengers, drivers and the like.

Horses

Horses were not then as common as we might think. They were transportation for the upper classes and professionals. Everyone else walked, hired a space in a coach or used oxen. Since horses required care, acreage in fodder, and tack (either saddles or harness), they were expensive to keep. They may even have required servants to take care of them. And they had other liabilities. They couldn't cover as much ground at a heavy pace, day in, day out, as a human could, for they would die. Since they were skittish, they were prone to causing or being involved in accidents. Bees, bears, smells, noises and lightning all were enough to cause one to break into a full and uncontrollable gallop, dragging whatever was harnessed to them behind. Because they moved quickly, they broke plows when they hit an obstruction in the ground. The gait run throughout the colonies was the WRACK, near a gallop, and unusually hard on a horse. Even though fast, it required so many rest stops to cover any distance that it made the average speed slow. One horse could effectively cover about twenty miles a day.

The horses brought over (most were from England; a few came from Spanish shipwrecks) beginning in 1609 were small. Today, by definition, a horse is 14.5 hands or more, but in colonial times the average seems to have been 13 to 14 hands. The colonists usually harnessed two horses for every one we would use today on the same job.

Thoroughbreds were just being introduced. The very first was developed about 1760, although the term soon became known here, if not used in the sense in which we would use it today. Horses were typed as being for the turf, for the field, for the road or for the coach. Turf horses were racehorses, especially popular in Virginia, where horse racing and hunts were the most anxiously awaited event of Sundays, with ministers even required to cut short their sermons if they ran over into race time. One minister was so fond of the hunt he kept his horse saddled and ready in front of the door of the church, so if one should ride by, he could run down the aisle, stripping vestments and leaving the service to be finished by a layman. Field horses were the heaviest draft animals, while carriage horses combined some of the characteristics of turf and field animals. Road horses were everyday fast riding horses and were the most common.

Owning a carriage was akin to owning a limousine and keeping a chauffeur on staff today. Those few horses that were gentleman's toys received exceptional care. Others, more numerous by far, were considered beasts of burden and cared for about as well as the average working pickup truck today. Unlike England, the colonies do not seem to have docked tails in the period.

Due to the problems of exhaustion of horses, the most efficient way to move mail and people was through an organized network of posts or stages at which horses could be changed when exhausted, much like the pony express later. Coaches and wagons were popular for this kind of service, for their greater capacity and thus profitability. POST HORNS were used to warn the stage of the approach of a post rider or stage coach, and the term "posting a letter" is related to this practice.

Saddles or small saddles were lightweight and English in design. Military, great or dragoon saddles (⚔ *page 287*) were more like the western version, designed with high backs and fronts to hold a rider in and protect him at the same time. Although details of bits, bridles and harnesses have changed, period gear is effectively like today's, with the observation that breast collars were more commonly used than modern horse or neck collars for draft animals, as the greatest use of draft animals was for gentlemen's carriages instead of farm carts. BRITCHING (breeching) was a harness strap that ran around under the wheel horse's tail to slow or hold back the vehicle, the force of which was passed to the shaft of the vehicle. The forward force of the horse was consolidated from the traces to the ends of a SWIVEL or SWINGLE TREE, a short bar of wood mounted in the middle to the vehicle, allowing give in the harness to match the horse's gait.

Horses and riders were not limited to roads in the early days. The great height of trees and absence of undergrowth in mature hardwood forests allowed riders easy passage.

Oxen

In comparison to horses, oxen (castrated male bovine used for work) were much esteemed and used. Slow, docile and incredibly strong, these animals proved better at the everyday tasks a farmer encountered. Their slow strength would allow a plow to break through an obstacle rather than be broken by it. They were not prone to being spooked and thus endangering the owner's life. And like the tortoise in the race, they got there just fine, even carrying heavier loads than a team of horses could. Instead of an expensive harness, they needed

190

only a wooden yoke the farmer could make himself, and they responded to verbal commands instead of requiring a bridle and bit. Oxen pulled the cannon captured at Fort Ticonderoga across the mountains to Boston in the middle of winter, and they drew the Conestoga and other wagons over the Great Wagon Road from Pennsylvania to North Carolina and over the mountains westward.

The following verbal commands are traditional, but not documentable: Go is "hip," turn left is "haw," turn right is "gee," stop is "whoa," back up is "back," to move the team apart is "put out" and to move them together is "put in."

Shank's Mare

Before we "forgot" how to walk, walking was the primary mode of transportation, and one could maintain a pace of four miles an hour for hours on end. In a ten-hour walking day that was forty miles, or twice as far as an average day's run for a horse. The term "shank's mare" derives from the idea that one's own shank, or leg, was his mare. The pace is described in the records: long and straight-legged with the legs swinging from the hips and the body leaning forward. In fact, the body literally fell into the next step, and the walker only kept upright by walking. Uphill, one leaned over more to keep falling up the hill. Downhill, one straightened up and fell anyway. It is helpful to realize shoes were better fitted and people more used to walking.

One infamous land purchase in Pennsylvania is called the Walking Purchase because the terms of sale were the amount of land a man could walk around in a day. A professional walker took in more than twice the land the Indians expected. The Indians called foul.

Roads

Serviceable roads were one of the first concerns of government in most places, although areas that relied strictly on water for long-distance hauling, such as the Chesapeake, Connecticut River Valley, Hudson River Valley and other areas near navigable rivers and bays, were behind in developing them. Here, New England, with its emphasis on formalized and centrally located towns, was more advanced than the South with its remote plantations located on rivers and creeks or connected by a loose thread of farm lanes. In the South, without centrally located towns, roads first connected political centers such as courthouses, churches and government towns. The presence or absence of roads was a determining factor in the presence of wheeled transport.

Exceptions to the rules, however, do exist. In the area of Norfolk, Virginia, within the Chesapeake where water was the major route of travel, roads were highly developed early on because it was shorter to go by road than by water. Other areas conformed to local needs as well,

191

and historical maps in libraries will show the old roads. Alternatively, a careful review of modern maps can suggest the early conditions.

The construction of roads was hindered in several ways. Bridges were considered the highest form of the architect's or engineer's art from Renaissance times, but large rivers and other bodies of water were difficult to bridge, and, if bridged, the structures were impossible to maintain. Ferries were used instead. Swamps were another major problem, as road foundations and bridge footings were difficult to place. It is no surprise that Lee made the Union cross the Chickahominy Swamp where he did. Virginia had been trying to keep a road across that area for almost 150 years. Travelers avoided that route because of the difficulty. Mountains were difficult not only because of construction and bridging problems, but because grades were difficult or impossible for burdened draft animals.

Some of the first major overland routes were turnpikes, operated by private developers who charged a toll for the use of the road and collected it at gatehouses covering obstacles (toll gates) in the road. The term gatecrashing derives from the practice of running through these barriers at high speed to avoid paying a toll.

Wheeled Transport

Wheeled vehicles were divided into three basic types: carriages, stage wagons and wagons or carts. The first were private vehicles, the second like our buses and the third like our trucks. Although some distinct types were known and different terms were used, the detailed definition of vehicle types associated with the nineteenth century had not yet developed. Carriages were not common in the early days of the colonies. Roads had to be developed and the population needed to get past the subsistence stage before they appeared.

The springs and suspension of early carriages were made of heavy stitched leather straps suspended from goosenecks, as the metal band spring had not yet arrived.

Carriage was a generic term that included two- and four-wheeled varieties: the four-wheeled varieties usually called coaches or chariots and the two-wheeled forms commonly called chairs. Some varieties of chairs were known as chaises, although the exact difference is not known and the term could also refer to a four-wheeled version.

Because carriage types did not yet have formalized meanings, it is difficult to know what is meant by a term. The table on page 193 provides some information to allow relative comparison of values.

Chariots appear to be lighter in weight than coaches, while phaetons were open-topped. Chairs were open-topped, single-axle vehicles not unlike but more substantial than a racing sulky. A calash appears much like a wheeled sleigh with a roof mounted on posts.

TYPICAL CARRIAGE TYPES, RANDOM TAX VALUES, OCCURRENCES

Term	Wheels	Horses occ = occasionally	Tax in pounds	Occurrence during colonial period
Coach	4	6, occ 4	40	throughout
Chariot	4	6	40	throughout
Chair	2	2 or 1	10	through- out, later
Chaise	4	4 or 2, occ 6	40	throughout
Chaise	2	2	10	
Phaeton	2 or 4	2, occ 4	30	1750s +

Many persons wealthy enough to own a coach also owned one or more smaller, lighter vehicles such as a chariot or chair, while persons OF THE MIDDLING SORT often owned chairs only.

The popularity of carriage types was localized. For specific details about carriages, consult estate inventories (available in the clerk of the court's office) for the area and dates of interest. Even if these do not provide precise descriptions, they will show local taste, availability and relative values.

Wagons and carts were work vehicles. The main difference was wagons had four wheels while carts only had two. One of the most famous wagon types was the Conestoga, which was developed in the Conestoga valley of Lancaster County, Pennsylvania. This wagon was favored because its curved bottom helped to keep cargo in, and its deep sides allowed for great carrying capacity. The Conestoga became available to the Southern colonies after Forbe's Road was built during the French and Indian War and as a result of immigration and commerce along the Great Wagon Road.

Hitches, Drivers and Staff

Horses were hitched singly between shafts of a cart; in tandem around a single shaft or with traces; in fours, with two in tandem (the WHEEL HORSES) and two more as the lead horses, and if driven from the box known as FOUR IN HAND, otherwise a COACH AND FOUR; and in sixes, with an additional pair in front becoming the new lead horses COACH AND SIX, LONGSET). Although it was possible to drive six from the box it was not easy, and many rigs utilized a postilion rider on the left or near lead horse to control the leading pair, with the remaining four driven four in hand.

The postilion also helped keep the team from bolting, and in fact came into being after the French royal carriage was scared off a ferry into a river with nearly fatal results. Longset with a postilion required a staff of three or more to run a carriage, who were either slaves or liveried servants. These were the postilion, the driver or coachman, who drove the team from the box, and one or more footmen who rode standing up on the back of the carriage and assisted in boarding and exiting, and were body servants on the road. The considerable expense of maintaining a proper coach rig is evident.

Taverns

Taverns were not places to go get drunk. They were hotels and restaurants combined. A tavern might be called an ORDINARY because it kept ordinary rooms, common rooms or public rooms. These were rooms with several beds in them in which the traveler might rent bed space. Occupancy varied greatly. In the larger towns, where competition was keen and the clientele upper class, attempts were made to keep it to two in a bed. In the remoter areas on the road, however, the available space needed to accept all the trade. It was considered possible to put six to a bed, heel to toe, "no boots or spurs, please," for obvious reasons. Equally obvious is why most ladies did not travel, except by way of a network of friends' homes. Women were generally too busy to have the opportunity to travel.

Most colonies regulated the maximum rates chargeable for common rooms. Unregulated were the PRIVATE ROOMS or PRIVATE SPACES, for which the rate was negotiable. These were truly private spaces, and some ladies did travel through these.

A LODGING HOUSE may have been the same as a tavern, or it might have used a different name to attempt to attract business from travelers with ladies in the party. COLD HARBOR was a tavern serving only cold meals. In the larger centers, a tavern with a great room or common room might rent it out for meetings, much as hotels do today.

WATER TRANSPORT

Water transport took many forms from the small canoe to the ferry to the oceangoing ship. Early, most transport was built in England. Some small but seaworthy boats called PINNACES or SHALLOPS were carried KNOCKED DOWN (disassembled) on the larger ships and assembled on arrival for duty in the coastal waters. In an emergency a reasonably sized vessel might be built in the colonies, as the thirty-ton *Virginia* was in Maine in 1607 and a ship and pinnace were by the shipwrecked *Sir*

George Sommers and *Christopher Newport* on Bermuda Island in 1610.

Although the English had the high-tech ship designs of the late 1580s, by the end of the colonial period they were behind the times, still utilizing essentially the same designs. Designs varied much depending on the function of the ship. The English round-ship design, on which the best Elizabethan galleons such as Drake's *Golden Hinde* were built, had a main hull shaped much like a modern submarine on which was built a tall, narrowing superstructure. Extremely seaworthy and maneuverable, they lacked great capacity and thus functioned poorly as cargo ships. Merchant ships traditionally were lower, with a greater beam (wider), and were slower and less maneuverable. Early ships had high forecastles and sterncastles, vestiges of the days when they were literally castles for hand-to-hand combatants. With the advent of serious naval cannon in the Battle of the Spanish Armada (1588), this function was made obsolete, and throughout the colonial period a gradual move to flat decks occurred because the high castles caught wind and interfered with handling. Fully flat decks were finally common around 1800. Still, even though smaller or nonexistent, castles retained their names.

The sterncastle was in the STERN (rear) and traditionally held the officers' quarters, the binnacle (housing for the compass) and steering tiller or whipstaff, which later was replaced by the wheel. The forecastle contained the crew's quarters and galley. Passengers, except for the wealthy or titled, were carried as cargo in the hold. The poop decks or quarter decks were located atop the sterncastle, the foredeck atop the forecastle. The head was the rigging junction at the bow (front end) of the ship, where the figurehead might be placed, and where the ship's sanitary facilities were.

Small Boats

Small coastal boats included Indian canoes (pirogues), small rowboats generically called bateau, and rafts, often made of full kegs of goods lashed together. Many times a reference was made to a small sailing rowboat called simply "the ship's boat." Longboats were long, rowing boats from the eighteenth century, after ship sizes increased.

Canoes were made of two principal materials: in the north the traditional birchbark and elsewhere hollowed trees. In a pinch other materials could be used for a covering, and Indians returning home from a winter hunt might construct a temporary canoe out of hides for a return down river. Birchbark was used as long as large enough canoe birches were available. This kind was like a modern wood-and-canvas canoe with cedar ribs and frame. Overlapping sheets of bark were sewn together with fine roots; the characteristic black lines on the white bark were from the resin or pitch that sealed seams.

In areas where birches were not available, canoes were dugouts, hollowed out by the process of burning and scraping the charred wood. Despite the crudity of the methods, prodigious craft could be built. In the early period on the East Coast, canoes seating up to eighty are recorded, indicating the size of trees available. Gum was a preferred wood for canoes (even being called "canoe tree" by the southern Indians) although it was extremely slow to work with using this technology. Cypress was also much used. In the early days many colonists utilized dugout canoes in areas where materials were available and the need adequate.

Englishmen had a greater tradition of rowing or sculling (rowing with a single oar facing backward through a hole in the transom, or rear board, of the boat). Most such boats were referred to as BATEAUX or DORIES. Local variations in design persist to this day and are the result of specific local needs. Read local materials if exact detail is required.

Ferries were a necessity for crossing larger rivers. They might be run by the government, but were more often licensed out to ferrymen who would often also keep a tavern on one bank. The ferry was either a barge or a raft and was pulled across small rivers, either by the ferryman or by horses or oxen on shore. On larger rivers, ferries were rowed or even sailed across. The flimsy construction and the low freeboard of many ferries resulted in a steady loss of life from storms, particularly quick-moving squalls that caught them midriver.

Large Vessels

Large vessels were employed in coastal or transoceanic trade. Unfortunately, it is difficult to demarcate the vessels used because anything over a small boat was used in the Atlantic trade. Also, as is the case with carriages, the formalized nineteenth-century terms for ships' rigs did not yet exist, and one ship may be referred to in the same record as a "bark," a "ship" and a "brigantine."

The greatest difference would be in those rigged fore and aft and those rigged square. Fore-and-aft rigs worked like modern sailboats and allowed sailing closer to the wind (more directly into the wind). Square rigs are the traditional picture of the tall ship and could only sail from about 120 to 240 degrees from the wind. Because most square-rigged ships needed to maneuver in close quarters, they almost all cheated a bit and carried one fore-and-aft spanker sail on the rearmost (mizzen) mast and might have carried one or two fore-and-aft triangular-shaped jibs on the foremast stays (guy lines) above the bowsprit. If a ship carried any jiblike sails between the masts, they were called staysails. For more details about rigging and sails, please refer to one of the books in the bibliography at the end of this chapter.

Ships, snows and brigs all seem to have been functionally inter-changeable terms in the eighteenth century. They stood for the largest, mainly square-rigged, civilian ships of the day. A good-sized ship drew (the DRAFT of a ship was its depth below the waterline) between eight and twelve feet of water, although some drew more. These were the ships of the major transoceanic runs. They were very large, up to three hundred feet long, compared to the early seventeenth-century ships, which ran fifty to one hundred tons and only some sixty feet long.

The smaller ships, which were also used in the transoceanic trade, were the sloops, schooners and ketches, mostly fore-and-aft rigged, narrower, faster and requiring far fewer crew. Many of these ships were owned by large planters, fishermen and small merchants. The larger of this type were favored by pirates and smugglers.

By about 1750 approximately half of the shipping was built and owned by colonists. A New England myth deals with the tall pines (King's trees) marked out as masts for the Royal Navy. The navy did mark trees, but far fewer were cut here than is commonly thought, because the lumber in the eastern Baltic was cheaper to ship to En-gland than that found in the Americas. The ready supplies of large timber, however, did not hurt the colonies' shipbuilding industry.

Military ships had specialized functions, and more is known about them than other types because of the government's fondness for records. Most important though are the ratings. The largest ships were called THREE-DECKERS, MEN-OF-WAR or SHIPS OF THE LINE. They had three gun decks and carried as many as seventy or eighty guns. These were the battleships of the day and comprised the first- and second-rate ships. As the ships got smaller, their rating increased. Frigates were smaller ships used for scouting, patrolling and running messages. A frigate the size of the *Constitution* would be rated about a 4, the *Constellation* about a 5. Ratings ran to about 7. Small coastal ships were not even rated.

Life at Sea

Duty at sea was divided into six four-hour WATCHES, each of which was divided into thirty-minute segments. Passage of time was marked by ringing the ship's bell, once at the end of the first segment of a watch, twice for the second, etc. Half the crew stood each watch, with one crew taking two watches at night so the other half could sleep soundly and also altering the pattern so they would get the next night off. "All hands on deck" indicated an emergency and meant what it said.

Food was dried and repetitive but heavy in fats and carbohydrates for energy. Hardtack or biscuits were most common, although a pound of dried peas per man every day was not an uncommon ration. Rum was a major and cheap source of alcohol, but it was watered down into grog, just enough alcohol to kill any bacteria in the bad water.

Sailors worked hard and faced the all-too-real risk of drowning, which led to a live-for-today attitude, but they had the opportunity to see foreign places that could be only legend to the average person. Thus there arose around them a certain mystique, which no doubt they cultivated. In the cold climes they wore heavy woolen clothing with the lanolin still in it. In warmer areas, they defied the styles of the day and wore next to nothing. Surprisingly, it appears many sailors could not swim!

The officers and passengers of status carried along all the pleasures of home, including musical bands, wives or mistresses, and the like, even from the earliest days on the smallest ships. The last anyone saw of Sir John Hawkins, who was lost at sea in a storm, he was sitting on deck enjoying a performance by a viola da gamba consort, a most unlikely instrument to take to sea.

Wooden ships required constant maintenance. When the bottom became foul, they were careened (drawn up sideways to the shore, emptied and rolled over to expose the bottom), which was then scraped, repaired and repainted. Seams in the planking required continual caulking, and something always needed to be scraped and painted. Rigging was painted with pine tar (hence the sailor's nickname) and sails were mended.

NAVIGATION

The two types of navigation are coastal and offshore. The problems associated with each vary greatly. While coastal sailing is fraught with more hazards in the form of shoals, etc., navigation is fairly easy. Offshore sailing is much more straightforward, but the navigation problems were insurmountable for much of the period. Thus, a course was SHAPED that involved simple ocean paths and much coastal piloting. Landfall (the sighting of land after a long sea voyage) was a most welcome occurrence.

Charts did exist, but they were limited in scope and accuracy. Real oceanic charts did not come into being much before the American Civil War. Most charts were local in scope, and ships relied on local pilots or intimate knowledge based on frequent visits.

A few fixed beacons were built in the mid 1700s, and some areas buoyed, but most beacons were houses or other distinctive landmarks. By the mid 1700s the first lighthouses were built at the entrances to major harbors like New York, and the first public building project of the new federal government was a lighthouse on the Capes of Virginia.

Coastal Navigation

Coastal waters are more treacherous than the open sea, because there is land to run into, and there may be dangerous shoals like the Outer Banks of North Carolina, on which the wind may force a less-than-maneuverable ship. But, as long as the sailor could see landmarks on which to take relative bearings and triangulate, he knew where he was. Even when he did not, the presence of land-based sea birds, flotsam, clouds, smells, water salinity, currents and the type and depth of the bottom (sand, gravel, color, etc.) could tell an experienced mariner where he was. All are clues recorded in period sources, such as *Hakluyt's Voyages* (see the bibliography at the end of this chapter) and numerous journals.

TAKING A BEARING was done by reference to the bow of the ship, which was on a known compass course, the bearing to the object determined by the compass degrees from the bow. TRIANGULATING two fixed points determined exactly where the ship was. CASTING THE LEAD or SOUNDING meant throwing a lead weight with a slight concavity in the bottom, in which soft wax was fitted, over the side on a long line (the lead line) knotted at intervals of one fathom (six feet). A bit of the bottom was brought up by the wax, and the knots allowed the measurement of the water depth.

The danger of shoaling cannot be overstated. After the land was cleared for agriculture using slash-and-burn techniques, water depths decreased rapidly from siltation. Hampton, Virginia, a major port at the turn of the 1700s, was silted up and unusable by 1750.

An uncommon but militarily important form of moving was KEDGING, named for the smaller of the many anchors carried by a ship (largest were bower, medium were stream anchors). If a ship was becalmed, the anchor was placed in a boat and rowed ahead, where it was dropped. The capstan, a rotary winch manned by the sailors, was then used to pull the ship to the anchor, which was raised and the process repeated. It was also used to pull a beached ship off, as after careening.

Offshore Navigation

Oceanic navigation is more difficult. Two measurements are used to fix a ship's position on the earth: longitude, or the variation east or west of an imaginary north-south line (the prime meridian) passing through Greenwich, England, and latitude, or a series of lines parallel to the equator that measure distance from the poles or equator.

Measurement of latitude is relatively easy. The astrolabe, backstaff, cross-staff and later the more precise sextant all measured the angle between a star like the North Star and the horizon, thus giving the latitude (uncorrected for atmospheric effects, optical parallax, etc.).

The sextant is still used for this purpose today. TAKING A SIGHT or SHOOT-ING the Sun or the North Star was the process of comparing this angle. All it required was the ability to see both the star and the natural horizon, and a known height above water level, although shooting any body other than the North star requires accurate timekeeping, as with longitude, below.

The real trick is measurement of longitude. The only effective way to do this is by comparing the local time, or angle of the sun or stars above the eastern or western horizon, and the absolute time that exists at the prime meridian. To do this, one must have a totally reliable clock (chronometer) that can be set to absolute time at the prime meridian and not gain or lose any time at all during the course of a year or longer journey at sea, referred to as a standard. Each error of a minute causes an error of about a mile. In the beginning of the eighteenth century, clocks were accurate to plus-or-minus twenty min-utes a day, and the only major improvement to the clock was the devel-opment of the long pendulum, which does not travel well on the jos-tling ocean. An accurate chronometer appeared only near the end of the colonial period. Before that, all longitude measurement was by guess and navigation by dead reckoning.

There were some aids to dead reckoning. Accurate tracking of the course and the time on a leg, compared with a check on the ship's speed obtained by using the log line, allowed an approximation of position, without being able to compensate for the effects of currents and tides. The log line was a board designed to remain stationary in the water after being dropped overboard; the board was attached to a long line with a number of knots on it, which was played out over a period of time measured by a sandglass and the number of knots counted, giving the speed in knots. Currents were generally accounted for by following known routes across the ocean.

The principal route to America, known as the Southern Crossing, was to leave England, move south to the Azores stopping for food and water en route to prepare for the ocean crossing, take the trade winds and westerly currents to the Caribbean, whence the Gulf Stream was gained off Florida for the return to England. En route the long stretches of ocean crossing were broken by areas where landfalls were frequent and large enough they were easy to find using clouds, smells and birds and through which coastal navigation could occur. Since, when dead reckoning, they could not know where they would hit, and thus which way to turn when they got in the area, it was wiser to aim off to one side and then turn and coast along until they found what they were looking for. The Caribbean and the American coast were perfect for this.

BIBLIOGRAPHY

Botting, Douglas. *The Pirates*. Volume of The Seafarers. Alexandria, Va.: Time-Life Books, 1978. A good blend of a historical overview with close-up vignettes of particular people and places in piracy.

Chapelle, Howard I. *The History of American Sailing Ships*. New York: Bonanza Books, 1935. Good for rigging plans, ship sizes and types.

Chapman, Charles F. *Piloting, Seamanship and Small Boat Handling*. Available at most libraries and boating stores in its latest revised edition. This is the standard work on small-boat handling. The basic principles still work, and the working glossary is an excellent starting point for details of rigging and handling.

Cipolla, Carlo M. *Before the Industrial Revolution: European Society and Economy, 1000–1700*. Third ed. New York: Norton, 1994. Provides much general economic background for Europe and the colonies.

Cotter, Charles H. *A History of Nautical Astronomy*. London: Hollis and Carter, 1968. More than you ever wanted to know about the tools and theory of celestial navigation.

Fishel, Leslie H., Jr., and Benjamin Quarles. *The Black American: A Documentary History*. Third ed. Glenview, Ill.: Scott, Foresman, 1976. Historical background on Africa and the slave trade.

Hakluyt, Richard. *Hakluyt's Voyages*. Edited by Irwin R. Blacker. New York: The Viking Press, 1965. Excerpted from a corpus totaling twelve modern volumes, these are first-person accounts from before about 1600 by people like Drake of the voyages of discovery. Wonderful for early detail and flavor.

Kirkland, Edward C. *A History of American Economic Life*. New York: Appleton-Century-Crofts, 1969.

McCusker, John J. *How Much is That in Real Money? A Historical Price Index for Use as a Deflator of Money Values in the Economy of the United States*. Worcester, Mass.: American Antiquarian Society, 1992.

———. *Money and Exchange in Europe and America, 1600–1775: A Handbook*. Chapel Hill: University of North Carolina Press, 1978.

McCusker, John J. and Russell R. Menard. *The Economy of British America, 1607–1789*. Chapel Hill: University of North Carolina Press, 1985.

Parry, J.H. *The Age of Reconnaissance: Discovery, Exploration and Settlement, 1450–1650*. Berkeley: University of California Press, 1981. Good overview of ships and navigation technologies.

Tarr, Laszlo. *The History of the Carriage*. Translated by Elisabeth Hoch, New York: Arco Publishing Co., 1969.

Many reproduction ships, living-history sites and museums have transportation artifacts. Almost all have materials on their collections, which can be consulted for more detailed local information.

Bay

20

5

5

...ay is very
...ll of Flatts
...n the Sea
...ngerous
...uk and
...ne
...
...for J
...d We
...tts in
...place of
...Veſſells and
...ar here.

↑ Rocky grount

Plymouth
Bay
Cedar P XI

Marks I.

4
7   10   30

4   Gurnet head
5   6
2   10
channelto way

7   Barnſtable.
Browns Sunken   reason of J
Islands   Run a Shoa

Monemeat
high Land

3

7 Note that th
Bars are bu
are ſet down
Water, and
7there is the

Plymouth

3

3   Barnſta
c.

ds Bay is very dangerous
y and Flowing is but small

3

Sandwich   12
7 F

Barnſt

XI

2

Bay

Barnſtable

Tucgguiſet
Woods Pt.

2

North Chann
3 Coarſe Sand 3
Southacks Chan.
Horseshoe ſand

...hole

...arpolin Cove

5   5
5

3

2

4
foot
3

2

3

5   2 Tucgguiſet Point

PART FOUR

Colonial Society

Chapter Twelve

Arts & Sciences

DECORATIVE ARTS
AND FURNITURE

ngland at the beginning of the colonial period was still in the late Elizabethan era. Archaeologists accustomed to working on sites dating only twenty years later are astounded at the Jamestown fort because the material culture is so unfamiliar, so Elizabethan. Within a very short time styles underwent major changes with the strictures of the Commonwealth, the introduction of baroque and High Renaissance styles at about the same time, the end of the seventeenth century, and a gradual simplification to the classical ideals of the end of the period. This section will try to outline these changes and the vocabulary that went with them.

Elizabethan culture was very modern at the highest court levels. Below that, the vast majority of the populace lived a life little changed from the late Middle Ages. The decorative arts show this combination of influences. The bulk of the population were from the lower classes and lived simply. Furniture was limited to a trestle table, which could be broken down when not in use to make room in the small houses for sleeping and other functions, and benches or stools to sit on. Chairs were rare, and beds and bedsteads so expensive as to be virtually nonexistent. People slept on mats that were rolled up during the day. Chests were used to store personal belongings, and these were usually simple, made of six boards nailed together, sometimes with a till or small box near the top to hold smaller, more commonly used items. The wealthy might use larger, bound chests with locks and might have cabinets. Cupboards or dressers were shelves used to store cups, wooden trenchers and cooking utensils. Glass was almost nonexistent. Pottery was mostly tin glazed and used in drug pots and dairy wares.

Leather JACKS and BOMBARDS were used for drinking and bottles for storage.

Early, each region had a distinct style of work. As time passed, this became more homogenized, but local shop traditions can still be identified, and even as late at the end of our period distinct styles of decorative work existed. During the Commonwealth a counterbalance took place at the higher levels, adding a gloss of simplicity which English culture was never to shake off completely.

Baroque forms were introduced to most of the populace during the reigns of Charles II through William and Mary, largely from their overseas contacts. These were derived from the mannerist style, discovered in Nero's Pleasure Palace in Rome in the 1480s and transported to England via France and the low countries beginning in the 1500s. This style took traditional classical forms and overlaid them with distortions, producing grotesque assemblages like women's busts with griffin's heads and ornate foliate and interlaced strapwork. Baroque style was organic, eccentric and dynamic. Because it used classical motifs and overlaid them with decoration, the two styles could exist contemporaneously. That is the key to understanding English material culture from then on.

Simultaneously with the arrival of the baroque, England was getting its first real look at classical forms. These were predominantly architectural in approach, symmetrical, balanced and restful. The baroque was the antithesis of this. Tensions arose as the result of combining these opposites. Over the next hundred years, English style can be seen as a gradual simplification from the excesses of the baroque to the core of classicism. In the process, England formed the end of the stylistic pendulum, inventing the neoclassicism that drove across Europe at the end of our period. In part, this may have been because of the Puritan influence, so strong in England, which tended toward frugality.

These various trends can already be seen in the furniture made in Massachusetts at the end of the seventeenth century. In the 1680s court cupboards and chests were heavily ornamented in a turned version of mannerist decoration. By the end of the century, geometric panels, either painted or framed with blocks, began to predominate as the classical underpinnings came out.

The most commonly known styles are those found in the eighteenth century. What today are called Queen Anne, Chippendale and Sheraton were not known by those names at the time. Most writers, specifying furnishings, asked for the latest fashion in some form or another. The later, classically influenced Chippendale forms were referred to as the "neat and plain style," distinguishing them from the earlier baroque and contemporary rococo forms.

Baroque style evolved from the highly convoluted styles of the

1680s, with heavy turnery, exaggerated changes in proportion, twisting vinelike decoration and C-curves, to a style that still utilized one of the key forms of the baroque, the S-curve, but simplified the decoration so that just the form itself was seen, as in the cabriole leg. Some vestiges of decoration were found, as the leg terminated in ball and claw or goat's feet, instead of the simpler pad or slipper feet, and there might be shell, lamb's tongue, acanthus leaf, C-scroll and even an occasional mask carving on the leg and its knee, but the overall effect was simplification. All this occurred within the first half of the eighteenth century. Furniture utilized the legs to create thrust, an animistic illusion of life in the mass. By mid-century, even simpler elements were at work.

On the continent these influences continued to be overlaid with elaborate decoration forming the rococo, which is most familiar from high French styles. Some markets existed for rococo items in the colonies, especially among the new merchants in Boston, who bought bombé chests, but the style was not common.

Legs became progressively plainer, finally becoming straight in the Marlborough leg. Forms became more perfectly proportioned, less dynamic. The neat and plain was here. The simple bachelor's chest is representative of this style.

Finally, largely as a result of the archaeological excavations of Herculaneum undertaken in the 1760s, a new classical vocabulary became common at the end of the period. The reigning symbol came to be the funerary urn, which was abstracted in many ways and used in chair backs, paintings, inlaid decoration, knife boxes and even, doubled, formed the bosses on drawer pulls. By the end of the century the urn, along with the weeping willow (after our period, seen, for example, in memorial paintings to Washington) became the symbols of the new cult of death which led to Victorian practices.

Other influences were felt during the middle of the eighteenth century. Chippendale provided designs inspired by the Chinese, the rococo and the gothic, the latter coinciding with the fascination with Satanism found among some English aristocrats.

Furniture also evolved during the period. The simple chests that sufficed to hold all of a person's belongings in the beginning of the period became inconvenient as material wealth increased. The till, used through the middle period to isolate small and frequently used items, became replaced by a single drawer under the chest, then more drawers until the chest itself disappeared. In the latter stages, two or more drawers might sit under the chest, which was faced with false drawers. Finally, the inconvenience of having to move items stored on top of the chest to gain access sounded the death knell for the simple chest. Roughly contemporary with this was a movement toward placing desks on stands, then filling in the stand with drawers.

Pair of knife boxes (ca. 1760) at Shirley Plantation, Charles City, Virginia, showing the typical form with inserts for cutlery, marquetry inlays and mahogany veneer with crossbanded trim. The urn-shaped brasses mark the beginning of the neoclassic revival. Note how the oval brasses around the escutcheon and on the plate supporting the lift ring are really derived from two urns placed top to top. This use of sympathetic shapes was common in the late period. Above, an eighteenth-century pastoral scene in an original frame.

The end of the seventeenth century saw a dramatic increase in the number of decorative Oriental and English pottery pieces available, and case pieces such as chests on chests with flat tops and even stepped display racks were made to display it.

COLOR

There is much confusion about color in the period. Although the earliest colonists did not have the profusion of synthetic aniline dyes that prompted the Victorians to the heights of gaudiness, they did utilize color to a degree not often recognized today. Natural pigments were available in a wide range of rich, saturated colors, and these were used to brighten lives otherwise dominated by greens and earth tones. Bright reds, blues and yellows were particularly common as paint applied to early carved furniture and as clothing colors. Even the Pilgrims utilized color in this way.

Approaching and through the middle period, the New England area would become fond of SAD colors—browns, grays and blacks—but this does not extend back to the early period.

Later, bright Prussian blue and green, often FLECKED OUT (trimmed) in white, as at Mount Vernon and the Governor's Palace in Williamsburg, became fashionable. Chippendale recommended pairing bright green with purple, a naturally occurring striking combination probably inspired by some period beans. Modern so-called "Williamsburg" colors, almost pastels, were the result of matching faded samples. Period fabrics and murals protected from light show vibrant and intense color, with all the richness of a good baroque painting.

PAINTING

The colonies produced a very few high-caliber portrait painters, or FACE PAINTERS, such as John Singleton Copley and Benjamin West, who traveled to England and succeeded there. A few second-rate English painters journeyed to the colonies. But most of the work done here was by self-taught colonists of moderate talent. The wealthy, particularly those who traveled to England on occasion, commissioned works from established English artists. Official structures used state portraits sent from England, which represented the highest standards. Some local artists were itinerants, working with stock pictures to which heads were added, while others painted the entire sitter. Almost all work was in oils and followed the conventions of the day, usually using a dark background to emphasize flesh tones and finery.

Murals were rare, but sometimes painted, often along stairs, overmantels and even entire walls. They might also be stenciled, but not as often as in the early nineteenth century. Their scarcity made them a source of comment.

The colonists were ravenous consumers of engravings, which they used to keep abreast of the latest fashions, for decoration and for edification. Early engravings were done on wood blocks. Later copperplate prints were popular, being cheap ways to obtain decoration and to see works of art one might not otherwise see. Many artists engraved their own paintings, as William Hogarth, or were copied by engravers. Many were published in black and white, but later many were done in color. Francesco Bartolozzi apprenticed in Italy, invented the stipple print technique, similar to a modern halftone but in color, and became engraver to George III.

SETS were popular, two of the most common themes being "The Seasons," four pictures of women attired, accoutred and aged appropriately, and "The Months," pastoral scenes depicting each month of the year. Some sets of the seasons were also painted on glass. Other sets included mythical subjects, allegories and travel pieces. Hogarth, the first bourgeois artist in England, became famous for his moralistic sets like "The Idle and Industrious Apprentice," "The Rake's Progress," "The Harlot's Progress" and others. Sets were hung en masse on walls, almost serving as wallpaper.

Little or no sculpture was executed in the colonies. A very few statues were commissioned from England.

MUSIC

For centuries music had been one of the liberal arts, almost equated to a science, because the mathematical problems associated with it (including a problem that required calculus to solve) were fertile ground for geometers and theorists. Music developed as an essential social grace rather coincidentally. All well-educated people were expected to be able to play an instrument or sing, both because doing so was a necessary entry into the mathematical discussions, but also because there was no music if people did not make it themselves. Singing work songs helped pass the time at repetitive labor and coordinate team efforts, such as the raising of an anchor on ship. Music also gave young people a chance to meet and court. And music is an exacting discipline, epitomizing other values.

Ladies did not generally play wind instruments, their garments being too restrictive and the necessary distortion of facial muscles considered in poor taste. They could sing or play keyboards, called generally clavier, or specifically harpsichord (strings plucked by quills in a jack on the end of the key), clavichord (which struck the string with a tangent of brass on the end of the key and was very quiet), organ (as today, but most commonly in the small chamber or positive forms, even church organs being very rare) and, very late, pianoforte (which hammered the string with a hammer thrown from the key).

Full-sized harpsichords such as you might see today at a concert were as rare then as nine-foot concert grand pianos are today. Most people had a spinet or small harpsichord. Earlier these would have been virginals, in a square box with the keyboard on the side. Later the keyboard was angled, and the instrument had a bentside like the tail of a full-sized harpsichord. Virginals are known, circumstantially, from as early as 1565 at Fort Caroline, near modern-day Jacksonville, Florida. A few spinets were made in Massachusetts.

Prior to about 1660 almost all instrumental music was written for whatever instruments were available to play it, in groups called CONSORTS. After this time, the composer began to name specific instruments, but colonists did not feel obligated to play only on those named. Elizabethan practice was to use broken consorts, consorts of mixed strings, or strings with a token wind, usually a flute.

The most common bowed string was (early) the six-stringed viola da gamba, "viol of the leg," played upright like a cello but available in a variety of sizes from treble (soprano, smaller than a violin) to bass. Members of the violin family were just becoming common around 1680. Before that (and even after in some circles) violins were played by itinerant street musicians and for dancing by fiddlers. John Utie, an early immigrant to Virginia, sued for libel in 1625 because a fellow passenger on the ship called him a "Fiddling Rogue and a Rascall." He did not contest the "rogue" but proved he played gamba, and won his suit. Gambas continued in England for a long time. VIOLINS (viola, violoncello) finally took precedence in orchestral music about 1680 and were the backbone of the orchestra to today. Violins hung in taverns for customers to use.

Other instruments which ladies played included CITTERNS, GITTERNS and GUITARS (ENGLISH GUITARS, no relation to the Spanish one, but rather a type of cittern, easy to learn because the strings were tuned to a major chord).

The broken consort of these and LUTES, ARCHLUTES and THEORBOS was replaced by homogenous consorts of viols in the mid-seventeeth century, only to be replaced by new chamber music forms, the solo or solo sonata, trio or trio sonata, concerto, or a solo instrument against orchestra, and others such as quartets and quintets. Near the end of the period classical forms like the octet (the military's Band of Music) became common.

Wind instruments were relatively uncommon early, when they were in Renaissance forms. Trumpets were the exception, used for signaling on ships and in the colonies by land troops. These were long, valveless instruments played like a bugle. Horns were used in dances, hunts and, late, chamber music. Cornetti, fifes, recorders, shawms and dulcians could be found. Later, after the French developed the baroque-style woodwinds in the 1680s, they were introduced to England and became popular. Hautbois (hoboys, hautboys, oboes) replaced

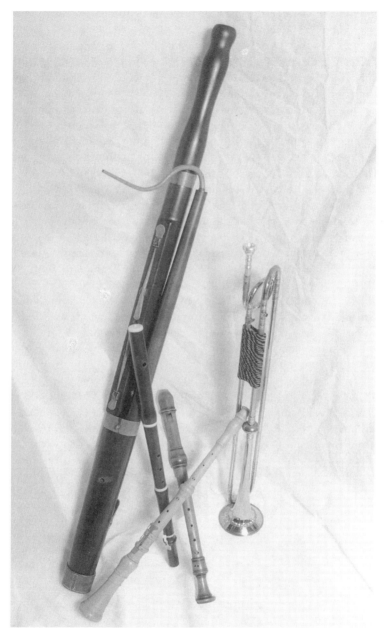

Some reproductions of common period wind instruments: An English-style bassoon of the second quarter of the eighteenth century, a German transverse flute (dark, one key) of the same period, a German oboe (light, two keys) of the same period, an English alto recorder of the first quarter and a trumpet in a style common to the entire period.

shawms and became the basis of the standard military music. They were common, hanging in taverns for the use of patrons. Recorders (or FLUTES as they were known in the middle period) became popular chamber instruments after 1680, often used in music denoting spiritual or metaphysical occurrences. Bassoon (fagots) were common bass instruments, used in church choirs to support singing in lieu of an organ. Flutes (queerflutes, German or French flutes) became common about 1730. These are the ancestors of modern flutes. Their popularity also marks a return of the fife to the military music about 1750. Clarinets were introduced by the English troops in the last period, but manuscripts from American bands in the Revolution indicate it was after our period that they became common here.

Music was played for ballad operas, festive events such as kings' birthnight celebrations, balls, as incidental music to plays and privately in chambers. Composers known in the colonies included Blow, Croft, Boyce, Tallis, Byrd, Green, Avison, Felton, Hebden, Hasse, Alberti, Handel, Vivaldi, Corelli, Purcell, Pepusch, Arne, Geminiani, Scarlatti, Giardini, Stanley, Schickhardt, Pasquali, Palma, Philadelphian Francis Hopkinson and Bostonian William Billings. The Moravians in Bethlehem and Winston-Salem had active and sophisticated musical cultures. A few top performers came to the colonies, some only to die from poor health almost immediately. Jefferson imported an Italian master to instruct him in violin.

In Charles Town the St. Cecilia Society, named for the patron saint of music, was formed in 1732. Annapolis's Tuesday Club, formed in 1745, included music among its many interests. In 1736 a benefit concert was given in New York for a Mr. Pachelbel, harpsichordist relation of the more famous composer, and in 1760 a series of subscription concerts was begun by Mssrs. Hulett and Dienval, local musicians and teachers. Pachelbel (the less famous one) later taught in Charles Town. In 1770 William Tuckey, choirmaster at Trinity Church on Wall Street, gave the first American performance of parts of Handel's *Messiah.* James Bremner, related to Scottish music publisher Robert Bremner, arrived in Philadelphia in 1763 and opened a school.

DANCE

Dance was the complement to music as an essential social grace. Balls were where the wealthy met and socialized after about 1700 and began with court dances like the minuet (🖙 *page 287*). These dances were performed in strict order of precedence, the ranking couple in the room dancing first, then down the social ladder. They were solo (one couple) performances, scrutinized by the other guests, and mistakes in the intricate choreography were noted. Excessive error could cause banishment of a dancer for the season, with attendant loss of prestige and social opportunity. After the formalities the floor was opened for the country or contra dances, which were commonly line and square dances with everyone participating and relaxing.

Two traditions of dancing were followed. In the aristocratic South, dances followed the French court models, favoring minuets, with dancing masters using English translations of Feuillet's treatise on dancing, available after 1706. In the Puritan North, dancers preferred Scottish reels and other country dances. During the Commonwealth court dance was forbidden, but Puritan John Playford's *English Dancing Master* (1651), immensely popular and published through the eighteenth century, contained almost one thousand country dances.

Dancing was a major courting ritual of the wealthy. It was considered a good way to determine others' physical soundness, as well as the state of their teeth and breath. It taught poise, grace and balance, especially important to women who had to learn to remain in their COMPASS, or the area of movement allowed by their clothing.

The importance of dances in the South cannot be overemphasized. Balls often lasted three to four days and took all day and most of the night. They were the primary means of socializing.

LANGUAGE AND LITERATURE

Writing was an essential skill for all but the lowest laborers. Literacy rates seem to have been high. It was not yet a crime to educate a slave.

The task of writing required certain tools. Pens were made from the primary flight feathers of goose or turkey, and the feather portion was trimmed to a narrow band, about half an inch wide. The nib was cut with a penknife, and small kits were made, fitting in a shagreen (sharkskin) case, containing knives and other tools for fashioning pens. Quill pens require a soft, spongy surface for the best results, so writing desks and tables were usually inlaid with a soft leather or covered with a green bays cloth or turkey work carpet. Writing stands were pewter or silver trays, like a condiment tray, containing one or more inkwells, often with holes to store pens, and a pounce pot to hold pounce (fine sand) used to pretreat the surface of the paper and after writing to dry the ink faster. Some inkwells were individual pieces, others were built into desks. Some desks contained wells for both red and black ink for accounting purposes. Inkwells were made of pottery, glass, brass, pewter and silver.

Pencils were made of lead bound in wood and were less common than pens. Tradesmen used chalk or a marking scribe or knife more than pencils.

Professional calligraphers or penmen were employed mostly for certificates and engrossing the fair copy of documents such as the Declaration of Independence. In the Germanic areas ornamented certificates were called fractures.

Letter writing was an important skill, for without it no communication was possible over a distance. In general, early in the period literary quality was high, even in mundane areas like court records. With time it deteriorated, becoming perfunctory and businesslike.

Archaic usages were obsolete by the eighteenth century. For example, "thee" and "thou" were long out of use except among Quakers, although they were used in the early seventeenth century. Read some primary sources to get a feel for the language in use at a specific time. Language varied widely with the part of England from which a person, or their ancestors, came. Interestingly, isolated pockets like Tangier Island and Guinea in Virginia still retain period English forms, as do overall regional dialects, such as the New Englander's silent *r* in car.

Spelling was not yet standardized, but phonetic. Many people imparted to their spelling their own local accents. For example, the authors of documents like inventories can be identified as Scots because they list bottles as "buttles" and other spellings following their brogue. Samuel Johnson's *Dictionary* was the first true dictionary. John Adams and Thomas Jefferson argued over whether the correct word was "inalienable" or "unalienable," with Adams winning, not on the floor of Congress, but by quietly "correcting" the printer before publication.

Because there was great variety in English spelling and pronunciation, scholars used Latin throughout the period, but with a general decline in the later period. Although men like Jefferson still employed Latin readily, it was beginning to decline in the face of increased standardization in vernacular English. Through about 1750 most colleges conducted lectures in Latin. Gravestones and other monuments were often, though not always, inscribed in Latin.

One thing that strikes modern readers as unusual at first is any person doing a trade could be designated by simply adding "-er." This resulted in job titles that are more like modern items, like dresser for one who trims something.

The period was good for literature. The seventeenth century saw a small general reading public, but things changed. The rise of an English two-party political system saw the replacement of official censorship with the doctrine of freedom of the press (1695), as both sides needed the press to sway the populace to their view. The publication of magazines such as *Tatler* (1709) and *Spectator* (1711) prepared the public for a new style of literature.

The novel was a new form in the period. Near the end of the period the earliest of our classics appeared. Early the forms were moralistic or instructive, as in Daniel Defoe's *Robinson Crusoe*. The satire was the preeminent early novel form. *Hudibras* by Samuel Butler, *Gulliver's Travels* by Jonathan Swift and Richard Brinsley Sheridan's semiautobiographical play *The Critic* are all good examples.

Johnson published his aforementioned dictionary, and Sheridan's partner-in-crime, James Boswell, set the standard for biographies with his *Life of Johnson*. Historical method was being developed, and David Hume published his *History of Great Britain*. Poetry was highly prized in the early and middle periods, and many amateurs' poems were published in local newspapers.

Even the spoken word had its champions. The classical art of RHETORIC was valued in the early and middle periods, later receiving less emphasis. Serious continental students included J.S. Bach and Frederick the Great. In the colonies, Patrick Henry gave speeches that compare favorably in poetry, evocation and inspiration to the finest work of Shakespeare and was said, in turn, to have been inspired by revival preacher Samuel Davies.

Shakespeare himself was not so favorably received. The middle and late periods saw a move away from the flowery, wordy prose of the late Elizabethans to a very concise, scientific style with a minimal vocabulary. The period from the 1680s to the end saw a flock of revisionists at work gutting his oeuvre. Most presentations of his plays were bastardizations. Still, the themes remained popular. French playwrights, including Molière and Voltaire, were highly regarded, read and studied by the literate (meaning those who read French and had time).

THE THEATER

The development of theater in America followed two distinct routes. The first was through colleges and schools, where plays were given for the purpose of advancing the student's rhetorical abilities. In fact, many of the "plays" presented by the students were really disputations and other practices of rhetoric. In the second course, professional touring companies came from England and visited large towns and cities throughout the new country. Late in the period a third medium arose, in which groups of officers from British regiments stationed here, and other gentlemen, put on amateur productions for the amusement of themselves and selected friends and occasionally for the benefit of some worthy cause.

Records of scholastic theatre begin about 1700, with performances at William and Mary, but references do not become common until the 1750s, when accounts name Philadelphia, the College of New Jersey and Yale. Dartmouth began to be mentioned about 1774.

Theater was a forbidden art form in most Puritan areas until the very late period and was particularly proscribed during the Commonwealth.

Professional theater was not readily available until the 1750s, although occurrences are known as early as the 1720s.

The Hallam Troop came from England to Virginia in 1752, where it opened in Williamsburg with *The Merchant of Venice* and Ravenscroft's *Anatomist, or Sham Doctor* on September 15. It spent a year, then toured the colonies, stopping for some time in New York the next summer. Its repertoire included *Othello*, Farquhar's *The Beaux' Stratagem*, Congreve's *Love for Love*, Steele's *The Conscious Lovers*, Addison's *The Drummer* and Cibber's *The Careless Husband.*

Lewis Hallam's widow married David Douglas in Jamaica in 1758, and they renamed his company The London Company of Comedians and set out on an American tour. Arriving in New York they built their own theater, wrestled with the authorities for a license and finally were allowed to run a short season including Farquhar's *The Beaux' Stratagem* and *Recruiting Officer*, Rowes's *Jane Shore*, Home's *Douglas*, *Othello* with a comic afterpiece, and Cibber's version of *Richard III*. Douglas moved to Philadelphia, where he was strongly opposed by religious leaders but built a theater and renamed his company The American Company of Comedians. He then moved on to Maryland, Virginia, Rhode Island and back to New York, building cheap, flimsy theaters at each stop.

One of Douglas's actors, William Verling, started a troupe called the Virginia Company of Comedians in 1768, and included in their repertoire *The Merchant of Venice* and *Henry IV*, Addison's *The Drummer*, Cibber's *Damon and Phillada*, Colman's *Polly Honeycomb*, Farquhar's *The Constant Couple* and *The Miller of Mansfield*, Garrick's *Miss in Her Teens*, Gay's *The Beggar's Opera*, Moore's *The Gamester*, Murphy's *The Old Maid*, Otway's *Venice Preserved* and *The Orphan*, Ravenscroft's *Anatomist, or Sham Doctor*, Townlye's *High Life Below Stairs* and the anonymous *The Honest Yorkshireman*, *The Bedlamites*, and *The Burgomaster Tricked.*

The above summary gives some idea of the range of drama available to the theatergoer in the late period.

The theaters themselves were small, without prosceniums, and lighted by candles in footlights. They tended to be firetraps. Entry was from the gable end, usually facing the street, with the pit between entry and the stage. Historical plays like Shakespeare were enacted in contemporary dress, costuming being limited to turbans and other identifying marks.

LIBRARIES

Libraries were one of the first educational institutions and served as a point of assembling books and scientific apparatus and forming clubs of intellectuals. The first and largest was the Library Company of Philadelphia, formed in 1739 and using a subscription basis to fund acquisitions. Newport, which had The Society for the Promotion of Knowledge and Virtue by a Free Conversation since 1730, added a library to it after a local benefactor visited Philadelphia. Charles Town founded the Charles Town Library Society in 1748. In 1756 Boston got its first circulating library of twelve hundred volumes with annual dues of £1.8. Many large planters amassed sizable and eclectic libraries and loaned out books within their circle.

SYMBOLISM

The use of symbolism, allegory and allusion pervaded the Renaissance intellect. Visual arts, legal argument, drama and virtually every other aspect of the arts contained a similar wealth of symbolism. The extent to which that symbolism pervaded a culture depended on education, religious background (Catholics would be more acquainted with traditional religious imagery) and how far the culture had progressed to the literal, scientific mode. The more medieval fundamentalist might see a bird's color as implying the work of otherworldly forces, while a more modern gentleman might simply see a new and colorful breed. Classical sources commanded a high status. The bibliography at the end of this chapter contains an excellent source to this subject by James Hall.

CALENDAR

England continued to utilize the obsolete Julian calendar (Old Style) for years after the rest of Europe abandoned it in 1582, because it was politically impossible for Anglican England to accept improvements to the calendar devised under the auspices of the papacy. Finally, on September 3, 1752, the improved Gregorian calendar (New Style) was adopted, redesignating September 3 as September 14 to compensate for errors and moving the start of the New Year from March 25 to January 1. In England there were riots among the lower classes, who believed they were being cheated out of eleven days of their lives.

WEATHER

Although farmers have followed and discussed the weather for centuries, only in the later part of the eighteenth century were many aspects of weather beginning to be understood. Most observers were meticulous, however, and their records allow us to understand events the witnesses did not. After about 1740 some had barometers and thermometers, but nearly all recorded wind direction and shifts, times and other conditions. John Winthrop of Harvard College recorded basic weather data three times a day.

Hurricanes, a discovery of the New World, appeared in the records with the first explorations, having influenced such events as the

217

destruction of Fort Caroline and the search for the Lost Colonists. Still, it was only in 1743 that Franklin, through correspondence with his brother in Boston, connected a northeasterly hurricane with a storm moving in the opposite direction from the wind.

Hurricanes were severe during the period, more like our "century" storms than anything else. They did extensive crop damage, destroyed many structures, uprooted thousands of trees, altered shorelines and the courses of rivers, and caused extensive damage to shipping and much loss of life in fishing fleets. Most major storms are listed in the Time Line which starts on page 6.

Equally important were northeasters, which probably did more damage to shorelines than did hurricanes. These storms rated much less attention, then as now, except in the isolated coastal communities they affected.

In recent history there has been a climatic cycle lasting approximately 150 years. We are just passing the peak of this cycle, but several notable events, including the Starving Time at Jamestown and the winters at Valley Forge and Jockey Hollow, fall near the bottom. Phillip Vickers Fithian's *Journal* records a killing frost in mid-June, 1775, on the Northern Neck of Virginia, where today the last chance of frost is officially mid-May. This cycle affected crops, military ventures and the earliest settlement.

Within the larger patterns of the weather, regions have their own infamous features. The Chesapeake Bay is known for severe squalls, usually formed by a line storm and contributing to many fatalities among watermen and passengers on ferries. The fogs of New England were well known and dangerous to those who made their living on the waters. Mariners avoided the offshore shoals of North Carolina's Outer Banks, with its onshore winds and frequent fogs.

As today, differing climatic zones influenced crops and growing seasons. In using modern sources, compensate for the cycle mentioned above, subtracting about four degrees, and present patterns should be fairly applicable.

Before rapid communications, weather prediction relied more on traditional methods like observing woolly bear caterpillars, wind shifts and clouds. Farmers were sensitive to the habits of animals, both domestic and wild, as they often indicated weather trends (for example, deer feeding in the middle of a snowstorm tend to indicate the storm will be long and hard).

TIMEKEEPING

Through most of the period clocks were rare and unreliable. Some Germanic pedestal clocks had existed since the sixteenth century, but the escapement (mechanism used to regulate the clock) common through the early period was only accurate to plus or minus twenty 20 minutes a day. A short pendulum clock was invented but was not much better. The long pendulum introduced about 1700 made the first really reliable clocks, which became known as tall case clocks. Some fine examples were made by South Jersey craftsmen, and Connecticut became known for its clockmakers, both near the end of the period. Before that time townspeople relied on the town clock, often in the church steeple, and travelers relied on sundials. Short-term timing was done with a sandglass (hourglass). Most farmers and craftsmen regulated their day by the hours of daylight, making long days in summer and shorter ones in winter.

PHYSICS

During this period Newton produced his work in areas such as mechanics and the properties of light, taking knowledge that light could be split into its parts with a prism and showing that it could also be recombined into white light. His work on the calculus rendered many earlier problems solvable. Of nearly equal mind was Robert Hook, whose explorations were at least as diverse. Philadelphian David Rittenhouse, in the late period, was a world-class mathematician and astronomer.

In the end, Benjamin Franklin's reputation for his studies in electricity, certainly his own most consuming interest, had a worth for the new country payable in muskets, francs, men and ships, for Franklin was esteemed in France above all others on the basis of his reputation, and his embassy there was highly successful.

During the Revolution David Bushnell built the first operative submersible, the Turtle, which sortied against the British fleet in New York harbor in 1775 but could not attach its mine to the British hull because of copper plating designed to protect the hull from worms. Bushnell then turned his attention to floating mines, and in 1777 he and Francis Hopkinson let loose a mine barrage on the British fleet in Philadelphia. As the mines floated down the river, the entire fleet fired to detonate them. The ensuing Battle of the Kegs was a major psychological victory for the beleaguered colonists.

CHEMISTRY

The colonial period saw major if fundamental progress in chemistry. Chemistry was already fairly advanced as a coincidental sideline to alchemy, whose ends were separate but whose experimental basis was similar. With the advent of manufactures and an increasingly technological society, chemistry passed from knowledge of a few ores and compositions to a more universal, systematic science. Most of this progress took place in the middle to late periods and would have been slow to reach the average person.

NATURAL SCIENCES

The natural sciences were one of the first to be systematically explored in the New World, and the colonies had their share of resident or visiting talent. Many discoveries were made by physicians, who began with the first colonists and continued to collect new plant specimens and interview Indians about medical properties. Naturalists active in the colonies included William Bartram, John Bannister, Cadwallader Colden and Mark Catesby.

Far more wild animals lived throughout the colonies than we are accustomed to think of. Wolves, cougars, black bears, bison (buffalo, east to near the modern-day District of Columbia and the Shenandoah Valley), deer, bobcats, lynx, foxes, raccoons, opossums, porcupines (south to the Potomac), alligators (north to North Carolina), skunks, otters, beavers, badgers, muskrats and many smaller mammals, several strange new snakes including rattlesnakes, water moccasins and copperheads, and a multitude of birds unfathomable to us today were common.

ACADEMIES

Scientific exploration of all kinds was sponsored or monitored by both English and French academies, and communicated to others. Cooperation between the English and French academies was so close that special arrangements through a surreptitious route were made to forward letters captured at sea during times of war, which implies well-known unofficial channels for other commerce existed.

BIBLIOGRAPHY

Burke, James. *The Day the Universe Changed.* Boston: Little, Brown, 1985. The accompaniment to a PBS series, this deals with changes in thinking and science through and beyond the period.

Dolmetsch, Joan D., ed. *Eighteenth-Century Prints in Colonial America: To Educate and Decorate.* Williamsburg, Va.: Colonial Williamsburg Foundation, 1979.

Fowble, E. McSherry. *To Please Every Taste: Eighteenth-Century Prints from the Winterthur Museum.* Alexandria, Va.: Art Services International, 1991.

Girouard, Mark. *Life in the English Country House: A Social and Architectural History.* New Haven: Yale University Press, 1978.

Hall, James. *Dictionary of Subjects and Symbols in Art.* New York: Harper and Row, 1974. Good browsing, great cross-references.

Hauser, Arnold. *The Social History of Art.* Translated by Kenneth J. Northcott. Chicago: University of Chicago Press, 1982.

Hindle, Brooke. *The Pursuit of Science in Revolutionary America, 1735–1789.* Chapel Hill: University of North Carolina Press, 1956.

Hogarth, William. *Hogarth: The Complete Engravings, by Joseph Burke and Colin Caldwell.* New York: H.N. Abrams, 196–.

Kaufman, Charles H. *The Music of Eighteenth-Century New Jersey.* New Jersey's Revolutionary Experience, no. 11. Trenton, N.J.: New Jersey Hisotrical Society, 1975.

Kirk, John T. *American Furniture and the British Tradition to 1830.* New York: Alfred A. Knopf, 1982. A comprehensive study of furniture with many pictures; design, carving and other details explored.

Lederer, Richard M. *Colonial American English: A Glossary.* Essex, Conn.: Verbatim Book, 1985. A dictionary of early terms, most with primary source examples. Good browsing, but the more obscure terms may not help your reader.

Ludlum, David M. *Early American Hurricanes, 1492–1870.* Boston: American Meteorological Society, 1963.

McCrum, Robert, William Cran and Robert MacNeil. *The Story of English.* New York: Viking, 1986. This companion volume to a PBS series contains good information about immigration patterns, literature and themes in language.

Miles, Ellen G., ed. *The Portrait in Eighteenth-Century America.* Newark, Del.: University of Delaware Press, 1993.

Moody, Richard. *Dramas from the American Theatre, 1762–1909.* Cleveland: World Pub. Co., 1966. Short introductory essays with scripts for a few early plays including *The Candidate*, a play written by Virginia Burgess about electioneering.

Thornton, Peter. *Seventeenth-Century Interior Decoration in England, France and Holland.* New Haven: Yale University Press, 1978.

Vaughn, Jack A. *Early American Dramatists: From the Beginnings to 1900.* New York: Frederick Ungar Co., 1981.

Wertenbaker, Thomas J. *The Golden Age of Colonial Culture.* Westport, Conn.: Greenwood Press, 1980.

Wright, Louis B. *The Arts in America: The Colonial Period.* New York: Charles Scribner's, 1966. Architecture, painting, decorative arts.

CHAPTER THIRTEEN

Farming, Fishing, Trapping & Laborers

FARMING

Despite the attention paid to craftsmen like the great cabinetmakers of Philadelphia and Boston, and the shipping businesses and merchants in New England, the vast bulk of the population were farmers. Farms were those producing food crops, including subsistence farms. Plantations, on the other hand, were simply any size farm that produced marketable crops such as tobacco. The subtle shades of meaning changed with time. Early, all the colonies were known as plantations; later, "farm" became a more common term up north, since, in fact, most small farmers in this region grew food and were often little above subsistence level. Those that did grow flax for textiles processed it before selling it as thread and lived off the food they grew, allowing "farm" to still be appropriate.

In a good year in a typical preindustrial Western society, it took seven farmers to grow food for every ten consumers. By comparison a typical hunter-gatherer spent about two hours per day providing food, so a strong incentive existed for wilding (going to live with the Indians). Changes were under way in agriculture, including the beginnings of crop rotation and early study of fertilizing, but these ideas were slow to catch on here, and it was almost the Civil War before any significant progress was made.

Both farms and plantations were generally small, about 250 acres maximum size, since more acreage could not be successfully cultivated by a single family. Larger tracts did exist but were in the minority. Fields on smaller farms were planted right up to the door of the house, as labor to keep the grass mown was expensive. If the farm kept sheep or goats, they could crop the lawn.

Cultivation tended to follow the Indian style of mounding up piles of earth with a hoe, then planting corn, beans and squash in the same

A barn raising at Quiet Valley Living Historical Farm in Stroudsburg, Pennsylvania. The practice of the community coming together to help in work too heavy for any individual to do alone spans the centuries just as does the costuming at this volunteer work session. The outer wall of the pegged barn frame is being lifted into place, and a heavy beetle or maul is being used to persuade one timber to line up properly. Meanwhile, the women would be working together on food or other essentials, making major social events of work.

mound. The corn grew out of the top, the beans used the corn as a pole and the squash covered the ground around the mound to prevent weeds from growing. By planting a fish in each mound, the crops were fertilized. Tending the field meant keeping weeds from growing on the mounds. The remainder of the field could be ignored, and tree stumps could be left in place. This saved labor. The mound system required only minimal tools: hoes (broad, for mounding; digging, heavier for cutting into the earth; and grubbing, or narrow for weeding among desired plants) and digging sticks. With these and an ax, saw and froe, a farmer could survive.

All but the poorest farmers, however, used other tools. Most had specialized axes, like the mortising ax used to cut narrow holes in fence rails, felling axes with wide bits to cut into a tree, limbing axes with a narrower bit for better control and broad axes for squaring timber. A bill hook (brush hook) was a J-shaped blade on the end of a handle, useful for clearing brush and small trees. Beetles (mauls) were made out of timber found lying around, by trimming out a handle while leaving a thick end as a hammer head. Splitting wedges were cut from wood.

If stock were kept, hay might be grown, and hay forks or pitchforks with two tines and dung forks with three were used. These were made out of saplings split at the end and splayed out. Shovels or spades with wooden blades and iron shoes (sheaths at the end of the blade) were also common. Hay and grains were cut with scythes or reaping hooks (sickles), bound into shucks or stacked, and cured. Placing green or wet hay in a barn caused spontaneous combustion. Most period stacks were made around a pole, and during the winter the animals would eat from the bottom until the stacks looked like giant mushrooms.

Tobacco was a labor-intensive crop. One man could cultivate only about three to five acres per year. Tobacco was also planted in mounds, placed about four to six feet apart. After planting, it was necessary to pick tobacco cutworms (large, white caterpillars) and tobacco hawks (yellow caterpillars with a single horn) off the plants and crush them between the fingers. This was a job for children. In Virginia only the top few leaves were picked, this being the best grade tobacco, comparable to what is used in pipes and cigars today. Elsewhere, with poorer quality production, planters picked the whole crop in an effort to increase their profit to match what Virginia could get from its few higher-priced leaves. Each acre yielded approximately five hundred pounds of tobacco if the entire plant was picked. After picking, the leaves were hung on poles carried between two people and placed in a drying barn to cure.

When fully dry, tobacco was packed in hogsheads carrying about nine hundred pounds for shipment to market. Small planters jobbed their product to large planters for consolidation. Tobacco wore out the soil in about three years, which required about seven years fallow to return. For this reason, small amounts of acreage were kept in cultivation at once, and new land was continually being cleared by cutting trees and burning over the underbrush. Crop rotation was not yet generally practiced.

Wheat, rye, oats, barley and other European grain crops were slow to catch on, only coming into their own in the middle and late periods and then only in the more northern colonies down to the Chesapeake. The use of plows was difficult in New England's rocky soil. In the limestone areas west of Philadelphia (Lancaster County), where the Germanics settled, and the coastal plains of the Jerseys, however, plows did work, and there European grain crops became a staple. These areas became the breadbasket of the colonies. Plows did not work well on newly cleared land, with tree stumps, roots and rocks, so they tended to be used later.

Rice and indigo were the two main crops of the Deep South. Rice

RICE EXPORTS FROM THE AMERICAN COLONIES, IN MILLIONS OF POUNDS	
1712	3.144
1726	10.754
1732	25.363
1740	40.447
1750	30.806
1760	53.342
1770	76.511
1783	30.987

was grown in those areas with swamp lands where tidal fresh-water rivers could be used to irrigate the swamps, commonly along the coast of Georgia and around Charles Town. Rice cultivation required some rather specialized constructions. Dikes were built to keep the salt waters out of the swamps. If a hurricane or other disaster allowed salt water into the rice fields, it was several years before a crop could again be grown. Refer to the time line to see a series of major storms. Muskrats and alligators, among others, often undercut dikes and allowed them to be breached. Within the large diked areas, smaller fields were set off, and these were divided with a series of canals for irrigation and drainage. Heavy gates, like the doors on locks, were mounted on the riverside to allow control of river waters into the fields.

Field preparation for rice growing began in January and February, with oxen used to plow and harrow the soft ground. Planting took place between March and May, when the fields were flooded and drained in a highly controlled sequence. Then came the harvest, when the rice was stacked into sheaves. A sheaf forty-five feet by twelve feet produced about one thousand bushels of rice. The season was broken while food crops were harvested. In November and December the rice was threshed and winnowed, dropped from a tower through a breeze to separate the chaff. Rice was primarily shipped to Iberia and the Mediterranean. Many Africans were conversant with rice cultivation and contributed their expertise to the process in the New World.

Indigo was not successfully grown in the colonies until Eliza Lucas's crop of 1739. Her first successful extraction of dyestuff was in 1744. She quickly distributed seeds to others in the Charles Town community. In 1747 South Carolina exported 138,300 pounds of indigo. In 1749 Parliament offered a bounty of six pence per pound on colonial production (effective March 28). A decline in production came in the

1750s as superior French and Spanish indigo became available, but the French and Indian War was a boon to the colonial planters. Indigo was probably the most profitable North American colonial agricultural product. Originally a partner for rice, indigo later moved inland independently.

Small plantations cultivated between ten and twenty-five acres in indigo, large plantations forty to ninety-five acres. A single slave could work between one and two acres, producing between twenty-six and one hundred pounds of dye. The plant, a perennial legume growing to about eight feet tall, produced three to five cuttings per year between March and November.

Indigo was extracted in a series of large (typically $4' \times 4' \times 12'$) vats, usually made of heavy timbers. One set of vats could handle the produce of seven to eight acres. Indigo plants were cut and placed in the first (steeping or fermenting) vat, where they were crushed under heavy timbers. A pump alongside this vat was used to fill the vat and rot the plant for between eight and twenty-four hours, until the brew effervesced strongly. Then the plug was pulled from the bottom of the vat, where it overhung the next vat, and the slurry drained into the second vat, called a battery (beating vat). A catalyst (human urine, lime water or, later, potash) was added. The mix was agitated by slaves using bottomless buckets like churns until sediment began to form. The sediment was then allowed to settle, the waste water tapped off the top and the remaining concentrate emptied via a bung into the third (evaporation) vat to thicken. Prolonged exposure to the vapors of this vat was believed to be fatal to workers. After the sediment was reasonably dry it was placed in conical bags and hung in the shade while water drained off; then the paste was put in boxes to dry, during which time it was turned three to four times a day to dry thoroughly while boys fanned it to keep damaging flies off the product.

The process stank, and it was difficult to place houses nearer than one quarter mile from the vats. Vats were usually placed downwind from habitations. Flies swarmed around the vats, tormenting animals and humans alike. Even chickens were difficult to keep on an indigo plantation.

Flax, the fiber from which linen was made, was an important domestic industry in New England, and cultivation was required by law at certain times.

Rats and mice were common problems to grain farmers, who used both cats and snakes to keep them at bay. Some granaries or corncribs were built off the ground, allowing easy viewing of pests trying to climb in, and some farmers would fence cats underneath. Blacksnakes were recruited by placing out a tray of milk, which attracted the snakes' prey. Birds destroyed grain on the stalk and so were vigorously hunted, with the take added to the stew pot. Still, huge flocks could strip a field bare in a matter of minutes. A single deer could devastate a cornfield, but, as long as the mast crop was good, they tended to stay in the woods.

Fences were erected to keep animals out of fields and gardens. In timber-rich areas like the South, snake or zigzag fences were common, using split rails laid directly on the ground and stacked one upon the other. These required little labor other than splitting the wood cleared off the land. Although the wooden fences rotted quickly, the tobacco just as quickly required new land to be cleared. In areas where stone was common, stones from the field were laboriously cleared, and dry stone walls were built. New Englanders joked about growing a new crop of stones each spring because frost heave and cultivation moved new ones to the surface. Stiles were openings in the fences or stairs over them constructed so people could pass through but cattle and horses could not.

Livestock was the basis of the diet. During the period the diet changed from a heavy reliance on mutton, traditionally a by-product of the woolen industry, to beef and pork. Wolves and panthers were still common, and sheep were easier prey than the larger cattle and more violent swine.

Most livestock was allowed to run wild, rounded up and harvested as needed. America's wild hogs are descended from European stock managed in this way; they also look like typical hogs of the colonial period. Islands were the preferred places to put stock, because predators could be eradicated and the stock could not range too far. Unseasonable floods could destroy an area's entire stock.

Many small farms had a milking cow. This usually required owning at least one other animal, be it goat, sheep, horse or cattle, as cattle are social animals. Milk cows were kept contained and required milking morning and night.

Cattle were classified according to breeding status. Oxen and steer were castrated male bovine used respectively for work and meat, while a bull was breeding stock. An adolescent male bovine was a kip, a juvenile bovine calf. A heifer was an unbred female, a cow one that had been bred. All milk producers were cows. These terms transferred laterally as slang for women.

Sheep were shorn each spring after the weather warmed, allowing them comfort during the summer and a reasonable growth of wool by fall. Tails were not docked, a practice that developed later to avoid the animals' soiling their own fur with dried dung. Children picked dung out of a fleece before carding. Already different breeds were being developed for meat and wool.

Goats were common at first, providing both milk and meat without the space concerns entailed in transshipment (to the colonies) by cattle. Goats are hardier than cattle; they also do not mind being alone the way cows do. A preponderance of female goats was preferred. Male goats go into must, equivalent to heat, and exude a heavy scent much like a skunk's that imbues anyone coming into contact with them.

Livestock was marked with ear and sometimes nose notches, which were recorded at the courthouse, so the herd could be properly divided. Each farmer in an area had his own pattern of notches. In the fall roundup new stock was proportionately divided. Brands were not yet common.

Farmers raised a large amount of fowl for the table and for eggs. Pigeons (squab), chicken, guinea hens, Cornish hens and ducks were all domesticated. They were kept in fenced yards with henhouses attached, or dovecotes built either as freestanding buildings or in the gable ends of stables and other outbuildings. Fowl were killed by wringing their necks or chopping off their heads, then the bird was scalded, plucked, cleaned and ready for cooking.

FISHING

The earliest immigrants were poor fishermen. Even in New England, where fishing would become a major industry, the Indians had to teach the settlers how to fish. Most fishing in the period was done from small boats, often rowed by a single fisherman.

By comparison, the exploitation of the cod found in the Grand Banks off Newfoundland was a major industry for both the west of England and the French from before the English colonial period. The Spanish, particularly the Basques, had been involved but were driven out by competition. In this area an ongoing fight ensued between factions in London intent on colonization and the fishermen intent on leaving the coast wild to promote the fisheries. The fishermen won, and by 1735 England was sending approximately twenty thousand tons of fish from this area, about 95 percent of which went to foreign, mostly Iberian and Italian, markets.

The major force that made salt cod profitable—and its profits never really collapsed—was the shortage of cereals in the market areas, which required a protein staple and found it in cod.

New England did not develop its fisheries quickly. Beginning in the 1630s, helped along by the instability of the Civil War, and developing strength into the next century, New England became a major fishing center. Earlier, New Englanders had done some subsistence fishing from small boats close inshore. Most New Englanders did not come from the areas of England with fishing traditions.

NEW NETHERLANDS FUR PRODUCTION (NUMBER OF FURS)	
1625	5,758
1626	8,130
1627	7,890
1631	7,126
1633	15,174
1656	35,000
1660	25,000

Most offshore fishing was done by small by-boats, stationed off the coast of Newfoundland, that caught the fish and then sold them to sack ships which delivered the product to market. Fishing was done with baited set lines and some nets.

The fisheries were seen as a major source of manpower for the British Navy. By law, one-third of the crew of by-boats must have been fresh men, either novices or one-year veterans, while sack boats were required to have 20 percent fresh. During times of war enemy navies preyed upon the fishing fleet, and there was stiff competition from the French fishermen through the 1720s. An occasional hurricane caused terrific loss of life on the banks.

A seasonal whaling industry also developed in the mid-seventeenth century along Cape Cod, where small boats within the Bay chased mostly pilot whales, using techniques similar to those used by the chase boats dispatched from the large factory ships in the heyday of whaling. Whaling was an industry dominated by the Dutch, however, who took thousands of whales each year and supplied most of the whale bone, oil or train oil needed by England for its cloth industries, lighting and soap.

Oysters and clams were harvested by tonging, using long-handled rakes doubled like pliers to grab the shells on the bottom and pull them into a small boat.

FUR TRAPPING

Furs were one of the major products of the colonies. The number of furs exported out of French and, later, English Canada greatly exceeded any exports from the East Coast colonies. The Dutch in New York were the largest exporters there, with Pennsylvania and then the Chesapeake next, although New England relied on furs briefly.

Fur had traditionally come from Russia and had been an upper-class product. During the seventeenth century the ready availability of American furs made them more of a bourgeois product. Beaver fur was felted into material for hats. Felting had centers in Amsterdam, Paris and, after 1629, London.

New England relied on fur early, it being one of the products that enabled Massachusetts to continue to operate. One man sent nine thousand skins to England in the five years ending in 1657. As population grew, it forced the fur-bearing animals out, and the industry declined.

In the South, deerskins augmented beaver. In the middle period when Virginia developed the fur industry, its annual exports ran about two thousand skins, but in 1712 it was forty thousand skins. After 1705 the major part of William and Mary's support came from a tax on skins. South Carolina in the same period averaged one thousand a year.

A conservative estimate has the Americas exporting about three hundred thousand skins a year by 1700, including those exported by New France (Canada). By 1704 overproduction caused prices to drop and furs to lie rotting at trading posts.

Much of the fur traded came from the Indians, and the Dutch and French liberally traded guns to them for the purpose of aiding the trade. The Dutch and French colonies' economies were based on the fur trade, not settlement. In fact, the two enterprises often opposed each other. Most English were aghast at the idea of trading guns to the Indians, fearing the Indians might use the guns against the English. Neither New France nor New Netherlands had large populations and so were less threatening to the Indians than the English plantations were. After England took over New Netherlands, the Iroquois and other tribes reacted strongly to restrictions on guns, and the English finally had to relent and allow trade in firearms. Most colonies enacted licenses to trade with the Indians, mostly with limited success. See the bibliography at the end of this chapter for more information.

SERVITUDE

"Servant" was a generic term used for paid staff, apprentices, indentures and slaves, all of whom were, in fact, servants. In general, servants lived and worked in a specific area. The experience of servants varied widely among areas and economic levels.

Most were employed in the field. On the smaller plantations, servants would live among the family in their one-room house and work alongside the family in the field. For these owners, a servant probably represented one to five years' gross income. Servants and slaves both

ESTIMATED SLAVE IMPORTATION FOR ALL THE AMERICAS, INCLUDING NEW SPAIN (ABOUT 66 PERCENT) AND THE CARIBBEAN	
1601–1650	373,000
1650–1675	368,000
1675–1700	600,000
1700–1800	7,659,000
Total	approx. 9,000,000

cost about five to six pounds to import. A slave might sell for thirty pounds or more, and estimates for indentures run as high as seventeen pounds.

On the larger plantations field hands might live in the field buildings or in quarters. Here, they were a relatively autonomous work force.

In the house, whether in town or on a plantation, servants lived where they worked. Servants slept in the passage outside the rooms they were responsible for, on mats that rolled up during the day. Kitchen staff lived upstairs in the kitchen, stable hands in the stable. Apprentices lived in the shops. On larger plantations and up north, many slaves became skilled craftsmen.

Because servants kept few journals, documentary evidence of their lives is scarce, and because they lived among the class that employed them, except field hands on the larger plantations, archaeological evidence of their existence is difficult to find. What evidence is found is intriguing. Even field hands tended to get hand-me-downs of pottery and other material items, so although the items were old, out-of-date and damaged, they were high quality in make. In the finer homes, house servants, footmen and the like were often dressed in fine livery (uniforms), well trained and educated, for all these factors reflected well on the owners. All this applies equally to slaves and other servants.

Indentured Servants and Slaves

Indentured servants or indentures were those under some form of contract (indenture) to work for a specified period of time in exchange for some advantage or other. Most signed indentures with a ship's captain to pay for passage to the New World, which was bought and assigned at the destination by a colonist. Others might work to settle a debt, be under court order or be a prisoner transported out of England. Indentures were considered binding, and the servants thus bound, or not free. The major difference between indentures and slaves was that indentures could hope to one day be free. Technically, indentures enjoyed more rights under the law, but in practice slaves had limited recourse in certain specific cases.

The similarity between indentures and slaves creates some great paradoxes. The conditions under which indentures came to the colonies were not much better than those under which slaves traveled. Colony-born slaves, having a natural resistance to local diseases, probably were more valuable and thus better cared for than immigrant indentures who were likely to die within the first six to twenty-four months. Since the owner of either had invested a considerable amount that he had to recoup, his chance of doing so was greater in the case of the slave, who might live seventy years, than in that of the indenture who might live two. On an economic basis, then, exploitation may have been worse in the case of the indenture. In some places indentures who ran away were punished with death, in others with a doubling or other extension of their period of service.

Colonies had different policies about the end of an indenture's service. In some, the headright system gave indentures land, while in others it went to the owner. In most cases law required indentures to be given a suit of clothing and an extra shirt, hoes, axes and other fundamental tools, some basic foodstuffs, and then their freedom. In practice, enforcement was lax, and some were simply turned out.

Not allowing for mortality, to maintain the numbers of servants working in the American and Leeward Island colonies in the 1670s required an estimated three thousand to four thousand new servants each year.

By the end of the seventeenth century, indentures were considered worthless compared to slaves, as indentures were often loathe to work and quick to die, and proportionate immigration dropped off considerably. Quality of life for all servants seems to have been determined by whether slaves or indentures were more common. In the early period, when slaves were uncommon, both were treated more as indentures; later, they were treated more as slaves. Slave importations rose only near the end of the seventeenth century.

The earliest Africans brought to the colonies in 1619 were sold as indentures, and the process continued until slavery became legally established. In the interim, some interesting twists occurred. While communities of free blacks continued through the Civil War, black indentures gradually became de facto slaves. In one case on the Eastern Shore of Virginia and Maryland, Anthony Johnson, a free black planter, owned African slaves before slavery was legalized and sued a white planter to obtain return of his slave property when that planter allegedly stole it under false pretenses. He won. Another case is known of a slave buying his freedom by purchasing indentures and assigning them to his master. Unfortunately, such exploits became virtually impossible after 1700.

On the large plantations that had separate slave quarters, slaves had slightly more autonomy than they would have had in town. In the slave quarters they were better able to maintain African traditions and some semblance of familiar life, which was impossible to do among the whites in the big house. Even though the material standards of living were better in the big house, going there meant cultural isolation, and the standards in the fields were not generally worse than in Africa. Quarters were usually set up after an African pattern of round fences and round tracts of land, not the geometric squares of the English.

Midway between the field and the house was the foreman, a slave placed in management over the other slaves. He generally received a separate cabin near the quarters and finer material wealth. But he, too, paid a price: He was no longer welcome among other slaves and was responsible for carrying out discipline including branding, whipping, slicing off ears or tongues, and the like. His was a solitary existence with nowhere to go.

Comparable to the foreman was the overseer, a white manager who ran a plantation for an absentee owner. These were most common in the Deep South, where economic factors contributed to a different kind of slavery.

In and north of the Chesapeake, slaves engaged in one-season cultivation or mercantile or craft work. In the deep South, rice and indigo were raised in rotation, one in summer and one in winter. Unlike labor-intensive tobacco, both crops were raised in large, swampy fields where alligators, snapping turtles, poisonous snakes, malaria and other diseases were prevalent. As a result, labor mortality was substantially higher, but the great returns from these crops allowed a steady purchase of new labor. Add in the concerns of the overseers to obtain a quick return, a portion of which was theirs, and get back to England before they died, and the result was a more exploitive, less humane situation. Slaves in the deep South did not live as long as their Northern counterparts.

UNSKILLED LABOR

Most laborers other than farmers worked in other occupations. Carters and teamsters loaded, unloaded and drove carts and wagons. Sailors sailed ships and loaded and unloaded them. Housewrights needed laborers to dig foundations, miners dug ores and axmen cut timber for sawyers, charcoal burners and others. The main distinction in purely laboring occupations is they were nonskilled, which precludes housewrights and other skilled trades from this classification.

COMMENTARY ON THE
TRADITIONAL VIEW OF SLAVERY

Common knowledge and documented law says slaves were not allowed guns for fear they would rebel. But archaeological work at Middleton Place, South Carolina—right in the most exploitive area—shows slaves were routinely given guns to shoot the vast flocks of birds that raided the rice crops. These birds in turn became a major source of variety in the diet of the slaves, as were turtles, muskrats and other game common to the swampy fields.

Similarly, the North would have us believe slaves did not exist there, but in fact the New England colonies legalized slavery before Virginia did. The middle colonies, where the Dutch were prevalent, had many slaves. Northern areas, particularly those with seaports such as Portsmouth, New Hampshire, are reevaluating the extent of local slaveholding and rewriting older interpretations as information grows that slavery in these distinct communities was often much more pervasive than previously thought.

Much of what we think we know about slavery is the result of propaganda circulated during the nineteenth century when crops, economies and conditions had changed substantially from the colonial period and the issue of slavery became a major political issue, much like abortion is today. Worst-case examples were described as common occurrences. Atrocities and mistreatments did occur, but they represented a statistically smaller portion of the population than some records suggest.

The instances of cruelty have counterexamples. Fithian records in his journal (see bibliography at the end of the time line) how Robert Carter, one of the wealthiest men in Virginia and a member of the governor's council, banned another gentleman from his plantation because the other gentleman chained his slave to his carriage during a visit. Carter ultimately manumitted (freed) his slaves, and his attitudes were not unique.

Restrictions were placed on slaves. Because slavery was only allowed against persons who were not Christian, allowing slaves to convert would have made it impossible to keep them in bondage. Likewise, marriage, as a Christian ceremony, was not allowed. Slaves continued with their traditional marriage ceremonies, including jumping forward together over a broom (divorce was jumping backwards), and attempted to form strong family groups. Unfortunately, although planters allowed the Sabbath off, during which slaves might walk many miles to visit family, slave families were not recognized by the owners. Many owners tried to keep families together, but death, economic pressures or discipline might require families to be sold apart. The better owners might attempt to sell locally to allow the family the opportunity to stay in touch, but this was not always possible.

Owners of slaves or indentures probably never amounted to much more than 10 percent of the population of any given area. Traditional Southern attitudes toward blacks can be traced to the period when the possibility of slaves being freed, and thus competing for jobs and land, became a real threat to the existence of the nonslaveholding classes. This was well after the colonial period.

The ethical questions about slavery grew throughout the period. In the colonies, under influence from Quaker activists in England and locally, distinguishing the fine line between holding property and holding people as property became important. The Deep South, most dependent on slavery, held out for economic reasons, but many in Virginia and north manumitted their slaves. The abolition of slavery became a major debate during the drafting of the Declaration of Independence but was finally dropped to ensure unanimity.

In sum, the efforts of the colonies' African population, whether voluntary or not, made major contributions to the growth of the colonies. In addition, although different from our current standards of living, the standards under which they labored were not all that different from the standards under which most of the European population lived and worked. Thus, with the exception of the unique legal (and sometimes, in the case of quartered communities, social) environment of slaves, what is valid in this book for the European commoners is equally applicable to Africans.

BIBLIOGRAPHY

Breen, T.H. and Stephen Innes. *Myne Owne Ground: Race and Freedom on Virginia's Eastern Shore, 1640–1676.* New York: Oxford University Press, 1980.

Davies, K.G. *The North Atlantic World in the Seventeenth Century.* Minneapolis: University of Minnesota Press, 1974.

Ferguson, Leland G. *Uncommon Ground: Archaeology and Early African America, 1650–1800.* Washington, D.C.: Smithsonian Institution Press, 1992.

CHAPTER FOURTEEN

Trades

APPRENTICESHIPS

S killed labor produced all the goods needed during this period. In the factories of England people worked at specialized jobs, becoming highly skilled at a very narrow, repetitive task. In the colonies this was not common, because labor was scarce and the market substantially smaller, so most craftsmen diversified.

A young man learned his trade by being apprenticed to a master craftsman, which as a contractual obligation bound him until its completion. Usually, he apprenticed between his fourteenth and sixteenth birthday and was bound until his age of majority (twenty-one). In exchange for teaching him his trade, the mathematics necessary to run a business, and how to read, usually stipulated as adequate to read the Bible, the apprentice lived with and worked for the master, who provided him with room, board, clothing and, upon completion of the apprenticeship, a set of basic tools and often a small cash payment.

About 1747 *The London Tradesman* was published to guide parents in selecting a trade for their child. It described physical requirements and other attributes. The young man had probably been running errands for a while and likely already had a preference.

As with other servants, the apprentice usually slept in or above the shop and was responsible for opening it, lighting a fire in the morning, gathering wood and water, and performing other necessary chores. At first, especially with younger boys, these were the only tasks other than some simple but labor-intensive operations. With time, as his overall familiarity with a trade grew, as well as his strength and manual coordination, he began to learn the trade, which took two to four years. Then he practiced, building up his skill and speed to commercial levels and repaying the master through his production for the time, materials and maintenance he had cost.

At the end of the apprenticeship he produced a proof piece, which, in England, would have been shown to the aldermen or elders of the guild for his trade. If it passed inspection for competence, he was awarded the title of journeyman (from the French for day) and free to work for anyone for wages, being paid by the day, hence the name. That he was free to journey in search of work was coincidental.

Under the guild system, he had to remain a journeyman for three to five years, after which he could produce a masterpiece for review. If this was found to be of adequate quality, the aldermen next reviewed the business environment to determine if their market had room for another shop. If so, the journeyman was accorded the title of MASTER, which conveyed the right to open a shop.

Because of the straitened economies of much of England, many journeymen could not become masters, and some were unwilling to marry the master's daughter (finding her, for one reason or another, unsuitable as a wife) and wait for him to die to inherit his shop. The master may have had a son in the business, negating even that. The lack of opportunity in England became the colonies' blessing.

Many journeymen could afford to emigrate to the colonies where they were needed. Here the guild system did not exist and any journeyman with the means could become a master. Even widows who inherited a shop could run it with the title of master as long as they did not remarry. In the South, where skilled labor was in especially short supply, a good craftsman could readily acquire enough wealth to purchase indentures, gain land and become a planter, where the real money was to be made. He could still fall back on his skills, and if he acquired slaves and taught them his skill, he could hire them out at a premium. Such self-made men had little respect for the stifling system they had experienced in England.

A good example is the "Poor Potter" of Virginia. Shortly after immigrating he began a brewery, then opened a huge pottery factory. By the time he died some 9 years later he was a member of the lower gentry.

Still, labor was the least expensive part of a product. The mass-production shops in England produced tools, shoes, textiles and other goods at lower prices than the colonies. As a result, much of the local trade was in repairs, the materials in the item being more expensive than the cost of labor to fix it. Within each region there still existed a need for made items and a pool of skilled artisans up to the task of providing them.

Three skills were essential to the colonists: blacksmiths, who made and repaired tools and implements, shoemakers, who made footgear, and coopers, who made wooden barrels and other containers. These skills were found in most settlements up North, and on the larger plantations in the South. Other trades, with more restricted markets, were found in the larger centers in both areas.

LEATHERWORKING

Tanning

Leather was to the colonists what plastic is to us. The primary raw material came from meat animals and was tanned, or treated by immersion in a slurry of tanbark containing tannin derived from (oak or chestnut) bark. The rather smelly process was usually located in tanyards outside of town, on the prevailing downwind side.

Tanners first fleshed the raw material (hard, like a dog's chew toy), removed the hair if desired, then immersed the material in succeedingly stronger baths of tannin. They also dyed and curried it with waxes or grease if desired. When finished they had leather. All leatherworkers risked potential exposure to anthrax (hoof-and-mouth) and tetanus (lockjaw).

Hides are from large animals, while skins are from small ones. The most common hide was from steer, as these were slaughtered for meat at prime, when the skin was best. Cows lived too long. Elk, moose and bison hides were occasionally tanned. Most everything else was a skin, and most everything else was used. Among others, calf, kip (adolescent steer), sheep, goat, pig, shark (known as shagreen), dolphin, rayfish, other fish, dog (used for the finest dancing shoes), snake, lizard, deer, bear, chicken (used for fans) and even human (rare, by consent, usually bequeathed in a will for covering a family bible), were all used during the period. SLUNK was unborn calf tanned with the hair on and was used for covering trunks and boxes. BUFF or BUFFLE was not bison but true buffalo, tawed in alum to produce a white surface (so buff really means white) used in military gear. RUSSIA LEATHER was calf or goatskin tanned in sumac, which gave it a particular color, and was used for covering chairs.

Shoemaking

Shoemakers were the most important leather tradesmen. A shoemaker was not the same as a cobbler, who was a simple repairman, usually itinerant. To call a shoemaker a cobbler would be insulting. Shoemakers had about five more years of training than cobblers had. Shoemakers made shoes and may also have made many other leather products. Saddles and harnesses required special knowledge.

English leatherworkers used blunt needles for sewing, which they could get from Germany where they were made. Some boot and shoemakers doing very fine (thirty to fifty stitches to the inch) work may

238

have used waxed ends or hogbristles waxed to the cord. Sewing was done with two needles attached to one waxed flax cord, centered in the first hole and then both needles passed through each hole from opposite sides. It looks like a machine stitch, but is four and a half times stronger. The holes were made by stabbing an awl (a diamond-shaped blade) through first, then immediately following with the cord before the hole could close up. Work was held by a stitching clamp (clam), a giant tweezerslike device held across one leg and under the other. Many museums will show a stitching horse, which is nineteenth century. A good craftsman could sew fifteen stitches a minute or more. Most stitching had between two and six stitches per inch, using cord twisted up from several individual threads. Flax is the raw material from which linen is produced and is very strong.

Seams were sewn lap (overlapped), butt (joined edge to edge with the thread making a U-turn in the leather via a channel cut with a curved awl), box (at ninety degrees) and skived (a lap joint with oppositely tapered materials so the surface thickness did not change). Channeling set the stitching into the surface of the leather to reduce wear. Hide or fish glue was used where necessary to tack materials together, not as a permanent bond, except in some smaller items like drawing-instrument cases.

Shoemakers used lasts (wooden forms) around which the shoe was made. Contrary to tradition, they used stock sets of lasts, which allowed a tolerance of less than a twelfth of an inch with further customization possible by adding leather pads. It was not necessary or cost-effective to have a custom-made last, except as an affectation. Soles could be stitched or pegged, using square wooden pegs in a hole cut by a round pegging awl. One blow of the hammer set the peg or else it would break off because it could not be moved.

Harness Making

Harness makers specialized in strapwork, including harnesses and springs for carriages. They usually also provided saddles, since their clients were those with horses. A set of harness was primarily comprised of three parts: the collar, which allowed the animal to pull the vehicle, the breeching, which stopped it and the reins, which allowed control of the animal. The remainder of the harness either transferred thrust or held an essential part in the proper place. Carriages used breast collars (straps across the chest), which cut into the windpipe, while draft animals used neck (horse) collars, which went around the neck and provided greater pulling strength.

Saddlers produced hunt (English) saddles; dragoon, hussar or military saddles (similar to Western); pack saddles; and, for ladies, side-saddles. If (lower-class) women rode, they did so on a regular saddle.

A wooden tree or frame, made by another craftsman, was padded and covered to produce the saddle. Saddles could be elaborately embroidered, often in silver wire.

Most leatherworkers also made a variety of other needed items. Portmanteau (portmantles) were suitcases, cylindrical in form with a handle on the end, designed to be carried behind a saddle or on a strap. Trunks were made over a wooden frame, lined with paper (often newspapers) and covered in leather. Riders might use saddlebags, hunters and frontiersmen used hunting and bullet bags. The military required cartridge boxes, bayonet and sword scabbards, cross straps, drum and musket slings, fife cases, hats and helmets, and pistolbuckets (holsters). Travelers needed bottles; taverns needed jacks, bombards and dice cups; craftsmen needed aprons; and homes needed fire buckets, wallets and puddinghead caps.

Tools included a head, round or half-round knife (which looked like an onion chopper), burnishers of bone to bring rough edges to a glasslike finish, gouges and punches. Skiving was the process of shaving the leather to thin it, and the word survives as a term for cheating or shorting someone. Jacking was the process of wetting leather, forcing it to take a form, either by pounding sand or a mold into it, and then allowing it to dry till it was quite hard. This method was used to make targets, jackboots and helmets to protect riders, and bottles, jacks and fire buckets, where the finished product was sealed with a coat of pitch from the pine tree.

METALWORKING

Metalworking covered a wide range of trades, from the production of raw materials to the creation of delicate and sophisticated products in precious metals. In general, any name with smith in it means to FORGE (hammer) the product. BLACKSMITHS hammered black metals (iron); WHITESMITHS worked pewter, silver or filed iron until it was bright, which was also called BRIGHTSMITHING; GOLDSMITHS hammered gold (and other precious metals). FOUNDERS cast metals, including its initial production; MACHINISTS tooled it without hammering. Certain specialty smithing trades used their product in the name, as LOCKSMITHS.

Producing Raw Materials

By the end of the period the colonies were third in the world in iron production. Iron ore was acquired by deep rock mining in northern New Jersey and by picking up BOG IRON in most other places, including

(Left to right) The bridge to the furnace, the furnace stack and casting house, the forge containing the water-driven trip hammers, and the rolling and slitting mill at Hammersmith Iron Works in Saugus, Massachusetts. This is only a portion of the large complex even a small iron-founding operation required.

Massachusetts, Pennsylvania and Virginia. Refined iron was derived either at a bloomery, where the impurities were hammered out at a forge, or, more efficiently, by smelting, where the impurities could be skimmed off the molten metal with a flux. Smelting was the process primarily used, as ample forests were available to fuel the tall, beehive-shaped blast furnaces. A foundry site was a huge operation, requiring collection and storage of the raw ore, charcoal to fuel the furnace and lime to act as flux, as well as the pattern-making shops for molds, the furnace site, usually on the side of a hill, the casting house and the labor force to work the site, including rebuilding the entire furnace when it stopped and slag cooled inside it. It also usually had a dam or falling river nearby to power the reciprocating bellows that provided a continuous blast of air to the furnace.

To keep one furnace in North Jersey IN BLAST required an estimated thirty acres of hardwoods converted to charcoal for every day of operation. Because of the cost of rebuilding a furnace, they were kept in blast as long as possible, until raw materials ran out or the water froze over. Thus, in a typical year's operation, this site alone would consume seventeen square miles of hardwood forest, and North Jersey had numerous furnaces through the later period. Furnaces were usually on the edge of the cleared zone, continually widening it.

The tap of the Saugus furnace, with casting tools and a "sow" and "pigs" in the sand. Note the scale from the footprints.

The charcoal burner's life was a veritable hell. The wood to be burned was piled into huge mounds covered in sod and dirt. The correct amount of air had to be allowed into the core to fuel the fire that burned off the impurities. If too much air got in, the wood would simply burn up. So the burners WALKED THE KILNS checking for leaks, which they sealed. They frequently fell through into the inferno inside. Those who survived lived in the woods year-round, supervising the burnings. They were sooty, sweaty and often worked nearly naked.

Castings like rendering cauldrons and firebacks were produced at the furnace site. Otherwise, the iron was drawn off twice a day into a channel cut in sand in the casting house, which led to subsidiary channels in which ingots of iron were formed. Because the channel structure looked like a mother sow suckling, these ingots were called pigs. Lead and other metals were also made into pigs.

Pigs were transported to mills where they were rolled, slitted or drawn into usable bar stocks that provided the smiths. Some furnace sites also had a shot tower, where molten metal was dropped into water, forming round shot.

Foundries also existed on a smaller scale, where craftsmen produced flatware, candlesticks, buckles, pieces for teapots and the like. Gunsmiths did some founding to obtain blanks that were then forged, as cast iron is weak and prone to fracture, while forging strengthens it. Silversmiths and goldsmiths cast whole pieces or component parts. Founding on this scale involved the use of a forge or metalworking hearth with bellows to force the temperature up to working limits, with the metal smelted in pottery crucibles, then it was poured into the molds made of (French) sand, cooled, removed, finished and often soldered together to make the complete product. The fine sand was carcinogenic and caused asthma and other respiratory diseases.

Utilitarian metals

Blacksmiths here tended to perform repairs, as the industrial shops of England produced name-brand tools and items of a generally higher quality at a lower price. Local craftsmen made or repaired all manner of iron tools needed by any other trade: axes, plows, hoes, froes, cutlery, gun parts, architectural hardware (including hinges, shutter dogs and locks), carriage fittings and, often in specialized shops called naileries, nails, which were quite cheap and common in all areas but the frontier. A good nailer could make three thousand nails a day. One thing blacksmiths did not do was shoe horses. That was the job of a farrier until the nineteenth century when industrialization threatened blacksmiths and they took up another trade.

Precious Metals

Silversmiths were more common than goldsmiths because the material was more readily available. Even then they were not common, limiting clientele to those wealthy enough to have good credit and be able to hoard what cash came their way. Silversmiths made items in silver, pewter, BRITANNIA METAL (a later lead-free pewter), GERMAN SILVER or TRADE SILVER (nickel, much used for trade items for the Indians), OCCAMY (an alloy that looked like silver) and sometimes BRASS, but emphasized their finest products. Silver in the home was a reserve treasury. Silver has been called the quintessential art of New England, and many of the finest American silversmiths operated there. They made teapots, coffeepots, chocolate pots, porringers (small handled bowls), caudle cups (double-handled porringers), tumblers (glasses with rounded bottoms that could right themselves), beakers, Communion service and censers, tankards, monteith bowls, bowls and covers, strainers (as for tea or wine), colanders, plates, casters (like saltshakers, but used for sugar and other spices as much as or more than for salt), trenchers, humidors, flatware, salt dips, bottle labels, jewelry, epergne, candlesticks, candelabra, chandeliers, clocks and clock parts. American silversmiths stayed in close touch with the latest fashions in Europe and derived their designs from European sources.

Other Metalworking Trades

Gunsmiths were among the most esteemed tradesmen in the period, because in one or another aspect of their work they did most other craftsmen's work. They founded, casting various gun furniture (fittings and other parts); smithed, hammering up the barrel from a flat piece of iron, welding it into a tube and then straightening it; machined parts, including the barrel itself, bullet molds and screws; case-hardened and heat-treated various parts, including the frizzen and the lock springs; carved, inlet (setting the barrel and lock into the wood) and inlaid the wooden stock; and finished all the components like a fine piece of cabinetry. They worked in silver, brass, iron, various woods, ivory and bone. When they were done, the work had to be worth the price, which was at least a year's wages for a skilled craftsman for any ordinary gun, and it had to work accurately and reliably.

Machinists were not common here but had screw-cutting lathes and versions of most other machines known today, only not as refined. The dates on many modern machines keep getting pushed farther back into our period, but they were specialized tools for specialized, usually English, shops.

Tinkers were itinerant repairmen of metal goods, particularly pots and pans. A tinker's dam was a brass patch placed over holes in pans, so not being worth one meant it was scrap.

Tools and Processes

Metals were joined in several ways. Welding was done at the forge, by heating the various pieces of metal to just below the burning point and hammering them together in the instant before they cooled. A flux of sand or borax was used to prevent scale (oxidized metal), from contaminating the joint and preventing bonding. Soldering and silver soldering were done with an alcohol lamp and a mouth blowpipe, on jewelry, tubing and the like. Brazing was similar but required more heat to melt the brass it used as solder. Iron, copper or brass rivets were also used. Many cutting tools were made of cheap soft iron with a piece of expensive steel (iron into which carbon was introduced) welded in for the edge.

The forge referred both to the smith's actual working fireplace with its bellows and tuyére (air channels) and to his entire operation. Most forges used locally mined coal or sea coal imported from England, but some used charcoal, particularly those operations with smaller volumes. Coke was made at the forge by slowly moving the coal from the edge into the firepan, allowing the impurities to bake off before being used to fuel the fire.

Forging was the basic process of hammering the heated metal into shape. A hand-operated bellows provided air, forcing the temperature of the fire from near eighteen hundred degrees to around three thousand degrees. A smith had to be able to control his fire to put the right amount of heat exactly where he wanted it, then understand the different colors the metal turned as it was heated. Most iron was forged between a bright cherry and a yellow-white heat. A black heat was below eleven hundred degrees, where iron does not radiate light. If sparks flew, it meant the metal was too hot and burning up. If the project was large, a smith might have his assistant double strike (follow his blows with those of a sledgehammer), and really large operations used massive trip-hammers, which were raised by a waterwheel and released by an escapement. Drawing out was the basic process of thinning the metal, making it flow into a new shape, while upsetting was the process of hammering the metal back upon itself to thicken it. Metal could be raised (given relief from the back), called repoussé work. It could be carved using chisels, chased (decorated with hammered designs) using special chasing tools and engraved using small chisels called gravers.

Hammers of various sizes and styles were used, including cross peen, straight peen, ball peen, riveting, chasing and planishing hammers. The shape and size were related to the purpose of the stroke. Anvils or stakes were used to provide the surface for hammering, functionally doubling the hammer stroke into two, one from above, one from below. Anvils came in different shapes to make different shapes, and the typical anvil included a horn (a rounded portion). Swages were special anvils, sometimes mated as dies, to form specific shapes. Punches were used to force holes in the metal, chisels (both hot and cold) were used to cut or score the metal allowing it to be broken. These fitted in a hardy hole in the anvil. Tongs were used to handle hot work and crucibles. They were made by the smith to fit a particular project if he did not have something around that did.

When the metal was heated, it was annealed (softened). Hammering the annealed metal work-hardened it (especially with silver and brass), making it brittle and requiring repeated heatings to keep it soft. Steel could also be hardened by quenching (dipping into water or oil). It was often too hard then, and had to have its temper drawn (softened) by being polished and then carefully heated until the surface of the iron showed just the right color for its intended use, from straw through blue, and then quenched again. Case hardening was a localized process of converting the surface of iron to steel by packing the piece in carbon and baking it in a crucible, allowing the carbon to penetrate the surface.

Planishing was a special type of hammering done by silversmiths. It used a flat hammer and stake to smooth the surface of the metal without removing any. A hand-planished surface shows subtle facets in the light but is smooth to the touch. Metal might also be finished by filing and further refined by polishing with a sequence of fine abrasives known in order of fineness as rottenstone, tripoli and rouge. Because cuttings, filings and polishing dust from silver and gold were extremely valuable, shops working in these materials covered their floors with a wooden grate that trapped the dust, allowing it to be recovered. Workbenches had special cutouts and workers wore aprons that caught filings. Surfaces could also be smoothed by burnishing with a smooth steel tool, rubbing a softer metal to smooth it.

Ingots (bars of metal) were turned into wire with a draw plate, a steel plate having various sized and shaped holes cut through it, and the use of a draw bench, a miniature torture rack that used a windlass to pull the wire through the plate.

Later in the period Sheffield, England, became known for its PLATE (hot-dipped silver-plated base metal), and tin was available as small iron sheets dipped in tin, otherwise known as HOT DIP.

Occupational hazards for metalworkers included emphysema, arthritis, and arsenic and zinc poisoning. They were not known by those names, but the symptoms were present. Burns, particles in the eyes, and other hazards were not common but not unknown.

WOODWORKING

Wood was the principal material, used for everything from building construction to tools and small boxes. The time period saw significant change in some of the woodworking trades.

Coopers

Coopers made items out of wooden staves, such as the barrels used to ship and store goods. Although this is the product with which coopers were associated, they made much more: buckets, churns, laundry tubs, powder buckets, piggins (small, scooplike buckets with one longer stave as a handle) and handbarrows (a wooden deck made of slats between two poles with a handle at each end). Some ships had coopers who traveled with them, especially those engaged in fishing or whaling.

Barrels were made in many sizes and with a variety of materials. Casks, hogsheads and pipes were some of the sizes. The material of choice was usually oak, which split well, but might vary. Vintners, in particular, were careful about the source of the wood because it was used to impart a specific flavor to the product. Those made to hold liquids were built to higher tolerances than those for solids. Iron or brass hoops and wooden WITHES were used to hold the staves together. Barrels were so important that Sir Francis Drake, in 1587, chose to destroy hundreds of thousands of staves drying on a Spanish cape rather than seek plunder. When the Armada sailed the next year, its

DRY MEASURE

Anker (anchor)	⅓ barrel
Arroba	25–36 pounds
Bole (oats, corn, barley, potatoes)	6 bushels
Bole (wheat or beans)	4 bushels
Chaldron (coal)	2,500 pounds (New York), 36 bushels (London)
Dicker (leather)	10 pieces
Dutch pound	18 ounces
Fanega (Spanish)	1–1½ bushels
Firkin (butter)	56 pounds
Hundredweight	112 pounds
Last (ships)	2 tons
Moy (salt)	15 bushels
Pottle	2 quarts
Quintal	112 pounds
Schepel (Dutch)	¾ bushel
Seroon	bale wrapped in animal hide
Strike	1–4 bushels

sailors quickly took ill from food and water spoiling in improperly seasoned casks.

To make a barrel, the wood was first split into billets of approximately the correct size. These were shaved down using first an ax, then a draw knife and shaving bench or draw bench, and finally tapered with an ax and jointer plane. The inside was hollowed with curved draw knives. The entire process was done by eye. All the staves were assembled in hoops up to half height, then a fire was built inside the cask to soften the resin and allow the other half to be drawn in to shape. A retaining hoop was placed on, then final hoops. The top and bottom were grooved with a router and the lids installed. The barrel was finished.

Dry and liquid measure and coopers' products were closely bound together. Many terms had different meanings, depending on the context in which they were used. See the accompanying charts on this page and the next for examples.

Lumber

Various craftsmen procured lumber products. Axmen cut trees, cedar miners dug them out of swamps, and sawyers sawed them into boards.

LIQUID MEASURE

Anker (anchor)	ca. 10 gallons
Barrel	½ hogshead
Butt	2 hogsheads
Chopin	1 pint (France), 1 quart (Scotland)
Dram	⅛ ounce
Firkin	8–9 gallons
Gill	¼ pint
Hogshead	63–140 gallons, depending on contents and usage
Hogshead (wine)	63 gallons
Kilderkin	¼ hogshead
Muche	⅓ pint
Noggin	¼ pint
Pipe	2 hogsheads
Pottle	2 quarts
Puncheon	83 gallons
Quarter cask	¼ hogshead
Quartern	¼ pint
Rundlet (a cask)	3–20 gallons

Pitmen stood in a pit that ran the length of the timber, like an auto-repair pit today, and pulled the heavy two-man saw (pit saw) down, guiding it. The sawyer stood on top, pulling it up. Instead of a pit, trestles could be used to raise the log off the ground. Logs could be squared by use of a scoring ax, which cut into the bark perpendicular to the grain, and broadaxes or adzes (an ax shaped like a hoe, used standing on the timber, swung toward the feet) to cut off the material between scores leaving a slab side. Some locations used up-and-down water-powered sawmills, but they were no faster than men. The circular saw was introduced to the general public about 1840, although it was secretly in use by the Royal Navy about 1740.

A froe was used to rive (split) wood. This tool looked like a giant straight razor on a perpendicular handle and was used with a maul or beetle, a club made from a section of branch, to drive it. Some work, as shingles, was finished when riven, but others used the process to rough out raw material. A good craftsmen could control the way the split ran by using a forked tree trunk as a jig to exert side pressure on the work.

Early the preferred wood was oak, but in a dark finish, not the "golden oak" finish of the nineteenth century. Other traditional woods included pine, sycamore, chestnut, ash, hickory, poplar and yew. Some woods were ebonized, stained black to look like expensive imported woods, and pine was usually painted to cover its grain. By 1680 certain native woods began to predominate: maple, walnut and cherry. After about 1730 imported mahogany began to replace all of these, and by the end of the period it was the most common cabinet wood.

Furniture Construction

A number of trades dealt in furniture construction. Joiners were artisans who made joined work, or that with mortise-and-tenon joints and floating panels, including paneled interiors, turned furniture and house frames. The term applied most in the early and middle period but continued in some of the rural areas. Later, carpenters did house framing and joinery. Undertakers were contractors, undertaking to complete work. The modern usage comes from the fact that many undertakers, and not a few cabinetmakers, also made coffins (simply a name for a box).

Joiners made chests; chests of drawers; Bible boxes; desk boxes, distinguishable from Bible boxes by locks and, later, a slanted top; desks; desk on stands; cupboards (three shelves with no enclosures); court cupboards with an open shelf below and a cabinet above; press cupboards with two layers of cabinets; hanging livery cupboards in which a ration of food (LIVERY) might be kept with a grille to keep the larger pests out; hanging cupboards; dressers (set of shelves) for storage of plates and kitchen ware; bedsteads; trundle beds that rolled away under a bedstead when not in use; cradles; candlestands on which candlesticks could be set, or with a threaded center post on which an arm with two candlesticks was set, allowing adjustment for optimum height; wardrobes called kas or schranks; candle boxes like a large domino box to keep vermin from eating the tallow candles, either sitting on a table or hanging from a wall; wallpockets; pipe boxes, narrow and deep to hold long-stemmed pipes; joined stools; low cricket stools (nursing stools); arm chairs; settle chairs and benches with high backs to reflect heat and keep the cold off the sitter; growning chairs; childbed chairs; triangular chairs usually turned and with three legs to even out floor irregularities; chair tables where the top swiveled to make the back of a chair, and which usually had a storage box under the seat; tables including the forms known today as gateleg, butterfly, trestle and tavern; and spice boxes with locks and interior small drawers.

Turners were those who turned wood on lathes. Many furniture styles through the 1730s used turned legs and other components. They also made banisters, balusters, newel posts, chandeliers, musical instruments and walking sticks. Bodgers were turners who worked with green wood, building their simple lathes in the forest. Their most famous product was the Windsor chair, made of turned spindles. Warpage as the green wood dried secured the parts together and is one reason the chairs were commonly painted. In the colonies, shops in town also made these chairs, which date from the later period.

Cabinetmakers were a more sophisticated crew, assembling their work with fine dovetail joints, inlay, veneer and other intricate constructions requiring higher tolerances. Originally, cabinetmakers made cabinets (⌦ *page 287*), ornate, high-priced pieces originally given (in the sixteenth century) as state gifts. These had many small drawers, secret compartments and extensive fine decoration. Cabinetmakers became more common from 1680, as common furniture became more sophisticated. The best joiners approached their level of work, blurring the line. From about 1730 on, regional cabinetry styles became well established in New York, Boston, Newport, Philadelphia and Baltimore.

Cabinetmakers made side chairs, sofas, wing chairs for the elderly, CHEST ON STANDS ("highboy"), the CHEST ON CHEST (a highboy with drawers instead of legs), CLOTHES PRESSES (highboys with shelves behind cabinet doors instead of drawers), DRESSING TABLES ("lowboys"), SHAVING STANDS, shaving tables, basin stands, COMMODE TABLES (lowboys not used for dressing), teakettle stands, desk on stands, desk on chests, FALL-FRONT DESKS (a chest on chest with the upper chest being a desk whose writing leaf lowers into place), SECRETARY DESKS with pigeonholes for papers, DESK AND BOOKCASES with shelves instead of pigeonholes, writing tables with a smooth soft leather insert to cushion quill pens, library tables, bookcases, card tables often with wells or ponds for the gaming fish (tokens made of mother-of-pearl often shaped like fish) and brackets for candlesticks, gaming tables with chess and backgammon boards inlaid, consoles mounted to the wall, tilt-top tables (usually round or diamond) that took less floor space, corner tables, tea tables with slides for candlesticks, dining tables, sideboards for serving food, BUFFETS (BEAUFAT) that held plates and plate warmers, knife boxes to store cutlery, GLASSES (mirrors), TORCHÈRES (CANDLE STANDS), GIRENDOLES (candle sconces), CHIMNEY PIECES (overmantels), picture frames, bedsteads, close stools to hold chamber pots, cabinets, organ cases and field furniture for the military.

By the end of the seventeenth century well-established joiners and turners were in many shops in New England, but especially along the North Shore, where several makers were prolific. RUSSIA LEATHER CHAIRS or RUSSIA(N) CHAIRS were made on the North Shore and sold throughout the colonies in multiples of six. They were quite common to about 1750.

Tools and Processes

Woodworking hand tools have changed little since the period. Layout tools including scribes, dividers, rules, squares and gauges were common, and much of the decorative work found up to about 1700 could be laid out with a divider alone.

Saws included modern crosscut, rip, dovetail, miter, fret and coping versions. In addition, frame saws were a two-man version with the blade held inside a square frame that allowed great control. With a wide blade called a veneer saw, very thin veneer could be cut. These thin layers of wood were used to cover less exotic woods or to create fanciful patterns and inlays. Thin slices across a round trunk could be laid side by side to create an oyster-shell effect.

Chisels and gouges were common, in a variety of sizes from small inletting chisels to large, heavy SLICKS for timber framing. As today, there are special varieties for bottoming, mortising, turning and finishing.

Planes were used, the smaller, roughing planes for knocking off the high spots before using a long jointer to smooth a surface. Jack planes were used with the blade ground with a slight curve so the corners would not dig in when making parallel cuts on wide panels, and such panels show the hollows when the light strikes them properly. Veneer or TOOTHING planes cut small grooves for a better glue bond. Rabetting planes had a narrow flat section and a snub nose, allowing them to be used across the grain to cut rabbets, or slots in which boards like shelves could fit. Molding planes came in a variety of sizes and shapes, from simple components that could be used to build more complex shapes to the full construction. The larger ones required a man or horse in harness to pull them. These were used for everything from the cove, which allows a table leaf to drop, to house trim. The most common were tongue and groove, used to mate panels, flooring and other edge joints.

Holes were bored using gimlets (a small drill on a hand-driven T-handle), augers (the two-handed version of a gimlet), spoon and shell bits in a brace or drill press, or a hot piece of iron that burned its way. Reamers were used to taper holes and enlarge them. They were common among wheelwrights, pipe makers and musical-instrument makers.

Hammers were similar to our own and came in the same variety of sizes. Nails also came in various sizes, including small BROADS or brads.

Screws were relatively uncommon but were made with a tap (which threads the hole) and a die (which threads the screw). When wood was threaded, a screwbox and tap did the job. Screwdrivers were as today.

Finishes were generally shellac or varnish. Stains came from a variety of natural materials. Some finishes included pitch as a kind of protective coating.

Lathes could be either spring pole (bodger's), with a rope wrapped around the work which was attached to a spring pole or tree limb and a foot treadle, or great wheel, which was a sophisticated belt-driven machine requiring substantial apprentice labor to turn the drive wheel.

TEXTILE MAKING

The making of woolen textiles was one of England's major industries and protected by the Navigation Acts. Nonetheless, the colonies soon passed laws requiring families to produce a certain amount of cloth, especially linen, made from flax. After the period, in the Industrial Revolution, New England would be known for its textile mills, but before then textile production was a home industry. The production of fabric first required the raw materials: fleece from sheep, flax, cotton or silk. Cotton was not to reign as king until the nineteenth century. Silk culture was tried unsuccessfully from the earliest days. Wool and flax were relatively inexpensive local products. India cotton and silk were valued about the same at the expensive end.

Fiber Preparation
Preparation of fibers for spinning was a job for the children, after the raw material was obtained.

Wool had to be sheared off the sheep, picked to remove dried dung and other debris, washed if desired to remove the lanolin or grease from the wool, and carded to align the fibers into rollags (cigarlike bunches of fiber) ready to be spun. If the lanolin was left in, the wool made a heavy, water-resistant yarn.

Flax had to be planted, tended and harvested. The seeds were removed with a rippling comb, a threshing flail, or by threshing over a small cask. The flax was then rotted (retted); broken open by braking on a wooden frame with interleaving teeth called a brake; scutched by laying the flax over a scutching board and using a scutching knife (a wooden machete) to make the fiber pliable and remove the tow (short, stiff outer casing); hetcheled (hackled or heckled), run through a series of hackles or combs made out of iron nails set in wood, of progressively finer size; then set up for spinning.

Spinning
Spinning was done by the mistress of the house, older children or a servant. A small spinning wheel was used for flax and sometimes for wool, but more commonly a great or walking wheel was used for wool.

Spinning could also be done with a drop spindle, an ancient toplike device worked by hand and gravity. Flax was dressed on a distaff to help feed it into the work. Spinning could be done in the late evening by the fireside, after too little light remined to do much else. In a day a good spinner could produce enough thread to weave a yard of simple fabric. The spun thread was wound on clock reels, which had a mechanical device that flipped up at the skein length. This was the "weasel" which went "pop" in the children's song. Spun flax was called line.

Dyeing

After thread was made, it might be dyed, which was done in vats with local and imported natural dyestuffs. Indigo, one of the principal products of the deep South, was a popular blue, and cochineal, a beetle from the deserts of Mexico, made a popular red still used in cosmetics today. Common dyes were marigolds, goldenrod and apple root, which produced golds; cranberries, pink; walnut husks, deep brown; onion skins, golden brown; madder root, reddish brown; cuprous oxide, green; blackberries and logwood, purple; and soot or lampblack, black. In the early period green was most common for textiles, in the middle period blue became popular, and later a variety of colors became affordable. Most dyes required a mordant (catalyst) to set them to the fabric. Alum and sig (stale human urine) were the two most common. Many housewives were skilled at dyeing.

Weaving

Weaving was done on a loom. The simplest were tape looms, a series of alternating slots and holes cut in a board, even occasionally the back of a chair. They were use to make tapes (ribbons) for fastening shoes and dresses as drawstrings, and the like. Looms for making fabric ranged from flimsy simple constructions that allowed only a simple weave to massive, cantilevered barn-frame pieces with as many as eight harnesses to allow forming patterns. The latter were not common in the average household.

Weavers were usually professionals, although in the early days, particularly in New England, most people may have made simple goods. In New England most weavers had shops where the locals brought their fibers to be woven. In the South, the shops tended to be on the large plantations, using either itinerant skilled labor or a slave or indenture who could weave for the plantation and the local community. A weaver could produce about six yards of basic material a day, exclusive of time spent warping (setting up) the loom with the long threads. Fabric was only as wide as a weaver could throw the shuttle carrying the weft (cross thread) between his hands.

An improved shuttle was invented in 1733 that more than doubled production speed by cutting duplicate motion, but it was only accepted in England near the end of the period and probably not used here.

Value

Cloth was very expensive. A fine eighteenth-century dress with twenty yards of fabric had a value equivalent to that of a minivan today. Most people owned only two or three changes of clothes. Dresses were intended to last fifteen years or more. Mending and updating the trim, cut and styling of clothes was a job for a tailor, seamstress, mantua (maker) or milliner (☞ *page 288*), who also made clothing.

Because clothing was so expensive, stores did not stock ready-made. Most MATERIAL ("fabric" applied to things like buildings) was imported from England. The latest fashion was shown with intricately detailed dolls and fashion plates, from which the customer selected a style. They then selected cloth and had the clothing made. Gentlemen were peacocks, finicky about their clothes, lace, embroidery and fine trims. It was not effeminate. It was ostentatious.

Many materials were available. One source lists ten pages of different materials available in Suffolk County, Massachusetts between 1650 and 1699. Outside of this sample, and later, other materials were common.

THE MOST COMMON FABRICS AVAILABLE IN SUFFOLK COUNTY, MASSACHUSETTS, BETWEEN 1650 AND 1699

Woolens

bays: a plain-weave woolen often with a nap, much used in green to cover meeting, casino and billiard tables

broadcloth: cloth made wider than normal

camlet: a cheap worsted, or a fine plain-weave woolen

cloth: any fabric, or a plain-weave woolen fulled, napped and sheared

cotton: a woolen with a long nap, fuzzy (not to be confused with real cotton)

flannel: a plain-weave woolen, not always worsted as today

kersey: a coarse, narrow worsted used for blankets and the like

mohair: usually silk with a close grain, similar to angora

prunella: a coarse twill weave

say: a sergelike bays

stuff: any fabric, or a worsted with warp and weft both combed

Linens

dowlas: from Germany, used for sheets and linings

holland: a fine, closely woven linen much used for tablecloths, napkins, sheets and clothing

kenting: from Ghent

locram: unbleached linen

oznabrigg: a strong coarse German linen

Scotch cloth: possibly a Scottish copy of oznabrigg

Cotton

calico: a painted, printed, glazed or plain India cotton

dimity: a heavy cotton on linen warp, sometimes checked

fustian: a woolen napped to a soft finish, or a heavy cotton

Silk

alamode: used for hoods and mourners

sarcenet: a plain weave of substantial weight, used for curtains

OTHER COMMON FABRICS

Woolens

bunting: a plain worsted cloth

cheny: wool with a crosswise rib

devonshire: a wool like kersey

domick: of wool and linen, sometimes with silk details

frieze: heavy wool napped into curls on the surface

linsey-woolsey: of wool and flax

plain: simple Welsh woolens

sagathy: combed wool from Somersetshire

serge: worsted warp, woolen weft; for curtains, upholstery and clothing

shagg: napped wool

shalloon: worsted, sometimes glazed, used for linings

woolen: combed, short-stapled wool, fulled to make it dense

worsted: combed, long-stapled wool, with a harder surface than regular woolens

Linens

buckram: a coarse linen imported from Holland and France

cambric: a fine linen from the French Netherlands

canvas: for sails, bed sheets and the ground for embroidery

diaper: linen imported from Ypres

flexen: linen

gauze: as today, sometimes silk

lawn: linen

Cottons

checked: India cotton like a picnic cloth, new and fashionable about 1770

muslin (India cotton): cotton from India

tammerine (vermilion): heavy cotton

Silks

bengal: of silk and hair

crepe: light, transparent silk

damask: a brocade of silk, wool or linen

grogram: of silk and mohair, imported from Turkey

lutestring: a taffeta given an extra sheen by a gum dressing, invented in 1656

paduasoy: silk

tabby: a coarse taffeta with a wavy pattern

taffeta: fine, smooth with a glossy finish, usually used for gowns and clothes

Miscellaneous Cloth Workers

Various workers finished cloth. The seed pods of teasels in a holder were used to raise a nap on woolen fabrics, and fullers cleaned and thickened it, using fuller's earth or alum to clean it. Wool was felted, wetted and dried with heat to cause it to shrink and close the grain. Cottons were copperplate printed with designs, painted or glazed with heat and pressure or resins. Linen was bleached in the sun with sheep urine.

Upholsterers covered not only chairs and sofas, but also the testers, headboards and footboards of bedsteads and provided drapes and covered window valances.

Carpets were tied with individual knots. For much of the period they were rare and used more on top of tables than on the floor, where they received excessive wear. Often they were called Turkey work, in imitation of Turkish carpets. The term rug was used for a bed rug, a bedspread.

POTTERY MAKING

Pottery was one of the trades specifically forbidden the colonies under the Navigation Acts, to protect the English pottery industry. The colonies did have a few potteries making largely local products. Potters used foot-powered wheels to throw wares and wood-fired kilns to fire them. In the kiln stacked pieces were separated by three-legged saggers. Many pieces cracked or warped and became wasters, which were broken and used for paving walks or discarded on-site. Glazes were made of several materials, and some had underglaze decoration. Various types of pottery were known.

Tin enamelware was soft-bodied and was called delft in the English world, majolica in the Mediterranean. Most commonly white with blue decoration, it could be very fine in many colors. Large and ornately decorated display pieces were prized possessions. Some pieces imitated Chinese porcelain decoration after that product became common. Delft was common throughout the period and used for drug pots, pap boats used to feed invalids, storage jars and tiles.

Stoneware came primarily from the Rhine valley and included Rhenish jugs, mugs and plates. It is almost like porcelain but has a dark body, not pearlescent. It was usually salt glazed.

Salt glaze was a hard-bodied stoneware glazed by throwing salt into the heated kiln. The salt vaporized, leaving a coating on the pieces. Salt glaze was most common in a gray-blue style with cobalt blue underglaze decoration. It was also made in a brown form and in clean white forms which look more like creamware. It was particularly common in the middle period.

Redware was a soft-bodied pottery with a red base. It was common in Germanic areas and in English sites in the early period. Redware was often decorated with a thick lead SLIP (glaze) poured on and rolled around like buttering a pan. The slip could be decorated by scratching through, called sgraffito, or with a trailed slip, an overglaze layer of thick glaze dribbled or trailed on the surface. This layer was thick enough to be seen as a ridge on the ware. Sgraffito was not found before the 1620s and most common in the later early period.

Porcelain was a very hard stoneware, made first in China and then imitated in England. It did not become at all common until the 1680s, and then only among the wealthy. The blue-willow pattern familiar from cheap grocery-store pottery was introduced in the last period and widely imitated.

Creamware was a soft-bodied pot glazed in off-white, hence its name. It looked much like porcelain and was common after 1700. Queensware was a design named for Queen Anne, with simple molded decoration. At the very end of the period, featheredge became common, with a blue, green or red featherlike decoration around the edge.

Late in the period transfer printing became available, which was an early form of decal. The picture was printed in small dots on cloth, then transferred to the pot before firing. This allowed complex decoration to become cheap enough for the average person to afford.

Potters made a wide variety of products, including alembics (stills); mugs; tankards; ewers; basins; drug, fireplace, paving and roofing tiles; colanders; milk pans; porringers; plates; bowls; teacups; teapots; chocolate pots; coffeepots; decorative figures; vases; candlesticks; drug pots and jars and crucibles.

TRANSPORTATION BUILDING

Various craftsmen built transportation. Carriage makers used woodworking skills to build the body of the carriage, blacksmithing skills to build springs and other fittings, and leatherworking skills for other springs, strapping and covers as well as upholstery. Often the shop was an assemblage of individuals with the necessary skills. One of these was the wheelwright, who built the hub and axles, the spokes and the rim. Obviously, the demand for these shops was small, relegating them to those areas with enough demand to support a shop.

On the other hand, shipwrights and boatwrights became one of the largest colonial industries. By 1750 nearly half the shipping serving the colonies was colony built and owned. Shipyards were built along many rivers and became targets for military action during the Revolution.

Shipwrights worked largely with AXES and ADZES, and it is said a good wright could do all the work with one or the other. For speed, many other tools were used. Iron fittings were kept to a minimum because they stressed the wood and corroded.

In larger cities ropewalks and sail lofts provided necessary goods for the nautical trade.

PAPERWORKING

Papermaking was an important, indeed strategic, trade. Papermakers were exempt from militia service. Without paper for cartridges and wadding, military rounds could not be made. Without paper, accounts could not be kept. Paper was made by creating a slurry of beaten and bleached linen fibers and then gathering them together on screens, pressing the sheets and allowing it to dry. Paper made this way is far superior to our own.

Bookbinders took paper and finished it into books. Sometimes these were printed, but as often as not they were blank accounting books. Binders used needles and thread to bind signatures of pages together, or a series of signatures were placed in a sewing frame and bound together. The bound signatures were trimmed with a plough, then the binding was stitched to the book. Bindings could be stitched books, equivalent in value to our paperbacks, or fully bound with cardboard and leather. Small cheap books were called chapbooks. Books were called by the portion of a sheet of paper which comprised a page. Folios were folded once, quarto twice, octavo three times. Leather bindings were tooled, or impressed with heated brass tools. The impressions were treated with an egg adhesive and then inlaid with gold leaf. If the leather was left impressed without gold, it was called blind tooling. Tools were both individual letters and decorative finishing tools and rotary dies (rolls) for making borders. Temperature of the die was judged by holding it near one's cheek.

Printing was an important trade. Printers first appeared in government centers and were strictly licensed in the early period as a form of censorship. One publisher in the 1680s in Virginia was fined for issuing an unauthorized edition of the laws of the colony. He later moved to Maryland, where he set up in a tavern at St. Mary's City, the capital. Then as today, governments needed forms, reports and more, and printers provided them. They also printed the laws. The printing press was a heavy, screw-driven device, with power provided by the pressman leaning on a long lever. Printers may have looked for stocky youths as apprentices, because the pressman needed his body weight to pull the lever. Slaves may have provided this part of the labor.

Type was composed or set up in a (composing) stick, set into galleys, then put into a chase, locked up and placed on a sliding bed where it was inked with leather-covered balls coated with ink from a plate. The inked type was covered with a frame containing a piece of paper, run in under the press and printed. As slow as the process was, two good pressman could produce 180 impressions per hour. More than one page could be printed at once, then the sheet folded and cut. Print shops were sometimes called chapels, because the English printer, William Caxton, set up in a chapel connected to Westminster Abbey in 1476. The shop gremlin (particularly good at mixing up type) was known as the chapel ghost.

Type was bought from typefounders in London and Scotland. William Caslon was one of the most famous, giving his name to a new typeface. Sets of type called fonts were stored in typecases and manually composed into text. This process took some getting used to, as the type was upside down and backward.

Colonial newspapers made their first appearance in the early eighteenth century. They quickly became a preferred place for merchants to advertise their wares. As the only medium, they carried mostly outside news. The local sections were more like small-town weeklies in their content but were very small.

Broadsides or broadsheets were small posters placed on doors and trees around the community.

GLASSBLOWING

Glassblowing was one of the first industries tried at Jamestown, in 1608. In the early period glass was extremely valuable. Adding breakage during shipment to the initial cost made it virtually unaffordable. The colonies had ample forests to fuel the industry, and good sand, but it was near the end of the period before successful industries began in Massachusetts and New Jersey. The wood-fired kiln (oven) took about three weeks to reach working heat and provided about a day of glass-making. Still, basic products could be made quickly.

Sand, soda ash (from burned seaweed), potash (from burned wood) and lime were combined in a crucible and heated till they melted. A small amount called a gather was picked up on the end of a blow pipe, which was rolled on a marvering table to form a slightly hard surface, then a bubble was blown and manipulated by drawing it out into a cylinder or other shape or cutting it open. Work to be opened was held on a pontil rod by a small dab of glass, which left a mark on the bottom of the work called a pontil mark. Other bubbles could be attached, building up the product. Dividers were used to pierce and open the work, with the pipe laid across the worker's lap on a bench. Bottles were blown into rough wooden molds, then finished by hand. A wet wooden board called BATTLEDORE could be used to shape the outside. When finished the product was placed in a LEHR

OVEN to cool slowly overnight, which prevented shattering. Glass is naturally a shade of green, but by the addition of certain trace metals could be turned clear (manganese oxide, rare early) or colored (red from gold dust, blue from cobalt, etc.).

MILLING

Mills were necessary to convert grains to flour. In settled areas with significant drops in elevation along waterways, water-powered mills were common. In coastal areas with strong offshore winds, windmills were more prevalent. In a few coastal areas with large bodies of tidal water connected by narrow straits, tide mills, water mills operated by the flow of the tide, were used.

Windmills were most commonly of the post type, with the structure balanced on a central post around which the entire mill was rotated to face into the wind. Old maps illustrate these throughout eastern Virginia, Maryland, North Carolina, Delaware and New Jersey. Mills could operate in winds between fifteen and eighty miles per hour, but the wind's course had to be steady, without radical shifts that would unbalance the mill.

Milling involved storing the grain in a hopper; feeding it between two stones, one stationary and one rotating; then removing the flour and sifting and grading it through a series of shaker screens into collection bags. The skills involved are in cutting the stones and adjusting the correct balance of feed and stone spacing to keep from burning the grain or having it run too coarse.

Milling was one trade in which barter was common, the miller taking out his fee in a percentage of the ground flour.

SURVEYING

Surveyors or LANDLAYERS did not make a product but were one of the most important trades in a country where land speculation was a major motive. It was also one trade which gentry could practice. George Washington was only one example.

Of interest to the question of mapping the new country are the extensive variations found in shorelines shown by successive mappers. Research correlating maps and hurricanes in the Chesapeake Bay indicates that whenever a new map showed radically different landforms, a major storm that perfectly fit the bill to cause such a change had occurred within a few years. This tends to indicate early surveyors and explorers were very good with the parts of the land they had actually seen.

It was the unseen land that presented problems with which many surveyors had to contend. Rivers, which were often used as boundaries in grants of land, did not necessarily go the direction people thought they did. The same is true of other features. As a result, surveyors and the courts were given the task of reconciling the realities of various conflicting grants with the theoretical intentions of those who issued them.

Those surveyors who dealt with the massive problems of drawing state dividing lines, such as English astronomers Charles Mason and Jeremiah Dixon, employed astronomical concepts and solved astronomical problems discussed in part in the section on celestial navigation. This was a far different class of work from a mundane surveying job and explains why in most colonies the surveyor general was closely tied to the institution of higher learning in that colony. In no small part these problems are the same as those inherent in projecting the curved surface of the earth onto a flat map and those trigonometric problems involved in changes in elevation, as from sea level to mountaintops.

Surveyors not only drew the boundaries of patents and grants, they were capable of LEVELING the land, or drawing contour maps. Surveyors worked with transits, levels and other tools familiar to us (until the advent of the laser age), but with the exception that all minute divisions were made with a mechanical vernier scale. Surveys were generally by Metes and Bounds method, in which a starting point is defined in relation to a monument, at the time usually a tree, intersection, rock or other natural feature, then by directions and distance until it arrives back at the starting point.

MERCHANTS

Although influential in terms of providing the goods employed by the colonists in establishing their culture, the communications networks that tied the colonies together and, to a greater or lesser degree, the underlying economy of the colonies, merchants made up a small part of the population. As the colonies moved, over time, from almost feudal landholding ventures to commercial enterprises more on the model of the renaissance city-states, the merchants gained influence until it was their interests that government reflected. The richer merchants gained a status second only to the richest landowners, many of whom also traded as merchants. Unlike the landowners, the merchants tended to create cities, which allowed for the creation of more established cultural institutions.

Merchants required good ITALIAN BOOKKEEPING (double entry) skills; fairly advanced mathematics, especially for navigation; a good communication net; the ability to raise capital by selling stock; laws to protect their contractual interests and their ability to collect on debts; insurance; and secure shipping lanes. They represent the beginning of the

LINEAR AND AREA MEASURE

Barleycorn	⅓ inch
Chain	66 feet
Dutch mile	4 English miles
Ell	45 inches
Erf	(Dutch) ½ acre
Hollands acre (Morgen)	2.1 acres
Link	7.92 inch or ¹⁄₁₀₀ chain
Margin	4 acres
Perch	1 square rod
Rod (Pole)	16.5 feet or ¼ chain or 30.25 square yards
Rood	40 square rods or ¼ acre
Run (yarn)	1,644 yards

modern world. Practical scientific advances were of interest to them, for they provided opportunities in new resources and better navigation and in other ways.

In addition, merchants became the sources of information about the rest of the world for a clientele who could not travel. Their ships brought the news as fast as any other means and might tie together a network as large as Boston, the Southern colonies, the Caribbean, Africa, some of the Spanish and Portuguese islands, and England.

Merchants, or clerks, were trained by apprenticeship, but most commonly represented an extended family raised to the trade. Their STORE-HOUSE or COUNTING HOUSE was usually set gable end to the street and constructed so the front two-thirds was the sales area, with an office in the rear. Storage for goods was upstairs and in any basement. Large merchants might have complexes of more than one warehouse. FACTORIES were large compounds, often containing industry, run by factors which serviced a region. They were more common in places such as Africa than here.

BIBLIOGRAPHY

Bivins, John, Jr. *The Furniture of Coastal North Carolina, 1700–1820.* Winston-Salem: Museum of Early Southern Decorative Arts, 1988.

Bridenbaugh, Carl. *The Colonial Craftsman.* New York: Dover Publications, 1990.

Bruchey, Stuart Weems, ed. *The Colonial Merchant: Sources and Readings.* New York: Harcourt Brace and World Inc., 1966.

Campbell, R. *The London Tradesman*. 1747. Reprint, New York: Augustus M. Kelley, 1969.

Coons, Martha. *Linen-making in New England, 1640–1860: All Sorts of Good Sufficient Cloth*. North Andover, Mass.: Merrimack Valley Textile Museum, 1980.

Hoag, John S. *Fundamentals of Land Measurement*. Chicago: Chicago Title Insurance Co.

Kane, Patricia E. *Furniture of the New Haven Colony: The Seventeenth-Century Style*. New Haven, Conn.: New Haven Colony Historical Society, 1973.

Kauffman, Henry J. *The American Pewterer: His Techniques and His Products*. Camden, N.J.: Thomas Nelson, 1969.

———. *The Colonial Silversmith: His Techniques and His Products*. Camden, N.J.: Thomas Nelson, 1969.

Little, Nina Fletcher. *American Decorative Wall Painting, 1700–1850*. New enlarged ed. New York: E.P. Dutton, 1989.

Madigan, Mary Jean, and Susan Colgan, eds. *Early American Furniture: From Settlement to City*. New York: Billboard Publications, 1983.

Moxon, Joseph. *Mechanick Exercises, or the Doctrine of Handy-works*. 1703. Reprint, with introduction by John S. Kebabian. Morristown, N.J.: Astragal Press, 1989. Includes instructions for various trades.

Neumann, George C. *Early American Antique Country Furnishings*. New York: McGraw-Hill, 1984. A wide variety of everyday items in all materials from furniture to crochet hooks and baskets.

Nutting, Wallace. *Furniture of the Pilgrim Century (of American Origin), 1620–1720, With Maple and Pine to 1800, Including Colonial Utensils and Wrought-Iron House Hardware Into the Nineteenth Century*. Rev. ed. New York: Dover Publications, 1965.

Russell, Carl P. *Guns on the Early Frontiers: A History of Firearms From Colonial Times Through the Years of the Western Fur Trade*. Berkeley: University of California Press, 1957.

Sack, Albert. *The New Fine Points of Furniture: Early American, Good, Better, Best, Superior, Masterpiece*. New York: Crown Publishers, 1993. This unique volume compares similar pieces and rates their design quality. It is an excellent way to compare rural and urban work of a type and from similar times, as well as to see a variety of early furniture.

Saint George, Robert Blair. *The Wrought Covenant Source Material for the Study of Craftsmen and Community in Southeastern New England, 1620–1700*. Brockton, Mass.: Brockton Art Center, 1979.

Shea, John Gerald. *Antique Country Furniture of North America*. New York: Van Nostrand Reinhold Co., 1975.

Trent, Robert, ed. *Pilgrim Century Furniture: An Historical Survey*. New York: Main Street/Universe Books, 1976.

Wroth, Lawrence C. *The Colonial Printer*. New York: Dover, 1994.

CHAPTER FIFTEEN

Professions

MEDICINE

Through the period medicine (physic) was at a turning point. Its practice through the colonies over the period was variable. Most physicians still subscribed to the old humoral theory, and it was only in the late period that the first modern scientific doctors began to practice. Medicine and medical theory were at the cutting edge of science, then as now, but did not yet enjoy the prestige of today. Physicians were technically internists; apothecaries practiced medicine and made drugs, while pharmacists only made and dispensed drugs. Apothecaries were the most common because of the need to diversify.

Many people, particularly those who could not afford a doctor's fees, treated themselves. Large planters treated not only their own slaves but also smaller local planters. A do-it-yourself book, *Every Man his own Doctor*, was published in Williamsburg and Annapolis in 1736.

Humoral Theory
In the humoral theory the body was held to be comprised of four HUMORS equating to the four elements. These were blood, black bile, yellow bile (pus) and phlegm. Personality was HUMOR (hence the HUMORING of a person); AFFECTS were individual emotions, the preponderant character of which created a humor. Personality was thought to be determined by the preponderant humor in a healthy body. Sickness resulted from an extreme imbalance in humors. The humors were given attributes, obtained by using two pairs of opposites: hot/cold and dry/moist. The humors and their attributes are detailed on the next page.

Cures concentrated on restoring the natural balance, both with physic (drugs) and direct measures such as bloodletting or expectorants. Diagnosis was made by examining the illness. Most infections

CONCORDANCE OF PSYCHOLOGICAL TYPES, HUMORS, ATTRIBUTES

Humor (Type)	Humor	Hot/ Cold	Dry/ Moist	Characteristics
Choleric	Yellow Bile	Hot	Dry	Violent temper, rash, wrathful, bilious
Sanguine	Blood	Hot	Moist	Confident, optimistic, bloodthirsty, full-blooded, ruddy
Phlegmatic	Phlegm	Cold	Moist	Indolent, apathetic, even-tempered, absence of excitability, calm, sluggish
Melancholic	Black Bile	Cold	Dry	Depressed

and fevers were hot and dry, revealing an excess of hot, dry yellow bile. Urine samples were also taken and examined in a LOOKING GLASS (a beaker-like glass). Color, cloudiness and other features were noted.

Once a diagnosis was made of the problematic humor, two distinct theories existed about how to deal with it. One, the doctrine of similars, used treatments similar to the problem: Feed a fever and starve a cold. The doctrine of opposites did the opposite to restore balance: Feed a cold and starve a fever. By the 1500s prescriptions might include twelve hundred drugs, six hundred ascribing to the doctrine of similars, the other six hundred to the doctrine of opposites. It became obvious to the profession that clinical results did not match the theory, which did not work. Unfortunately, by this time the theory was Church doctrine and to question it heresy. In large part, the application of the scientific method to old medical theories fueled the Reformation, then the Age of Reason.

Treatment to balance the humors might use a lancet to pierce a vein, a scarificator (spring-loaded set of razor blades with a depth control) to cut the surface of the skin, leeches, or BLISTERING (CUPPING) (☞ page 287), the use of a hot glass cup to cause a blister around a wound, which could then be pierced. Expectorants, diuretics and emetics were also used, depending on the humor to be purged. The emphasis on bloodletting hampered the body's natural defenses, contributed to shock and often resulted in death from bleeding alone.

Throughout the period, the doctor was the often legitimate butt of many jokes. As John Milton put it, "Diseases dire, and Doctors still more banefull.'' That little difference existed between a true doctor and a quack made for good theater, including plays by Molière and popular ballad operas.

Modern Theories

In the late period a number of doctors began to practice without the old humoral precepts. These doctors were utilizing drugs, rest and natural processes for recovery. They were the beginning of modern medicine.

Bacteria (van Leeuwenhoek's "little animals") were discovered only in the middle early period and were yet to be associated with disease even as late as the Revolution. Consequently, surgical instruments were not sterilized, although they were cleaned. Few if any effective antibiotics were employed, although some herbs were reasonably effective, but coincidentally, not by design. Circulation was discovered and the explanation published by William Harvey in 1628, and respiration was a new study in the late middle period.

Surgery

Surgery was undertaken at the patient's home. Because there were no anesthetics, limited ability to control blood loss and no ability to replace lost blood, surgery was done very quickly. Most operations took less than five minutes. Contrary to Hollywood, alcohol was not given before surgery, for it was known to thin the blood and cause faster bleeding. It also could cause vomiting, which complicated the procedure.

The surgeon employed assistants or family members to hold the patient in place, usually on the kitchen table, while he operated. Patients could be given a lead ball to bite during surgery, and balls with tooth marks are commonly found around hospitals on military sites of the period. Most patients simply fainted. The procedures, painful as they were, did not kill the patient. Sepsis was the biggest killer.

The tools of surgery varied little from those used today, as a review of antique and modern surgical instrument catalogs shows.

Training

Surgeons, doctors and apothecaries were trained by apprenticeship. They suffered from a lack of precise anatomical knowledge, because dissection was generally forbidden throughout most of the period. Those doctors who obtained such knowledge often did so by grave-robbing and dissecting furtively. A few criminals' bodies were condemned to dissection (or bought), particularly in the later period.

267

Drugs

Drugs were not regulated. Apothecaries sold both components and finished concoctions. Advice cost extra. Many drugs were obtained from the garden and the woods, and several local products were relatively large exports. Others, such as opiates, were imported. Herbal remedies were still used, but the number of ingredients in a prescription were often so extensive as to render a listing unwieldy.

Treatment by drugs employed a wide variety of materials, including herbals, animal parts and metals. They were presented in different ways. Many essentials were distilled, then combined for treatment. Tinctures were suspensions made with alcohol, extracts were distillations, tisanes were teas, and poultices were applied directly to an affected area. Ingestible treatments were ground in mortars, combined with binders and rolled out on a pill tile, then cut and given final form. Pills were round; lozenges were oval.

Many of the drugs used in the period are still in the pharmacopoeia today. The foxglove plant, from which we derive digitalis, was used for heart conditions; ipecacuanha (ipecac) made into a syrup was a powerful laxative; Jesuit's bark (quinine) was used for malarial conditions; chalk (calcium carbonate) settled upset stomachs.

Other drugs commonly used were: ginseng as a cordial and to settle the bowels; rattlesnake root (dandelion) in a tincture for the gout, dropsy, worms, pleuritic fever and the bites of both rattlesnakes and mad dogs; balsam of tolu; licorice; orrisroot as a binder; knitbone or comfrey for helping bones heal; wild onion for colds; mugwort for dysentery; hepatica for convulsions; sumac for dysentery; currants for gravel and urinary trouble; hemlock for hemorrhages; peppermint for stomach ailments; chamomile for stomach ailments and as a sleep aid; yarrow for poultices for wounds and as a tisane for an expectorant; lamb's ear roots as a purgative and the leaves for soothing the stomach.

Diseases

Common diseases of the time were the flux (dysentery, particularly common in military encampments), ague (fevers), dropsy or cachexes (a morbid condition with accumulation of water in body cavities and connective tissue), consumption (tuberculosis), gout, scurvy, intermittent fever (malaria), pleuretick fever (pleurisy), scarlet fever, measles, mumps, king's evil (scrofula), whooping cough, quinsey, griping (flatulence), colick, palsey (stroke), epilepsy, yellow jaundice, diabetes, stone in the bladder, gravel (kidney stones), rupture (hernia), yaws (properly an African disease with raspberry-like excrescences on the skin, but usually confused in the colonies with syphilis) and cancer. Epidemics of yellow fever and pox (smallpox) ran through the country.

Yellow fever, known as Barbadoes fever or black vomit, was usually limited to a small area near the docks where the mosquitoes that transmitted it lived. When cold weather came, the mosquitoes died and the outbreak stopped. The worst months were August and September, but outbreaks could occur between June and frost. Doctors thought the disease was contagious. Symptoms were yellow-tinted skin accompanied by severe vomiting, usually black from internal hemorrhaging. Many thought it was caused by earthquakes, large runs of shad or other natural phenomena. Attempts to stop it included quarantines, escaping the affected cities and, in New York, spreading quicklime and coal dust and burning bonfires to cleanse the air. These latter probably caused as much death as the disease.

Smallpox or VARIOLA decimated Indian populations, which had no natural immunity, killing 90–95 percent. For Europeans, mortality among those infected ran about 25 percent. Symptoms included splitting headaches, backaches, chills, fevers, nausea and sometimes convulsions and delirium, which lasted for several days before fading as the characteristic deep rash appeared, which left pocks on the victim. Some survivors were left blind or infertile. Smallpox was either inhaled or spread through infected mucus and had an incubation period of about two weeks. Unlike yellow fever, smallpox intensified in colder, dryer weather, thus outbreaks might continue for two years. Many people fled towns for safety, although inoculations were begun early.

Mental Illness

In the early period mental illness was still considered by the bulk of the populace as indicative of demonic possession or similar evil. Later, a person suffering from mental illness was known as a NATURAL, in the sense that they were from nature and unlearned. They were often confined and hidden in a basement or attic at home. If restraint was deemed necessary, it was used. At times the insane were imprisoned, usually in cells with female criminals, who were considered more natural (in the sense of Eve) than men, and thus akin. The first institution solely for the insane in the colonies was the Public Hospital in Williamsburg, erected in 1773. Before that the Pennsylvania Hospital had devoted the basement to the insane. Both were little more than prisons.

PRACTITIONERS AT LAW

English custom distinguished between attorneys, solicitors, barristers and scriveners. The colonies did not. American legal practice was loosely organized, relatively informal and dominated by nonprofessionals. When the typical judge, including those sitting on the highest courts, was untrained in the law, and with little respect for precedent and the legal literature, it was unwise for any practitioner of law to argue, and thus presume to know, more than the judge. John Adams and Thomas Jefferson complained of the difficulty of obtaining a proper legal education in the colonies, in part because of the lack of books. Of some 150 volumes of English law reports, only about 30 were available here, and even those were little attended. Standard procedures were often ignored for want of understanding. Most people represented themselves in criminal matters, and the judges preferred to deal with the questions in as straightforward and pragmatic a manner as possible. The practice of law, then, was largely confined to matters of land title and other concerns of the wealthy, and disputes between the citizenry and the government.

A few sons, particularly from Virginia, were sent to the Inns of Court, the highest courts in England, to obtain a legal education. They likely found life frustrating here afterward if they used the opportunity for more than an introduction to the court establishment in England.

BIBLIOGRAPHY

Blanton, Wyndham B., M.D. *Medicine in Virginia in the Eighteenth Century.* Richmond, Va.: Garrett and Massie, 1931.

Colonial Society of Massachusetts. *Medicine in Colonial Massachusetts, 1620–1820: A Conference Held 25 and 26 May 1978.* Boston: Colonial Society of Massachusetts, 1980.

Inglis, Brian. *A History of Medicine.* Cleveland: World Publishing Co., 1965.

Kohn, George C., ed. *Encyclopedia of Plague and Pestilence.* New York: Facts On File., Inc, 1995.

Singer, Charles, and E. Ashworth Underwood. *A Short History of Medicine.* Second ed. New York: Oxford University Press, 1962.

Stokes, Byron, M.D. *A History of the Colonial Medical Education: In the Province of New York, With Its Subsequent Development (1767–1830).* Springfield, Ill.: Charles C. Thomas, 1962.

Walker, Kenneth. *The Story of Medicine.* London: Hutchinson, 1954.

CHAPTER SIXTEEN

Religion

eligion was an important part of life throughout the colonial period, but we should not place too much emphasis on it or view its importance with twentieth-century eyes. Although dying was a regular part of life, and the issue of man's mortality was always present, religion was of major concern only at certain times and places.

In general, religious matters were more important, and laws enforcing religious activity more strictly enforced, in the early period than later. In part this was due to the uncertainties of life in the New World. Mortality rates as high as 75 percent annually in some of the early colonies did not hurt the appeal of religion. Later the importance of religion faded, both because the outlook became more hopeful and the realities of a diversified population made toleration more general, although religion still kept a strong legal position because of its association with the state and its role as caretaker of the poor.

How much religious language in laws and charters was pro forma or intended only to deal with truly recalcitrant individuals and how much was intended literally is difficult to determine. In Virginia laws passed in 1612, missing church once in a week cost the settler their daily food ration, twice resulted in a public whipping, and three times led to "rowing the galleys" for six months. If the missed service was on a Sunday, the offender lost their ration for the entire week; a second offense meant another lost ration and a whipping; if three Sundays were missed in a row the offender was put to death. Blasphemy or taking unlawful oaths resulted in having a bodkin (sewing awl) thrust through the tongue; a third offense resulted in death. Questioning a minister was considered heresy and could result in death. As with sex offenders, it is questionable whether these laws were enforced as strongly as they were written, but they do show the official stance.

Because most religions were directly tied to a state, the history of the various religions is the history of the politics in the various colonies

271

and, as such, is too extensive to include here. Consequently, I have attempted to give an overview of the real everyday religions, not the political reality. For example, in most of the states where Anglicanism was the official religion, it was not in practice. Either the laws establishing it were essentially dead paper, or they reflected a political situation imposed by the monarchy but not actively followed by the people.

Despite the variety of religions, church buildings had some things in common. During this period they had high box pews, with seating around the edges of the pews, not all facing forward. The walls of the pews were high enough (four to four and a half feet) to allow families to bundle together for warmth in the unheated buildings. Families often carried FOOT WARMERS, iron and wood boxes in which a heated brick was placed to put under clothing and generate some extra heat.

Starting in the 1730s and reaching a peak in the 1740s, the colonies underwent the religious revival known as the Great Awakening. The Presbyterians, based among the Scots-Irish and Germanics, capitalized on the excitement created by Theodorus Freylinghuysen, a Dutch Reformed minister in central New Jersey, and, armed with the ministers trained at the Log College, drove a revival throughout the middle and southern colonies, which included among its accomplishments the creation of the College of New Jersey in 1746. It was bitterly opposed in Virginia, but the revivalists' preaching in support of the French and Indian War turned the internal strife into coexistence. New England experienced a contemporary but parallel revival under the leadership of Jonathan Edwards.

All the revivals were based on similar circumstances. Everywhere, church membership was reserved, implicitly or explicitly, for a very few. The rest of the population were outside the church, even if they attended services. The revivalists spoke to these people, through the form of pietism, based on personal experience, and not through an organized church hierarchy. The New England revival did not happen until pietistic elements were introduced into the Calvinistic theology. The rise of the Baptists at the same time was not accidental.

CATHOLICISM

When Henry VIII split from the Catholic Church, the new Church of England was virtually identical in all but name and titular head. Edward VI made it less Catholic before Mary Tudor reintroduced Catholicism. Under Elizabeth I's reign the Catholic Church was again repudiated, and Elizabeth's strong aversion to Catholicism resulted in acts against practitioners almost like a religious fatwa today. Several incidents served to strengthen anti-Catholic laws in England, and the Gunpowder Plot of 1605 against James I confirmed England in the belief that Catholics were dangerous to the stability of the country. By this time, severe criminal penalties accompanied acceptance of the Catholic faith in England.

Nonetheless, the vast majority of Catholics in England were wealthy, politically connected men who practiced in secret. With time, even Charles II and James II would espouse Catholicism privately while publicly practicing as Anglicans. Thus, Catholicism exerted a strong counterbalance on the Anglican Church to keep it from becoming too fundamental.

Early in the seventeenth century several wealthy Catholics considered the possibility of building a refuge for their faith in the New World, much as the Puritans had done in New England. From this interest came Maryland, the first English colony where Catholicism was widely tolerated. Although in 1689 toleration was granted to members of Protestant sects other than the Anglicans, Catholics were never tolerated except in Maryland and those colonies like Pennsylvania with preestablished toleration.

Because of the persecutions suffered by Catholics in England, Maryland was quite sensitive to religious discrimination, and even passed a law making religious slurs such as "Roundhead," "Separatist" and "Papist" illegal. Still, relatively few Catholics emigrated to Maryland compared to Puritan immigration to New England.

With the establishment of the Anglican Church in Maryland, the colony's Toleration Act was revoked. After 1704 it was illegal for a Catholic priest to say mass. The population, Catholic and Protestant, were so incensed at the bill it was suspended and later annulled. Thereafter priests could celebrate masses as long as their services were private. Rooms for services were soon attached to the priest's houses. In 1756 a Maryland Father Superior estimated seven thousand practicing Catholics in Maryland and three thousand in Pennsylvania.

ANGLICANISM

The Church of England was the state church since its head was the reigning monarch. In practice, it formed a moderate Protestant church, balanced on the one side by Catholic elements, on the other by Puritans. It spoke for the bulk of the official population, including the wealthier merchants, craftsmen, shipping magnates, bureaucrats and many government officials. Church membership was essential in most royal colonies for the franchise. Even in those colonies where it was established, it was not necessarily dominant. In many colonies taxes were collected by the church for the care of the poor.

The common feeling held by most puritan sects toward the Anglicans was they were a profligate, lazy, orthodox people without any

Westover Church in Charles City, Virginia, (ca. 1730). Churches like this, without tower or transept, were the norm throughout the rural Anglican South.

personal morals. This view was not valid but was easy to keep from within the confines of one's own territory. Travel tended to mitigate these regionalistic feelings. Unfortunately for the new country, travel was largely unheard of for the average person until the Revolution.

The Anglicans experienced one problem throughout the period. Postulants were forced to return to England to be ordained, as North America had no Bishop. A large number of highly trained young men were lost at sea in the course of traveling to England. The campaign for a bishop, exercised primarily by the middle and New England colonies, developed in the 1720s and continued to the Revolution. It was opposed by New England's Calvinist and the middle colonies' Presbyterian ministers as an attack on their institutions. By the time the movement gained steam after 1765 the Anglican Church was seen, almost universally, as just another instrument of royal authority, even in the South. Because there was no Bishop, there was no cathedral, no reserve sacrament and no genuflecting in the colonies.

Virginia was the only colony with an established Anglican Church that was fairly solidly Anglican. The climb up the political ladder began with membership on the church vestry. Maryland continued with a strong Catholic population and various other minorities, all of whom cherished their freedom of conscience. The Carolinas and Georgia sought immigration from a variety of Protestant sects, and basically ignored the Anglican establishment. There was some alliance in New York due to the closeness of the Dutch Reformed Church and the Anglican, but there were still large numbers of Congregationalists and others. Elsewhere, as in New England, the Anglican Church fought for recognition, even after the colonies became royal.

One factor that spread the Anglican Church after 1701 was the Society for the Propagation of the Gospel, a missionary group active in many colonies. It also sought to convert blacks to Christianity. The New Englanders were offended by the implication that theirs was a wild region without religion because missionaries acted in their territory.

Anglican churches reflected the political nature of the religion. Unless the church was built by a local patriarch, wealthier members vied with each other to obtain private boxes on the walls, with windows cut for their own use, almost like a theater.

Services in Anglican churches tended to be short compared to the Puritans'. In Virginia the local vestry had the power to appoint the ministers and relished the power it gave them, accounting for why a large number of Anglican ministers supported the Patriot cause during the Revolution. With this power, sermons were ordered to be no longer than about twenty minutes. If the minister kept going, he risked losing the congregation (they would walk out) and his job.

Many churches now named with a saint's name were not so named in the colonial period. More prosaic names like "Old Brick," parish names (sometimes with "Upper," "Lower" or "New") and "Chapel of Ease" (for second churches built within a parish), and location denominators ("Eastern Shore") were common.

METHODISM

Methodism was a late, and relatively minor, occurrence wholly within the Anglican Church during the colonial period. John Wesley sent his first missionaries to New York and Philadelphia in 1769, but most Methodism was the domain of lay preachers who depended on the established Anglican clergy to provide the sacrament to their following. The movement swelled in 1775 when Wesley's assistant Thomas Rankin visited Virginia and toured with Anglican minister Devereux Jarratt, the major force in the area.

LUTHERANISM

The Germanics, including the Swedes, brought Lutheranism with them. This was the religion that first threatened the Holy Roman Empire, under the political leadership of Swedish King Gustavus

METHODIST ACTIVITY IN VIRGINIA AND NORTH CAROLINA

Year	Circuits	Members
1774	2	291
1775	3	935
1776	5	1611 for 1 circuit
1777	7	4,379 of 6,968 in colonies, or 68 percent

Adolphus in the Thirty Years' War. Lutheranism was halfway between the Calvinists and the Catholic/Anglican groups. Lutherans utilized a mass, but it was much truncated. They were closest to the Anglicans, and over time many congregations became Anglican. When the Swedes surrendered to the Dutch, expediency made Stuyvesant consent to the Swedes keeping "the freedom of the Augsburg Confession, and one person to instruct them." Immigration from Germany and Switzerland created small pockets of Lutheranism in virtually all the colonies. These were often from differing sects, with differing basic creeds. As a result they never organized a national structure.

The major force in American Lutheranism was Henry M. Mühlenberg, who arrived in Charles Town in September 1742, then continued to Pennsylvania where he arrived November 25, 1742. He removed discredited ministers and unified the Lutherans in his area. He later assisted in clearing up problems in New Jersey, and in 1774 and 1775 arbitrated a dispute in Georgia. In 1748 he formed a synod, although opposition between 1754 and 1760 caused it not to meet. His children were influential, one becoming a general in the Revolution, another the first Speaker of the House of Representatives.

By the end of the colonial period about seventy congregations were in and near Pennsylvania, and thirty were in Virginia and the Deep South. Still, many German settlers were without churches.

QUAKERS

The Society of Friends, popularly known as Quakers, started when George Fox began preaching in 1647. In America, Quakers were most common in the middle colonies and New England, especially Rhode Island. The Southern colonies, with mainstream English political ties to Anglicanism, were suspicious and harassed the Quakers. Fox and missionary William Edmundson traveled to Virginia in 1671 and stayed until 1672, trying to negotiate better treatment with Governor Berkeley but with little success.

The official view was understandable in its own context. At the time, Quakers were prone to active civil disobedience and refused to take oaths of allegiance to the crown, and hence to Anglicanism. To a society that had just endured the political instability of the Commonwealth, caused by a similar group of people, the threat was palpable. In addition Quakers practiced in secret meetings and often refused courtesies to officers of the government and the courts, such as uncovering (removal of hats) in court, which were mandatory in a society based on formalities and rank. Even in language the Quakers set themselves apart. The Quakers retained the antiquated speech of King James' day long after the use of "thee" and "thou" had passed.

The Quaker nonviolence and tolerance for others with differing views went a far step beyond the norm of the day. These feelings did make colonies like Pennsylvania and New Jersey, which had large Quaker populations, havens for persecuted peoples from all over the world. Often, those with conviction to stand against the norm in their own country proved to be movers and shakers when they got to the colonies. Strictures against idleness and many forms of entertainment created a people with a strong work ethic, and they prospered.

Quakers did not rely on an established clergy and held monthly Meetings in homes until plain Meeting Houses could be built. Meetings were for handling temporal affairs connected to the practice of the religion and the Quaker society. Delegates were sent to Quarterly Meetings where larger matters of coordination were discussed. Doctrine included personal communion, frugality, modesty, industry, sobriety and plainness in dress and speech. Members who did not ascribe could be expelled from the Meeting, or congregation.

In the eighteenth century Quakers lost their political zeal and became more interested in social issues. They came out early against slavery, for the Indians and for organized education.

MORAVIANS

The Moravians were one of a number of small Germanic sects that established communities in the colonies. They had ties to the Lutherans and Methodists but varied significantly from both. The major influence of the Moravians was through the influential communities they established in Nazareth and Bethlehem, Pennsylvania, begun between 1741 and 1744, and those in North Carolina around Salem, established in 1752. Because all work was considered religious, these communities were driving economic forces, with large-scale agricultural production and numerous trades. As music was a major portion of their liturgy, which revolved around the blood and suffering of Christ, their musical establishments were among the most advanced in the colonies.

Many other small Germanic sects were established here, like the Shwenkfelders, Dunkers and Ephrata Society, the distinctions and local history of which exceed the scope of this book. For more, please refer to the bibliography at the end of this chapter.

PURITAN SECTS

Today the word "Puritan" is used to speak specifically of the (New England) Congregationalists. Historically, the term applied to all those religions that sought to purify the Anglican establishment of many of its Catholic holdovers. The Puritan following tended to come from the lower and middle classes, although there were notable exceptions.

Puritans were Calvinists. The Presbyterians were the model for English Calvinists, but strict fundamentalists disagreed on the specifics of many things. The largest concern was that the Presbytery, with which the Presbyterians replaced the prelate of the Anglican church, was a centralized governing body the Congregationalists could not tolerate. They split off, the first of many such schisms.

Most of the Puritans followed the Old Deluder Satan doctrine, which held that each person, as they were personally responsible for their actions and beliefs, must be educated to read and interpret the Bible themselves, or risk allowing themselves to fall under the sway of a corrupt (under the influence of Satan) minister or priest who could tempt them off the path of the righteous. As a result literacy and education figured heavily in Puritan society.

Almost all the Puritan sects sang only psalms in church and did not allow the use of organs. Hymns at this time were for the Lutherans and Anglicans. Psalms were LINED OUT (sung one stanza at a time) by the minister or a lay reader, then repeated by the congregation. This process tended to slow to a lugubrious pace.

In the mid-seventeenth century, when so much of English politics was driven by the Parliamentary force (an alliance of Presbyterians and other Calvinist sects against the Anglican/Catholic aristocracy), the term Roundhead became a common slur for Puritans, because they cropped their hair instead of wearing the curls and wigs of the Royalists.

Religion was probably most significant as a factor in government (in the broad sense of shaping people's lives outside the church environment) among the Puritan sects of early New England. This area and emphasis received much study by the group of historians based in New England who wrote the first real national histories after the Civil War. Their histories reflected, to a greater or lesser degree, the views, political interests and biases of the victors in that conflict. Modern work has

Characteristic New England church architecture, the First Parish Meeting House in Hingham, Massachusetts, built 1747.

shown pockets where religion was not a major factor in New England life, except as imposed by law. Modern social interpretations also place more emphasis on the stresses created by the power struggle between the old religious theocracy and the new merchant power block, which reached a peak about 1700, after which the traditional New England religious structures declined.

Presbyterian
The Scottish Presbyterian state religion gave birth to the Congregationalists. In the colonies, it also came full circle and derived from the

279

Congregationalists. After about 1700 the Congregationalist churches became more Presbyterian, and most New Englanders who left that region to settle in the Jerseys, Carolinas and elsewhere established full-blown Presbyterian churches on arrival. Here they were joined by Presbyterian immigrants from Scotland, often by way of Ireland. Immigration often represented a substantial portion of the population of the home territories (50 percent in the case of Ulster), and these immigrants formed the bulk of the Presbyterians in the colonies.

By 1700 there were twelve Presbyterian churches scattered throughout almost all the colonies but no Presbytery to organize them. Such a group was formed in 1706 in Philadelphia, largely through the efforts of Francis Makemie, a Presbyterian missionary based out of Virginia's Eastern Shore. This organization created an advantage over the Anglicans, as Presbyterians could locally license and ordain ministers for the colonies.

Later in 1706 Makemie was arrested by Lord Cornbury, the governor, for preaching without a license and was tried in 1707. He was acquitted in a case that proved the Queen's instructions to the governor invalid as law and toleration as implicit because New York had no established church. The case apparently led to Cornbury's recall.

In 1716 the first synod was formed, comprising four presbyteries. By 1720 the number of organized churches had grown to thirty-seven, and soon the Presbyterians took over all the Puritan congregations in New York and New Jersey. By the eve of the Revolution there were several synods, numerous presbyteries and hundreds of churches throughout the colonies.

Ministers were trained to the highest possible standards at several colleges, including Yale, Harvard and, later, Princeton. Log Colleges were formed near the frontier to train ministers.

Congregationalist

The Congregationalists split from the Presbyterian church because they believed the Bible required churches to be governed from within each congregation, not from an organized power structure as the Presbyterians did. Shortly, numerous theological and political quarrels arose. Some members wished to separate from the Church of England, others to reform it. The Plymouth Colony was founded by a congregation of Separatists but included some non-Separatists and outsiders.

In a form of predestination, members believed a limited number of Chosen, Elect, Saint or Select souls were in the world, and that the church existed only for them. Unlike strict Presbyterians, the Congregationalists believed God could raise any person to sainted status. Membership in the church required each individual to have had an intense, personal conversion experience to prove Select status.

The basis of the Congregationalist doctrine was a covenant (they were also called Covenanters) or contract drawn up between God and a specific congregation, setting out the congregation's obligations to God. Each congregation policed itself and did not recognize a higher, judicial court.

Several congregations contested the idea that only the chosen could participate in church, and other fine points of doctrine. As each issue was raised by individuals preaching their views, the established organization tried and exiled such practitioners and their followers. In this way Rhode Island, Connecticut, Long Island and New Hampshire were settled. Because the religious issues were closely related to political events, these issues have been thoroughly studied for New England.

The political strength of the Congregationalists in New England was such that they were able to ignore royal orders that they tolerate Anglicans and allow them the franchise.

Dutch Reformed

The Dutch Reformed were a Calvinistic sect that was the official church of the Protestant low countries. It was most influential in New York and, since it was established before the English took over the area, contributed to a tolerant attitude in New York.

During Dutch rule the church was state supported, and immigration swelled its ranks. When New Netherlands surrendered to the English, the terms allowed that the Dutch would not be considered Dissenters, nor would they be comparable to the Church of England. This unique status led to passage, by a Catholic Governor and largely Dutch legislature, of New York's Charter of Liberties and Privileges, in which freedom of conscience for all Christians was guaranteed.

The Classis in Holland required all persons wishing to be ordained to return to Holland to stand examination and be ordained. After losing two brothers at sea on separate voyages to be ordained, John Frelinghuysen defied the Classis and began a seminary in Raritan, New Jersey, in 1752. By then the only tie to Holland was the religious chain of command.

Considerable toleration and cross-fertilizing occurred between the Anglican and Dutch churches, but the Dutch held their own identity. The Dutch Reformed Church finally settled its financial problems related to paying ministers, and with a local source of ministers was able to survive. Into this century services in the Raritan Valley of New Jersey were held in Dutch.

Baptist

The Baptists began in the early seventeenth century in England and numbered twenty-thousand by 1644. They were an extension of the various Puritan sects who believed infant baptism was not endorsed by the Scriptures, and later, that Christ died not just for the select but for all people. Although many Congregationalists gained such views, they were considered dangerous, and when Roger Williams began to preach them in the Massachusetts Bay Colony he was exiled to the wilds of Rhode Island.

There Williams established a haven of religious toleration extending outside his own views. Williams's *Bloudy Tenant of Persecution*, published in England in 1644, attacked a pamphlet by Massachusetts clergyman John Cotton, resulted in a pamphlet war and became a major manifesto for groups embracing full separation of church and state.

Because Williams viewed church establishments as an act of governance, and thus forbidden under a strict separation, American Baptists placed little emphasis on either church buildings or organizations. Although a Baptist church was organized in Providence, Rhode Island in 1639, it is not known when the first structure was erected.

Although some became highly placed during the Commonwealth, associating directly with Cromwell, most Baptists were found among yeoman farmers in the more rural areas. This was because the Baptists required minimal training for preachers and allowed significant autonomy to local churches. In many ways Baptists were like the Congregational churches of New England, except they tended not to produce leaders or engage in controversies.

In 1644 Massachusetts made it a crime punishable by banishment to refuse to present an infant for baptism, and in Plymouth a public controversy resulted in the flogging of Obediah Holmes, which inspired a great number of converts. Henry Dunster also signed on, and when his resignation as president of Harvard College was refused on the grounds of his success, he made a public spectacle of interrupting baptisms so the authorities had no choice but to remove him. This attitude was finally reversed in 1718 when Baptists were granted toleration and exemption from taxes for established churches, and as a result a wealthy English Baptist gave the largest donation to the college in the colonial period.

Outside of New England, Baptists flourished in Pennsylvania by the turn of the eighteenth century with over eight churches, Virginia had three by 1756, Charles Town two by 1700, and several were in New Jersey. After about 1760 membership rose dramatically as part of the Great Awakening. The Baptists also appealed to the black communities. The Harrison Street Baptist Church in Petersburg, Virginia, organized in 1776, was the first black Baptist church in the country.

In many ways the Baptists were similar to, and interacted with, the Mennonites from the low countries who immigrated to many of the Germanic areas of colonization.

JUDAISM

Judaism existed in small, scattered pockets, mostly in the later middle period and after. Jews were not allowed in England until after Oliver Cromwell readmitted them during the Commonwealth. A community was established in South Carolina, others existed in Providence, Rhode Island, and in Norfolk and Richmond, Virginia. Touro Synagogue in Rhode Island was the first in the colonies. The leader of the South Carolina group, Francis Salvador, was elected to the Provincial Congress in 1775, the first Jew to hold elected office in the country. Shortly thereafter he was killed in a skirmish of the Revolution. Probably more Jews, like the Dutch, ran taverns and shops as individuals, without forming noticeable communities, but the records are not clear.

AFRICAN RELIGIONS

Because slavery was only lawful if the slaves were heathens, conversion of Africans to Christianity was not only not sought, it was implicitly forbidden. With time the tensions inherent in this doctrine resulted in the admission of blacks to Christianity, particularly in New England, which may have contributed to the abolitionist movement. Before that time slaves, particularly those on the large plantations, preserved African customs and religions in their communities. These would vary with the tribal origins of the individuals or the balance of the community.

NATIVE AMERICAN RELIGIONS

Little is known about most Native American religious beliefs. Almost without exception, the earliest settlers had no interest in understanding or recording foreign beliefs that to them were at best heathen and at worst satanic. The Native Americans quickly learned to keep their own views quiet, in part to protect themselves from the sacrilegious attitudes and acts the newcomers used to reject them and in part to protect themselves from the anger such disclosures repeatedly brought out in the colonists.

Although individual tribes had their own beliefs, including the Leni-Lenape who had a hieroglyphic record of their long creation story, certain fundamentals were common. Each individual aspect of creation had a spirit, whether it be a rock, spring, animal or plant. By showing consideration to that spirit (usually asking for its help, apologizing for hurting or killing it, or making a tobacco offering), the Native American could utilize the physical component and the powers of the spirit itself. Certain proto-spirits might become dream helpers, a kind of guardian who guided a person through dreams and granted certain powers or skills. These were usually anthropomorphic animals who bridged the worlds of the two-leggeds and the four-leggeds, wingeds, no-leggeds and others. Along the lines of dream helpers were the larger deities of the corn, or the hunt, who governed a whole type of being, such as a specific species. The settlers had the greatest conflict with these deities, as they often had horns, cloven feet and other features that smacked of the demonic in European theology.

Consequently, almost every colonization effort included a mandate to convert the heathen to Christianity. Until the late period, the attempts were rarely effective. Early, for every Native American who converted to Christianity and European ways, something on the order of fifty colonists WILDED and adopted the Native Americans' society or religion. Still, neither group numbered many people, until whole tribes were converted, often by Germanic settlers in the late period.

HOLIDAYS

Religious holidays varied widely from sect to sect. Among the Puritan sects, Easter (the first Sunday following the first full moon after the spring equinox) was more important than Christmas because it celebrated the death and resurrection of Jesus, while Christmas was an unavoidable biological necessity. Celebratory firing of guns at Christmas has evolved into our New Year's Eve firecrackers. Christmas trees appeared in Germany about 1600. A very few might have been found among the Germanic settlers in Philadelphia or New York, but the first known American tree is after the period.

Among the Anglicans, Twelfth Night (January 6), or Epiphany, also known as Boxing Day, was more significant than Christmas. This was the traditional date of the arrival of the magi and was celebrated by giving presents, usually a new piece of clothing or money (in a box, hence the name) to the servants, and other relatively minor gifts among the family. It was primarily a day for weddings, dancing and other merrymaking. A heavy Twelfth cake was baked with a coin in it. The finder was assured luck in the coming year. Catholics and Anglicans kept a formal liturgical calendar and noted saints' days appropriate for their faith.

Fast days or days of thanksgiving were special days of prayer and fasting ordered by the local government in response to some national or local disaster or danger, or in thanks for some beneficence, including safe arrival in the New World. What we now celebrate as Thanksgiving was a common autumn festival known as a harvest home, celebrated after the harvests were safely stored for the winter.

The birthnight of the king or queen, the announcement of new heirs to the throne and the celebration of treaties and victories all occasioned festivity, balls, illuminations with cressets (baskets of iron holding resinous wood) and bonfires (illumination did not often include candles in the windows), parades, disbursement of bumbo to the crowds from official residences, and the like. Announcements of the death of a monarch or heir were solemn public events but might be delayed or followed by parties if times were difficult for the colonists or politically unstable.

WITCHCRAFT, SATANISM AND SADISM

Nowhere are the tensions created by the changes in society more evident than in the belief in witchcraft, and nowhere are the differences between the religious colonies of New England and the economic colonies elsewhere more apparent.

By comparison to Europe, American witchcraft hysteria was minor indeed. In Europe the phenomenon had existed for over 150 years, and the death toll ran to millions. In the colonies, it was most evident at the turn of the eighteenth century, as the modern world replaced the old, particularly in New England, where the old religious theocracy was being replaced by a secular bureaucracy.

Studies have shown witchcraft was usually a crime charged by the establishment against those who were distinctive: spinsters, barren women, the ugly, the extremely successful, the independent, the reclusive, the litigious, the willful and the like. Only after the Salem hysteria escalated to the point of implicating numerous leading citizens did the theocracy awaken to the problem and put an end to it.

Contrary to popular belief, most witches here were hanged, not burned.

While the religious establishment in New England accepted the possibility of witchcraft at face value, the secular humanists of Virginia saw the accusations for what they were—essentially slander. They passed a law in the mid-seventeenth century making it a crime punishable by a fine of fifteen hundred pounds of tobacco (about a year's production for a small planter) for anyone to accuse another of witchcraft and not be able to produce substantive proof. Most cases were dealt with on the local level and resulted in apologies to the accused. Only one, Grace Sherwood (ca. 1705), achieved notoriety, only because Sherwood refused to deny it. Even so, the General Court, on review of the fact that her accusers had all been sued by her, refused to hear the case as a capital matter.

Despite a widespread European aristocratic fascination with sadism, Satanism and masochism during the mid-eighteenth century, few if any occurrences are known here. Presumably, the colonists had too many real concerns to be bothered.

BIBLIOGRAPHY

Because religion and politics were so closely tied together in the period, state and regional histories also contain a fair amount of material on religion. Also, although I have dismissed witchcraft above, the preponderance of it in the bibliography is because modern studies have concentrated on the religious and social environment that made such charges possible, and thus closely study the prevalent climate.

Sources of information on both Native American and African religions present special problems. Both have differences among both tribes and regions of the country. Most Native American religious materials that are readily available are heavily influenced by the Plains cultures, which have survived somewhat intact, and into which many exiled easterners were integrated. The best materials are incorporated into volumes on specific groups, be they Native American (Powhatan, Iroquois, etc.) or African (Ibo, Ashanti, etc.). Identify the tribe or nation in which you are interested and look in studies of those peoples for more information.

Booth, Sally Smith. *The Witches of Early America.* New York: Hastings House, 1975.

Boyer, Paul, and Stephen Nissenbaum. *Salem Possessed: The Social Origins of Witchcraft.* Cambridge, Mass.: Harvard University Press, 1974.

Demos, John Putnam. *Entertaining Satan: Witchcraft and the Culture of Early New England.* New York: Oxford University Press, 1982.

London, Hannah R. *Portraits of Jews by Gilbert Stuart and Other Early American Artists.* 1927. Reprint, with appreciation by A.S.W. Rosenbach and introduction by Laurence Park. Rutland, Vt.: C.E. Tuttle Co., 1969.

Ruether, Rosemary Radford, and Rosemary Skinner Keller, eds. *The Colonial and Revolutionary Periods.* Vol. 2 of *Women and Religion in America.* San Francisco: Harper and Row, 1981–. A survey of women and religion through primary writings with introductory essays.

Simpson, Alan. *Puritanism in Old and New England.* Chicago: University of Chicago Press, 1955.

Sweet, William W. *Religion in Colonial America.* New York: Cooper Square Publishers, 1965. Confusing at times, not through any fault of the writer, but because the subject is confusing. Deals more with institutional events than day-to-day practices and dogma.

Weisman, Richard. *Witchcraft, Magic and Religion in Seventeenth-Century Massachusetts.* Amherst, Mass.: University of Massachusetts Press, 1984.

APPENDIX: FILM REFERENCES

Three Musketeers

This and the companion *Four Musketeers* were heavily researched. Virtually anything you see can be documented. For our purposes, please remember this is Paris at the height of its glory and much finer overall than what you would find in the colonies. Still, there are many useful references, especially to costuming.

balloon curtains: Being raised in the background, while Richelieu interrogates Mr. Bonacieux.

cabinet: Behind secretary reading transcript of Queen's conversation.

closet: Buckingham's shrine to queen.

comb: Milady uses comb as weapon against Constance.

cupping: Athos has sword wound treated.

enfilade (architectural): Buckingham walks through mansion, dressing after hunt.

hunt: D'Artagnon arrives at Buckingham's.

military saddle: Athos is dragged from well.

minuet: King opens ball. This dance is not a solo minuet, but clearly shows the idea of the leading couple leading off the dance. It is based on an original painting, and may represent a courante. I cannot vouch for the steps.

palladian window: Balloon curtains cover one where Richelieu interrogates Mr. Bonacieaux.

swept-hilt rapier: Presentation by Buckingham in billiard room. One with dagger in handle (authentic).

tennis: Decision to leave for London is made.

Four Musketeers

bandoliers: Planchet picks up, after picking up muskets, leaving bastion.

billiards: Casino scene.

breastplate: Richeleiu at La Rochelle.

busk: Milady is dressed.

cabosset helmet: "There's the outer bastion cleared of rebels, General."

case bottles: Athos's story. On table between Athos and d'Artagnon.

cup-hilt rapier: Brigand on shore in ice battle.

French farthingale: Milady is dressed.

gabions: Protestants fire cannon at bastion in front of La Rochelle.

matchlocks and loading sequence: Huguenots shoot Rochefault (spy).

pair of bodies (bodice): Kitty, during affair with d'Artagnon.

portcullis: Escapes from La Rochelle after rescuing Rochefort.

stays: Milady is dressed.

sword breakers: Final duel, Rochefort breaks d'Artagnon's sword.

wheel lock pistol: Red Dove Cote Inn, Aramis and Milady.

Tom Jones
This does an excellent job of portraying the dichotomies of mid-eighteenth century life, including the character types of Squires Western and Allworthy (the Southern colonies seem to have had more Westerns, the Northern more Allworthies) and the contrast between city and country. Costuming is excellent for the 1740s. The country interiors are older in style, as is Western's clothing. The fashionable city interiors are neoclassic, and Tom is outfitted at the milliner in the latest fashion. Only the church interior is not authentic.

coal grate: Tom's London lodging.

cock fight: Tom's arrival at tavern with Mrs. Waters.

dressing table with gauze: Bellaston receives Tom's proposal.

lacing stays ("tight lacing"): Sophy in mirror.

making a leg: Tom leaves Sophie and Bellaston.

milliner: Tom is dressed.

purple powdered wig: Tom in new clothes.

snuff ritual: Tom before Sophie comes in at Bellaston's.

triangular gallows: Tyburn.

Joseph Andrews

Another well-researched film. Costuming is fine, with sack gowns worn by Lady Booby in the scene after the arrest of the Gypsy and buying the commission. Macaronis make an appearance, and fan language is correct throughout. Wedding customs shown are generally correct, as are the women's sinks or courtesies (curtsies). The country dance scene at Bath is one of the most accurate anywhere. Keep in mind this is decadent, aristocratic English life, and tone it down for the colonies.

firebuckets: Background, Booby releasing Joseph.

The Scarlet Letter

Regardless of its adaptation of the novel, this is accurate in its visual images. It portrays several issues such as the change of New England society in the later seventeenth century, witchcraft as a social complaint, attitudes about solitary living and the tensions just before King Philip's War very well.

BIBLIOGRAPHY OF FILMS

Barry Lyndon. Produced and directed by Stanley Kubrik. Actor: Ryan O'Neal. 185 min. Hawk/Warner Brothers, 1975. Videocassette.

Cyrano de Bergerac. Produced by Stanley Kramer. Directed by Michael Gordon. Actor: Jose Ferrer. 112 min. United Artists, 1950. Videocassette.

Four Musketeers. Produced by Ilya Salkind and Alexander Salkind. Directed by Richard Lester. Actor: Michael York. 108 min. Twentieth Century Fox, 1975. Videocassette.

Joseph Andrews. Directed by Tony Richardson. Actors: Peter Firth, Ann-Margret. 99 min. 1977. Videocassette.

The Scarlet Letter. Produced and directed by Roland Joffe. Actors: Demi Moore, Gary Oldman. 135 min. Buena Vista Pictures, 1995. Videocassette.

Three Musketeers. Produced by Ilya Salkind, Alexander Salkind and Michael Alexander. Directed by Richard Lester. Actors: Michael York, Oliver Reed. 105 min. Twentieth Century Fox, 1974. Videocassette.

Tom Jones. Produced and directed by Tony Richardson. Actor: Albert Finney. 121 min. Woodfall Film Productions, Ltd., 1963. Videocassette.

INDEX

Academies, 220
Accessories, 118-119
Accounting, 213, 262
Act for the Naturalization of European Protestants, 14
Adams, John, 16, 214, 270
Adultery, 127
Affects. *See* Humors and humoral theory
Albany, New York, 6, 41, 53, 61-62, 78
Albemarle region, 29, 37, 38
Allen, Ethan, 51
Andros, Sir Edmund, 10-12, 31, 35, 40, 42, 44-47, 49, 54-55, 59-60
Anglicanism and Anglicans, 31, 39, 43, 54, 122, 142, 147, 273-275, 278, 280
Animals, wild, 65, 79, 137, 220, 225-227, 233
Annapolis, Maryland, 212
Anne, Queen of England, 13-14, 56, 62, 182, 258
Apothecaries, 268
Apprentices and apprenticeship, 132, 147, 230, 236-238, 259, 263, 267
Architecture, 29, 72, 89-106, 272
Armor, 112, 116, 129, 162-163
Art, 15, 25, 138, 208-209
Artillery, 157, 163-167
Assemblies, 31, 35, 40, 43, 47, 50, 54-55, 58, 64, 67, 70, 146-149, 154

Bacon, Nathaniel, and Bacon's Rebellion, 11, 151, 184
Baltimore, Lord, 7, 35, 36-37, 146
Baltimore, Maryland, 15, 35, 250
Baptists, 31, 46, 48, 54, 272, 281-282
Barter, 181
Battle, 172-173
   of Blenheim, 14
   of Bloody Marsh, 16, 71
   Braddock's defeat, 17, 172
   at Lexington and Concord, 20
   off the Capes, 21
   of the Spanish Armada, 163, 195, 246
   of Yorktown, 21, 37, 171, 176
Bay Psalm Book, 8
Beer, 39, 80, 87-88
Berkeley, Lord John, 10, 55-56
Berkeley, Sir William, 8, 11, 277
Bermuda, 33, 195
Bethlehem, Pennsylvania, 16, 58, 212
Beverages, 86-88
Bibliography
   of Films, 289
   General, 22-23
   See also bibliographies at end of each chapter
Birth rates, 129
Blackbeard (Edward Teach), 186

Blacks, 21, 29, 128, 232, 282-283. *See also* Slavery
Blacksmiths, 29, 237, 240, 258
Bloody Tenent of Persecution, 8, 282
Blue laws, 155
Boats. *See* Shipbuilding
Bookbinders, 182
Boston, Massachusetts, 8-17, 19-20, 39-40, 43, 45, 78, 126, 129, 176, 191, 250
Boston Massacre, 20
Boston Tea Party, 20
Bradford, William, 6-9
Breeching, 115, 131, 190
Brown University. *See* College of Rhode Island
Bundling, 123
Burgesses, 31, 147
Burial customs. *See* Funeral customs
Burlington, New Jersey, 56

Cabinetmakers, 69, 249-250
Cabinets, 92
Calendar, 17, 217
Cambridge, Massachusetts, 8
Canada, 2, 6, 8, 12, 18, 61, 152, 167, 174-175, 229-230
Canals, 38
Candles. *See* Lighting
Carolinas, 3, 10, 12, 37-38, 65, 70, 274, 280. *See also* North Carolina, South Carolina
Carriages, 164-165, 190, 192-193, 239, 258
Cartagena, Colombia, 16
Carteret, Sir George, 55-56, 68
Catholicism and Catholics, 11-12, 28, 31, 36, 43, 72, 272-274, 278, 281
Cavalry, 117, 158, 163, 167
Censorship, 12, 259
Charity School, 16
Charles I, King of England, 7, 9, 40
Charles II, King of England, 9, 11, 48-49, 55, 58, 86, 115, 205, 273
Charles Town, South Carolina, 13-15, 17, 20-21, 65, 67-69, 72-73, 112, 126, 171, 176, 187, 212, 225, 276, 282
Chemistry, 219-220
Chesapeake Bay, 29, 37, 63-64, 218, 261
Chesapeake region, 121, 126, 128, 185, 188, 191, 229, 233
   overview, 28-38
   population, 30
Children, 83, 109, 120, 125, 127, 130-137, 165, 227, 236, 252
China, 29
Chocolate, 49, 86-87
Church of England. *See* Anglicanism and Anglicans

290